French Muslims in Perspective

Joseph Downing

French Muslims in Perspective

Nationalism, Post-Colonialism and
Marginalisation under the Republic

Joseph Downing
LSE European Institute
London, UK

ISBN 978-3-030-16102-6   ISBN 978-3-030-16103-3   (eBook)
https://doi.org/10.1007/978-3-030-16103-3

This Palgrave Macmillan imprint is published by the registered company Springer Nature Switzerland AG.
The registered company address is: Gewerbestrasse 11, 6330 Cham, Switzerland

For my partner, Gina

Acknowledgements

I was a relative latecomer to France. My first trip to the hexagon started with a missed flight from Fez in Morocco in 2007, where I remember standing in front of the departure board with two options to get me closer to home in London—Paris or Marseille. This is one of the few times where Paris won, and resulted in a very expensive royal air maroc flight to the city of light. After a daunting RER B ride from Charles de Gaulle airport through high-rise estates into the intimidating Gare du Nord, I was in Place de Clichy—and slightly bemused by the prospect of four days in the French capital without a travel guide, map or a working knowledge of the language. Little did I know that through interesting twists of fate I would spend most of that summer in Marseille in a 'hotel meublé' in Belsunce, 'hotel triomphe', and eating mostly in the 'la Goulette' Tunisian restaurant a few streets away. My fascination and passion for the streets of Belsunce and Noailles would actually get me fired from my job that summer due to absenteeism. This would be the beginning of a love affair with the Mediterranean port city that would change the course of my life and lead me to PhD study and the academic career that I now treasure.

The journey from that abrupt introduction to Paris to this book has involved living and writing in many cafés in many places—Leipzig station's breathtaking Starbucks in Germany, café clock in Fez, Morocco, and even the illustrious 'Les Deux Magots' in Paris. All in all, not a bad run for a working-class, council-estate kid from Northolt who left the UK for the first time at the age of 20. In fact, it was my relative and enduring fascination with all things suburban and deprived stemming from my own early life that would first pique my interest in France when the riots broke out in 2005. The dress of the rioters, their demands and the grinding poverty and geographical isolation of suburban estates was all too familiar to me having spent countless cold mornings trudging to Northolt High School through the racecourse estate, and later in life, spending hours on the N7 bus getting home from nights out in London. Northolt is still the last stop on this night bus route—and indeed like many deprived and neglected places the world over is also the last stop for many peoples hopes, dreams and their lives. The stories emerging from Clichy-sous-Bois in 2005 reminded me of those of friends and family. However, both the architecture and the ferocity of the unrest shocked me—but it was nearly a decade later that I would first visit Clichy to conduct fieldwork and experience first-hand the shocking state of the housing in those infamous concrete blocks. The estates of Northolt are by no means a social housing utopia, but I never witnessed such total degradation of high-rise housing stock like I have seen in France. Indeed, the private sector unfortunately fares little better—many times I have mused in Marseille that the state of the buildings reminded me of Havana in Cuba. This observation was eerily bought to life with the collapse of a government-owned building that I frequently walked past, at 63 rue d'Aubagne, that claimed eight lives and brought to light just how bad private housing in France can be if you are poor and/or working-class.

In thinking about the acknowledgements for a book like this the names of people, institutions and places that have contributed to my intellectual and physical journey are long and diverse: Peter Giles and the basketball gyms of West London that would teach me mental and physical toughness and how even when exhausted you have keep pushing; Northolt High School for paradoxically teaching me the undervalued skill of ignoring those in authority when they tell you what you can and can't do. More positively, in particular the chemistry teacher Roger Moore was so instrumental in getting many of us to university when he stepped into the chaos and incompetence left by a colleague to get us through the

A-level chemistry syllabus in only one year; Kings College London, which accepted an unpolished, hoody-wearing teenager into its historic hallways and set me on the path to social mobility. Here, Dr Peter Moore of the life sciences division often welcomed me into his fascinating, sundrenched and memento-adorned office in waterloo just for a chat and a catch up—something that made me feel at ease in a world I knew nothing about; SOAS, which took a natural scientist and turned him into a critical social scientist. In particular, Charles Tripp and Laleh Khalili were instrumental in providing the instruction and inspiration to pursue a field of study that inspires me to this day; the London School of Economics for a 'baptism of fire' of graduate study, with opportunities to teach and learn beyond my wildest dreams. Here special mention needs to be made to the wonderful Jennifer Jackson-Preece who has encouraged me and taught me to think about security, minorities and politics in new, imaginative and incisive ways. The late Maurice Fraser also contributed hugely with his encyclopaedic knowledge of French politics and culture.

A greater list of colleagues have also been hugely helpful at LSE: To name but a few Esra Özyürek, John Breuilly, John Hutchinson, Claire Gordan, Sue Haines, Manmit Bhambra, Jessica Templeton, Steen Mangan, Spyro Samonas, Michael Farquhar, Joseph Lane, Antonia Dawes, Sarah Zouheir and countless others would all do their bit in providing emotional support, obscure references and sometimes work opportunities in my hours of need. Outside of the LSE I have been very lucky to meet some amazing scholars who have proved to be extremely influential in the work contained within these pages in their own ways—Wasim Ahmed, Richard Dron, Sylvie Mazella, Salman Sayyid and Fiona Adamson to name only a few. Also, my many students have been truly inspiring over the years with their questions, comments and anecdotes that have widened my view of the world in so many ways, in particular, Jacqueline Ménoret who has been a real help with my recent research.

I am also very lucky to have a supportive cast of friends and family who have been there with financial support, encouragement and good times when the going has been tough—Deborah, Tony, Jason, Shahid, Faz, Heleno, Sam, Charles, Lydia and many others have been invaluable. Most of all, my partner Gina has been a rock through sickness and health, and through moments when I didn't think I could go on, whether it was through financial and physical difficulties or the rather more privileged problem of jetlag.

Academia is no joke, and quite often I have felt like I would not be able to go on. However, I could not, and would not, give up nor choose to do anything else with my life. Education has given me literally everything and it has been an honour, a pleasure and a blessing to be able to contribute back to a system that continues to provide transformative experiences to so many. One of my chief inspirations Jalal ad-Deen Rumi, whose work was my point of entry to a spiritual life many years ago, is quoted as saying "Let yourself be silently drawn by the stronger pull of what you really love" which to me sums it up nicely. To further quote his work, which fundamentally changed my life, I endeavour to remain committed to the mantra of "sell your cleverness and buy bewilderment" in the face of a world which continues to be fascinating, bewildering and enchanting.

London, 2019   Joseph Downing

Contents

1

'French Muslims' and Banality: Beyond Essentialism, Exceptionalism and Salaciousness

1.1 Introducing Banality, Essentialism and French Muslims

On 7 January 2015, two masked men entered the offices of the French satirical magazine *Charlie Hebdo* and, after killing 12 people, declared that they had avenged the prophet Mohamed in the name of Al-Qaida in the Yemen. It transpired that these two men, the Kouachi brothers, were French citizens born in Paris to Algerian parents. One of them had indeed travelled to Yemen to study Arabic and to train with Al-Qaida affiliated militants. However, this event did more than simply illustrate the international nature of Islamist inspired terror attacks, it also placed France's Muslim population even more firmly in the spotlight that it had been subjected to repeatedly over recent decades.

Here, the symbolic importance of an attack on a satirical magazine by two French citizens claiming to defend the legacy of a holy man over 1300 years dead, on behalf of a fundamentalist religious organisation based in the Arabian Peninsula, is hard to overstate. Indeed, while *Charlie Hebdo* had hardly been popular in France up to this point, having nearly folded several times, it suddenly became the symbol of all that was right

© The Author(s) 2019
J. Downing, *French Muslims in Perspective*,
https://doi.org/10.1007/978-3-030-16103-3_1

1

about liberal values. On the flip side, the attack then became epitomic of all that is wrong with fundamentalist religion. Such an attack on a satirical magazine only in existence to test the boundaries of free speech was too neat a fit with the 'clash of civilisations' paradigm not to add fuel to the already raging fire of anti-Islam rhetoric both in France and in Europe more widely. By the time this attack happened, the so-called 'failure of multiculturalism' was already old news (Kimlicka, 2010), and bordered on being a political and intellectual tenet of unquestionable truth. However, it would be wrong to think that the focus created by this incident draws on debates that discuss 'religion' and 'cultural' problems in Europe in abstract and universal terms. Rather, it has become clear that Muslims are the focus of constructions of the securitised 'other' within this discourse (Cesari, 2013). Here, Muslims are constructed as presenting European states with 'communities of fear', portrayed as outside the remit of European values that require integration and regulation (Kaya, 2009). Thus, Muslims have become the threatening internal other par excellence, who present not only an existential threat to physical security through terror attacks, but also a far wider and diffuse threat to the liberal democratic order of things in a Europe that still struggles with home-grown, nativist fascism.

However, what has been obscured by the horrific violence and bloodshed of recent terror attacks in France has been how exceptional individuals such as the Kouachi brothers actually are. It is hard to comprehend, given the disproportionate space dedicated to Muslims as threats to security and liberal values in discursive realms such as the mass media (Brown, 2006), just how fringe such individuals and acts are to the daily Muslim experience. The number of French Muslims is estimated to be nearly 6 million, with violent extremists estimated to be only in the few thousands at most (Dell'Oro, 2015). At 11:30 that morning, while gunshots rang out in the Charlie Hebdo offices, the rest of this community of 6 million individuals from a diverse set of ethnic, racial, cultural and doctrinal backgrounds would have been getting on with far less exceptional, but sociologically important, daily lives. Whether working in banks, or in the case of Ahmed Marabet, who was killed outside the offices by the gunmen, patrolling the streets of Paris as a French policeman, defending with his life the values of freedom, democracy and security so dear to European democracies. On a more banal level, the staff in the many excellent couscous restaurants of my adopted home city of Marseille would have been frantically preparing for the lunchtime rush, where they would warmly serve French customers of all religious, political and cultural backgrounds the tasty, simple meal of grain, vegetables and slow cooked meat that has become a French favourite. In many of these establishments in Marseille and across France an extensive wine list is offered, with the Muslim waiting staff refilling the glasses of their customers as they clear away the dirty plates. Indeed, many other French Muslims would be in the process of fulfilling a large variety of social roles explicitly condemned by the religious extremists bringing a premature end to the lives of satirists in Paris. No doubt some French Muslims would have been making rap music, selling drugs in the open air drug markets of the large French housing estates, and even playing roles in the production of the adult movies openly and enthusiastically advertised and sold in the kiosks dotted around French streets. Magazines that would have carried erotic depictions of French Muslims, interviews with French rappers of Muslim origin and exposés about the state of the suburbs would have jostled for shelf space alongside the very issue of *Charlie Hebdo* which contained cartoons depicting the prophet Mohamed that triggered the hostility. The paradoxes, nuances and diversity of the French Muslims' experience highlighted by this 'rogues gallery' of magazine publications should not be dismissed lightly as polemic. Rather, they set the tone for the basis of this book's attempts to draw a broad narrative arc across a diverse panorama of the multitude of ways in which French Muslims exist in French society.

Thus, these opening paragraphs are not simply an idle wander through my musings on more than a decade of living, working and holidaying in various parts of the hexagon, and indeed eating a lot of couscous. Rather, they make a fundamentally important, yet in these times of dramatic events, neglected, sociological point—that the presence of Muslims in France has been, and remains to be, marked by overwhelmingly banal forms of existence across all social domains and functions of French society. Banal here should not be interpreted as 'boring' or unimportant, as there are indeed many important sociological insights to be made by taking this banal approach, if indeed this book does justice to them.

Paradoxically, adopting this problematic and mis-deployed socio-political category of 'Muslim' and connecting it to a thorough investigation of the numerous and often banal ways that it interacts with French politics, norms, culture and social relations is actually an important and contrary stance to take. This is because of the plethora of voices across all shades of politics, and indeed even within the academy, that seem to be convinced that the terms 'French' and 'Muslim' are somehow destined to never be reconciled. Here, they are juxtaposed like two English neighbours that have fallen out over a boundary fence or ill executed loft extension. However, while Nicolas Sarkozy was preoccupied with creating the ministry of national identity to formalise what Frenchness actually means, Marine Le Pen was lambasting praying in the streets as akin to Nazi occupation and Andrew Hussey was busy writing about a 'long war between France and its Arabs' (Hussey, 2014), the lived experience on the streets of Paris, Lyon, Marseille and across towns, cities and villages across France tells a very different story.

This brief and woefully incomplete sketch of the daily lives of French Muslims and the importance of narratives of banality within it is not simply included to entice readers to dip further into this book, which I hope it does, but to make a very serious sociological point that will be one key thread that will weave through what will be an interdisciplinary and mixed methods account of a social grouping. This is the all too often neglected empirical reality that French Muslims and their historical, cultural and social realities are extremely diverse and require a nuanced treatment. This approach enables both understanding from a scholarly perspective and also for this understanding to be disseminated into the public realm, where in France and overseas this realm often gets to peak only into the dark, exceptional and salacious aspects of the French Muslim experience. Within this, it is important to look beyond the overtly and obviously 'Muslim' issues such as the regulation of religious symbols or women's dress. While these are undoubtedly important facets of understanding the French Muslim experience, and extremely worthy of scholarship, they can only illuminate small parts of a much bigger story. Reuters made a very valid journalistic point during the 2005 riots where, regardless of pressure from some of their readership to label the riots as 'Muslim' riots, the lack of any overtly 'Muslim' claims from the Muslims who participated in the unrest meant that they did not feel justified in labelling them 'Muslim rioters', but simply rioters (Heneghan, 2007). Journalistically, this argument undoubtedly has merit and is commendable for its commitment to truth and rejection of salaciousness. However, the sociological logic of this book seeks to take a countervailing logic in that it makes the argument that one can only begin to understand the experiences and lives of Muslims anywhere in the world by looking beyond the obviously 'Islamic' facets of their lives and into the much broader social contexts in which they exist. The Reuters article makes the important argument that Muslims are also men, women, music fans and football supporters (Heneghan, 2007), and should be examined at times by putting these identifications in front of any conception of being Muslim. This may sound obvious, but these are facets of Muslim experiences across the globe which are unfortunately neglected in favour of the more dramatic, and perhaps within the political economies of the news media, policy circles and perhaps even academic funding bodies, more profitable aspects of the Muslim experience such as security, terrorism and radicalisation. Recent attention lavished on French Muslims is no exception. However, this book seeks to make important points by putting these secular categories into an analysis of French Muslims to demonstrate the diversity of their social roles and functions. Thus, rather than inaccurately labelling rioters as Muslims and further securitising a minority population, this books demonstrates that Muslims are also police officers, musicians and indeed porn stars.

However, not all journalists and public intellectuals have taken this path in trying to be nuanced and empirically grounded when discussing French Muslims. The anti-Islam rhetoric of the far-right leader Marine Le Pen of the 'Reassemblement National', the former 'Front National', is well documented. Indeed, a wide range of sentiments that view French Muslims and Islam more generally with suspicion exist across French society. There even exists a political youth movement, 'Génération Identitaire', which overtly claims to battle against mass migration and the 'Islamisation' of France. Looking deeper into how Islam and Muslims are constructed in France it is important to argue that these sentiments are not limited to the fringes, but rather have become rather mainstream pillars of intellectual life. An example of a public intellectual who has pushed such an agenda is Eric Zemmour, who has written numerous books in the reactionary right-wing tradition, and has criticised Muslims in France numerous times. His works include books which address the existential anxiety about the 'self-destruction' of France (Zemmour, 2009, 2014, 2018). Zemmour sets this argument against a far broader context than simply the presence of Muslims in the hexagon, following in the typical right-wing trajectory of mixing post-colonial nostalgia with anti-globalisation and even viewing feminism as a key force destroying the fabric of French society. A sense of an 'impotence' in the face of the Muslim threat has become a common trope in this French intellectual vein, as it has across much of Europe, where arguments are made that a form of cultural insecurity is being caused by immigration, globalisation, Islam and the 'elites' (Bouvet, 2015). This is also argued as extending as far as 'Islamaphobia' being a lie (Bruckner, 2006, 2018), and the resulting guilt being an important means by which Muslims are manipulating the West into its own destruction.

Other authors in this intellectual vein have gone on to make several kinds of arguments that seek to depict a France, and indeed a 'West' or a 'Europe', as under attack from a wide range of Muslim aggressions (Caldwell, 2014). These include those who discuss the lost territories of the republic that situate the suburbs as Islamised places, vectors of threat, which exist outside of French control and where anti-semitism and sexist acts run rife (Brenner & Bensoussan, 2015). What is important here is not denying that the suburbs have security problems, but rather than seeing them constructed as banal, structural problems of a lack of policing or municipal neglect (as correctly highlighted in works such as Wacquant, 2007), it is the religion of Islam, and French Muslims, who are to blame for creating a kind of ideologically driven insecurity. However, the truth about the nature of xenophobia is much more nuanced in France—in the case of anti-semitism the roots are long, and include such abhorrent events as the Dreyfus affair and the deportation of French Jews to the death camps of the Second World War by French collaborators. Indeed, in 2018 the number of anti-semitic events in France was said to have risen by 74%. This increase was due to a wide range of issues—including Islamist inspired incidents, but also due to the French nationalist far right, and also even as a product of action by some of those involved in the yellow vest (gilets jaunes) protest movement (Couvelaire, 2019). This demonstrates the necessity of being empirically grounded when discussing anti-semitism in France or in any other context, and not simplifying Jewish–Muslim relations due to the recent history of the Israel-Palestine conflict. In Belsunce, an immigrant-rich area of central Marseille, Jewish and Muslim merchants have shops side by side and sell similar items, including the famous 'bleu de chine' garments, which are worn in Marseille or exported to North Africa for resale. An Algerian Muslim Oranaise baker in Noallies, the city's central market, bakes Sabbath bread for Jewish customers. These examples are not meant to deny that some French Muslims are xenophobes and anti-semites, just like their French-Christian or French-atheist co-citizens. The point being made is that discussing these issues as specifically Muslim is both empirically incorrect and dangerous in terms of constructing French Muslims as having specifically anti-semitic tendencies. Indeed, the French comedian Dieudonné M'bala M'bala (who is not a French Muslim) was given a jail sentence for anti-semitism in 2015, due to comments made at a show in Belgium— demonstrating that the issue runs across race, class and religious lines in France as it does in other European contexts.

This dovetails with other empirically unfounded notions that situate perceived contemporary problems in France as specifically the result of French Muslims. This includes proclamations made about the 'end of assimilation', caused by Muslims making claims against the central state (Tribalat, 2017), which make little reference to other groups, such as Bretons, the Provençals or the Basques as also making claims for kinds of cultural and linguistic rights. Rather, again it is Islam and Muslims which are singled out as somehow being specific, ideologically driven, threats to the French order. Thus, the perfect storm of a decadent and out of touch elite has left France abandoned to an Islamic encroachment, where a connection is made between women wearing the veil and halal meat and somehow the loss of a national identity (Mamou, 2018). These kinds of voices are not limited to lofty debates in the latest provocative monograph, but also filter down into public policy. The municipality of Marseille, seemingly disinterested in the state of housing to the point where a municipally owned building collapsed on 5 November 2018, managed to be concerned with lowering the number of kebab shops, telephone boutiques and 'bazars' in the same city streets, where their neglect of 63 Rue d'Aubagne claimed eight lives. The municipal resources that went into the so-called 'plan anti-kebab' Max A (2017) would have been much better spent on making day-to-day life safer for the inhabitants of the city. This is a sentiment which could be applied to many of the works above, where public intellectuals make grandiose sweeping statements about the 'out of touch elites' that they themselves are part of, while their work neglects the more complex, far less marketable and less sound-bite worthy banal social concerns that confront France.

However, these sentiments have not only found their expression in books which directly address 'real world' politics and society. They have even spilled over into works of fiction set against a France which has become 'Islamised'. One example is the novel *Submission*, which depicts France as being taken over by Muslims and the republic having a Muslim president (Houellebecq, 2017). Houellebecq does not see this book as simply using such a possible future as a literary tool, but rather as depicting something which he sees as possible, due to the perceived changes he has seen in France in the past 20 years (Bourmeau, 2015). In this book, an unholy alliance between the Socialist Party and a new French 'Muslim brotherhood' party means that non-Muslims are banned from teaching at the Sorbonne and women are banned from working. While a work of fiction, it remains important to highlight how Houellebecq conflates Islam with a dangerous, totalitarian political ideology that forbids women working and non-Muslims teaching at universities. There is a clear way that this fiction builds on the recent reactionary intellectual tradition that juxtaposes the existence of France on one side, and Islam and French Muslims on the other, and never shall the two be compatible. One of the key aims of this book is to demonstrate that not only are the two compatible in the abstract but also already are living happily alongside, and within, each other. The banal reality of French Muslim daily life demonstrates this.

However, this book needs to acknowledge that it takes a huge conceptual gamble in using this term 'French Muslim'. Indeed, out of the more than 90,000 words which make up this book, these are the two words over which the most sleep was lost. Academics are prisoners of terminology because we need to make definitions that are inherently overly simplistic, even when at their most nuanced and complex. Whether we discuss class, gender, sexuality or any other category that involves the possibility of lassoing a diverse group of people and corralling them into a fixed and cramped terminological pen. There is an argument to be made here for the use of the designation 'Muslims in France' as possibly less limiting than 'French Muslims'. This is because 'Muslims in France' would perhaps enable the capture of the discrepancy in citizenship status between those who have been born in France and those who have arrived more recently, and indeed those who are in France illegally and are 'sans papiers' (without papers). However, 'Muslims in France' also contains within it a connotation which is inaccurate. Going back to the analogy of the English neighbours falling out over the boundary fence, saying 'Muslims in France' risks depicting what is a very settled and very French community as wrongly being unsettled and somehow existing in France but not being 'of France'. This would not only be erroneous and also misleading, but would also echo the rhetoric of far-right politicians such as Marine Le Pen, who seek to peddle the agenda that somehow French Muslims not only live apart from society but have no interest in becoming part of it. This is paradoxical, because anyone that has spent even a weekend city break in Paris would have, perhaps even unconsciously, witnessed the integration of French Muslims into a range of social, economic and political functions in France that demonstrates that they are an integral part of the fabric of contemporary France. This is neither a recent nor impermanent development, and French Muslims will likely be French for generations to come, like their French-Italian, French-Jewish and French-Portuguese co-nationals who arrived several generations prior. It is little understood, and yet essential to understand, that French Jews, and even Catholic French Italians, were recipients of very similar marginalising rhetoric in France in the past. There is much to be gained from seeking to understand the current discourse around French Muslims in comparative perspective with the similarity of language used around the 'Italian invasion' of Marseille in the nineteenth century. This is because doing so would enable a greater understanding of the fact that not only are French Muslims unremarkable in many of their social functions, their discursive marginalisation is also not unique. As the Marseille rapper Akhenaton says in his song 'Métèque et mat', when referencing his Neapolitan origins, 'I am one of those that Hitler called the niggers of Europe'.

Even using the term 'French Muslim' still carries with it an entire set of baggage which requires unpacking. This is because it could easily degenerate into the ontological 'cardinal sin' that any book on this subject must avoid—what social scientists and philosophers call 'essentialism'. This is the belief that social categories have 'an underlying reality or true nature … that gives an object its identity' (Gelman, 2003). Here, there is no one central reality or nature that is the key that unlocks the truth about French Muslims. Paradoxically, if there is one 'essential' nature or truth about French Muslims it is their diversity, dynamism and complexity; and rather than one central truth, there are currently somewhere around 5.7 million 'truths' that sum up the French Muslim experience. Telling all those stories is clearly beyond the scope of this book, and as in all social science studies, generalisations have to be made and categories have to be created that enable the analysis of a large and diverse social group in a way that enables transferable points to be made. It is the hope of this book that these generalisations are made in conscious and intelligent ways and that categories of analysis are created in ways that do justice to the complex social realities of a diverse social group. As mentioned already, it is in the appropriation of this category, as highly securitised and stigmatised, that enables the telling of a very different set of stories and experiences. Thus, it is the purpose of this book to broaden this discussion and for this to be a starting point for those who are interested in France and its Muslims to begin to understand the nuanced and multifaceted nature of their experiences. It must be added at this point that no single humble book can do this in its entirety, and I sincerely hope that it inspires and acts as a launching point for other scholars in the field to shine a light on the many aspects of French Muslims' social experiences that had to be neglected here.

It is not just the 'Muslim' part of the 'French Muslim' construction that we have to be careful about essentialising. Essentialism can occur against any group, not just those of non-European origin and at the thin end of a power differential. Rather, it is possible to essentialise white populations, European countries and European identities in the same way it is to essentialise the Muslim world, Arabs or black people. France, especially in the anglophone world, can sometimes seem to occupy a sacred position at the pinnacle of European achievement—a refuge for artists, and a country with the best food in the world. Thus, there exists a current in French studies obsessed with certain essential understandings of what constitutes French culture, and a subsection of France experts obsessed with the elite chatter of the 'grand salons de la capital'. France is an extremely diverse country and Frenchness a construct which includes both the chic parts of central Paris and the classic works of Molière, but also the rural Catalan-speaking areas of the South West and the literature of the French-Spanish-Italian Marseillais crime writer Jean-Claude Izzo. On a pejorative note, it can also be constructed as innately racist, anti-Muslim, backwards and stuck in its out-of-date and quaint ways. Again, any of these statements make either positive or negative generalisations that can be unhelpful—yes, there is racism and marginalisation of Muslims in France, as there is in the UK or indeed in Saudi Arabia or Pakistan. Rather, in investigating such phenomena we need to be specific in which contexts we are seeking to understand any given process and also avoid the all too easy and tempting, lazy generalisations. Perhaps the best quote I have come across that sums up these paradoxes of either negative or positive constructions of difference was a meme on nationalism from a French rap Facebook group—which gave the definition of nationalism as 'the belief that your rubbish country is better than someone else's rubbish country'. Thus, when examining questions of French Muslims, it is both France and being French as well as Islam and being Muslim that we must avoid essentialising.

1.2 How to Investigate French Muslims? The Centrality of the Symbolic and the Discursive in This Book: Methodological Approach and Statement

An important starting point of any piece of academic enquiry is a discussion of the methodological and conceptual approach employed. Whether we like it or not, we are engaging in a discussion about the philosophy of science and the very nature of knowledge production. However, as this is absent from many works of scholarship, it is important to ask, as Gorski (2013) does, why should we care? This could be double emphasised here as I am predominantly an empirically orientated social scientist and not a theorist. As an empirical researcher this is something that I have mused over for quite some time. An important starting point is the observation that scholars don't often outline their epistemological or ontological positions, they have to be guessed at. Also, the biographies and positionalities of authors is only often explored in ethnography. This does not mean that expertise has to be experiential—that only a working-class person can be an expert on the working classes or only someone with African ancestry can be a professor of African studies, while acknowledging the importance that these perspectives can bring to the studies of these areas. The reason I am including a discussion of this here is partly out of admiration for the frank honesty of the anthropologist who gives a biographical statement about positionality in the outset of their detailed works. However, it is unescapable that my intellectual and social influences do play a role in defining this piece of scholarship, and if it was not for my grounding in Middle Eastern studies as an MSc student, I would not have the tools to approach the discussion of French Muslims from the comparative social studies of Muslim societies, the knowledge about theories of colonialism and post-colonialism and indeed an understanding of the traps offered by orientalist scholarship and perspectives.

Additionally, with the pitched battles that continue to rage around approaches in the social sciences, it is important for a work to situate itself in these debates and be clear about where it stands. These battles have, in large part, been driven by the somewhat unfortunate obsession with those who rank universities and departments with publication metrics and impact factors, where the highest impact factor journals are largely based on the positivist approaches to understanding the social world borrowed from the natural sciences. This rationale centres on the need to 'prove' relationships with recourse to statistical tests that rely on complex models and the 5% confidence level. It is doubtless that this approach has massively furthered social knowledge and provides valuable and valid methodological tools in the hands of social scientists to undertake the investigation of pressing social problems. However, it is my observation that the privileging of these methods over others is also generated by the inevitable insecurity of the adopter rather than the creator of methodological approaches. As the social sciences took these methods from the natural sciences, the social sciences can be seen as somewhat the zealous converts, seeking to constantly and overtly assert their pious scientific credentials often, with disdain for the backwards 'folk' religion of the qualitative researcher. As someone with a natural science background, I can attest that in my experience those in the natural sciences do not have such a need to assert their scientific credentials, and being 'scientific' is something that is done intuitively and securely. There is something to be said for the methodological distinctiveness of the human sciences that require greater degrees of nuance to understanding the complexities and peculiarities of the human condition (Moon, 1975).

This is especially pertinent for a book of this nature. In seeking to understanding the diverse experiences, compositions and lived experiences of a group in French society, one single methodological approach, be it humanist or inductivist, would be neither sufficient nor advisable. That is why each chapter, with its specific focus, will use different tools from the social toolbox to examine the phenomena to be interrogated. They are, however, united in their focus on the discursive and symbolic, and the means by which meaning is rendered through social construction, whether this is to be found in the discussion of war memorials as a means to explore the various ways in which the French colonial legacy has been handled symbolically at home, or through the examination of popular culture forms such as rap music and pornography to understand how the various, often orientalist, essentialist and indeed securitised, gender roles for French Muslims are socially constructed by these cultural artefacts.

It is also important to briefly pause here and be more specific about what kind of social constructivism is to be employed and to acknowledge some of the conceptual baggage which it carries. Social constructivism has a long and storied history in the social sciences since it was coined by Berger and Luckman (1966). The conceptual underpinning of this school of thought contests that reality is socially situated and that knowledge is constructed through interaction with social stimuli in works such as the invention of tradition (Hobsbawm & Ranger, 1984). This is a conceptual tradition that is strongly rooted in the relational nature of social experience, where the meaning that we render to the social world and its wide and diverse range of actors and artefacts comes from our social experience of how meaning should be interpreted. This is not to say that social constructivism does not come without critique, and it has been critiqued in its more extreme forms as promoting the idea that constructions take place instrumentally by those with an interest in reality being shaped in a particular way (Hacking, 2000). This has clear Marxist overtones of a 'ruling class' perpetuating consciously a 'false consciousness' for nefarious ends. It is also true that a vulgarisation of social constructivism insists that social constructivists do not believe in any 'objective' facts, and is thus an unrealistic and 'floppy' postmodern thought that holds that everything is a construct. This is an erroneous, and unfortunate, caricature of a theoretical position that has underpinned massive advances in the social sciences, including the opening up of gender roles to criticism and interrogation (Beauvoir, 2011).

This book cautiously adopts a more 'realist' view of social constructivism advanced by scholars such as Elder-Vass (2013) and Gorski (2013). This seeks to combine the beneficial aspects of social constructivism with the realist work of scholars such as Bhaskar (2008), to bring the role of social reality and social structures back into the work of social constructivism. Thus, as advanced by this book, employing a socially constructivist stance does not mean that 'everything is a construct', nor does it argue that 'nothing is real', but rather it is concerned with understanding the relationship between object occurrences and the subjective meanings ascribed to them that is the essence of social constructionism. A masterful example of such scholarship can be found in the discussion of how the stories and myths around the Zulu king Shaka were embroidered and enhanced through the retelling of these stories by individuals who did not consciously engage in the processes of social construction but were rather simply telling stories (Hamilton, 1998). This is a pertinent point to make in that actors in any given situation constructing and reconstructing reality are diverse, as are their interests, indeed if they have any, in constructing reality in particular ways. This is a ready observation applicable with the direct empirical concerns of this book that two examples highlight very well. Flags exist in the physical world and people die in acts of mass violence, but it is our rendering of meanings that tells us that this is our national flag that has this meaning, and also that an act of mass violence like the Charlie Hebdo shooting is an act of terrorism. This is where advances in critical realism also become highly useful and extremely complementary to social constructivism, in that critical realism seeks to highlight that the nature of the social world may be very different from the way that humans perceive it (Gorski, 2013). Thus, here it is about looking beyond the observable and into the processes which go on behind the scenes to understand why an act of violence is constructed as terrorism in the same way as an arrangement of rectangles of colour are reified as the national flag.

1.3   Who Are They? French Muslims, Names, Numbers and Confusion

Defining the entirety of 'French Muslims' will clearly present some analytical and conceptual challenges to overcome the obvious pitfalls of essentialising an extremely diverse group of approximately 6 million individuals. The use of 'approximately' here highlights the first and perhaps most obvious 'pitfall' we face, specifically in the French context—namely that we have no reliable statistics on exactly how many French Muslims there are, nor what their ethnic or religious statuses are. However, even in contexts with reliable numbers, such as the UK, discussing a Muslim whole, or specific Muslim sub-groups runs up against the issues of homogenisation and essentialisation of groups into monolithic wholes who think, act, practice and believe in the same ways. Clearly, this runs completely counter to the rationale for this book and to aid in overcoming these issues it is necessary to consult the existing literature on Muslim identities. This should be the case for those not just in the French context but in the broader contexts of Muslim migrant communities in non-Muslim societies, and also on the diverse social, political, religious and cultural variations in Muslim identities in the Islamic world.

In terms of numbers, the French state defines the collection of statistics on racial, ethnic and religious origins of its citizens as unconstitutional under article 1 of the French constitution of 4 October 1958, which states that the republic will 'ensure the equality of all citizens before the law, without distinction of origin, race or religion. It shall respect all beliefs' (Assemblé Nationale, 2018). Clearly, the development and deployment of this principle requires greater unpacking, which will occur later in Chap. 2, when this book turns to the discussion of identity categories under the republic and how they are formally operationalised by the various levels of the French state. However, here the observation that this clause has been interpreted as incompatible with the collection of any statistics that would give us a clear idea of how many Muslims actually lived in France opens up a big enough can of empirical worms to keep us occupied. Therefore, in the absence of statistics we are forced to rely on estimates. The Pew Research Centre estimated the French Muslim population to be 5.72 million in 2016, 8.8% of the population (Hackett, 2017). As mentioned, this cannot be proven or disproven by any official source, so the number is open to all kinds of contestation and uncertainty from those both on the left and right of French politics. The salacious and attention-seeking world of aspiring to elected office unfortunately rarely has time for sober and reasoned estimates that do little to grab headlines. In this vein, in past decade both Azouz Begag, researcher at the CNRS (French National Centre for Scientific Research), and the far-right political party the Front National both argued that a more accurate estimate of the Muslim population in France was between 15 and 20 million, or between 22% and 30% of the French population of 66.9 million (Begag, 2011; Jacob, 2016). While they have clearly very different political agendas to their large estimates of the numbers of Muslims in France, the situation of uncertainty means that it is not possible to prove or disprove these estimates either way. Additionally, this situation of confusion around numbers is not something that simply sits in the academic or political spheres of discussion, and this uncertainty is not lost on the generally French population. A poll has shown a tendency to overestimate the Muslim population at around 31% of the population, so around 20.74 million Muslims (Jacob, 2016). This confusion and contestation over numbers does not stop at the more general level of estimating the size of the 'Muslim' population of France. Even estimating the numbers of the far smaller and more specific subset of radicals, terrorists or ultra-conservative Muslims throws up similar confusion between various estimates. However, these difficulties do not stop politicians and scholars making estimates about the numbers in France. Manual Vals, when he was prime minister, estimated that there were 15,000 individuals being monitored in France for radicalisation, yet only 1400 are currently under judicial prosecution for terror offences (France 24, 2016). However, as the issues with the terminology are numerous, and Vals also does not give further details on these numbers, they mean very little. Samir Amghar, researcher at the University Libre de Bruxelles estimates that there are between 20,000 and 30,000 'ultra-orthodox' Muslims in France—less than 1% of the practising Muslim population of France (Dell'Oro, 2015). This figure of ultra-orthodox does not in any way suggest that these French Muslims are violent or likely to commit acts of jihad. Thus, the number of jihadists in France, even if it was as Vals states at 15,000, is less than 1% of the French Muslim population. Thus, this corroborates with Khosrokhavar's (2014) findings that radicalisation is an 'ultra-minority' phenomenon that remains at the fringes. This ties strongly to the observations made at the start of this chapter that the discussion of French Muslims requires significant banalisation and nuancing, given the disproportionate attention that this small, unrepresentative fringe is subject to from the media, politicians and scholars alike.

Beyond the statistics, and somewhat complicating them, is indeed the differential nature of the citizenship status of Muslims in France. This presents quite a problem in regards to claims here made about taking an analysis from the angle of 'French Muslims' because many of those caught in the conceptual net of 'Muslim' deployed by politicians, the far right and indeed scholars, on a de jure level are not French in the sense of having official French nationality. Indeed, when this book turns to examining the role of French Muslims in the French security services from the colonial era onwards, this is further complicated by the hierarchies of colonialism that grant differential citizenship statuses to those under colonial rule, dependent on their ethnic and religious characteristics. Indeed, it was argued by some theorists of the colonial enterprise that Muslim 'Arab' North Africans could never fully 'evolve' into Frenchmen like those black Africans from Senegal could (Camiscioli, 2009). Like many questions to do with migrants and minorities there is no simple answer to this conundrum (Jackson-Preece, 2005; Roe, 2004). This is where this book seeks to subvert the category of 'French Muslim' and use it to move beyond both a notion of citizenship and religion, because sociologically this category is deployed to mean many different things discursively in France. Thus, this book, with some important caveats of course, seeks to use the term 'French Muslim' in a deliberately diverse and dynamic sociological way that should not be seen in terms uniquely as conferred by a certain passport or by adherence to a particular religious orthodoxy. Indeed, thinking about the discourse created around French Muslims, as threats to the state and social order, does not discriminate on the basis of citizenship status, ethnic origin nor degree of religious practice when lumping 'Muslims' together in one homogenous whole. As such, taking this term, this book seeks to take this homogenising logic and flip it upside down to actually describe, discuss and analyse the heterogeneity of French Muslims in both social functions and discursive entities.

This is only the first conceptual and empirical issue that this book faces. A far larger and more complicated sticking point, and indeed the biggest conceptual, ontological and epistemological headache, of writing a book of this nature exists precisely in the essentialising logic set in train by writing a book on 'French Muslims'. This title instantly suggests that there is actually a coherent group of French Muslims around which such a work can be based. This would fall into the traps of essentialism in assuming that 'categories are real ... they are discovered (rather than invented), they are natural (rather than artificial), they predict other properties' (Gelman, 2003). This logic is extremely dangerous for a number of reasons, most notably because the assumptions that they exist out in the social world in a homogeneous form can be used to predict other properties that are undesirable and untrue. In short, being a French Muslim is being something that is natural and inescapable and could mean that you are likely to become a terrorist. The Copenhagen School labels this kind of logic as 'securitising', because assumptions of group homogeneity enable far easier construction of an entire group as a security threat based on the violence of a tiny number of the heterogeneous group's members (Buzan, Waever, & Wilde, 1997; Huysmans, 1998; Rumelili, 2013). This logic, however, has unfortunately not only taken root in France (Cesari, 2013), but also more widely across Europe (Cesari,

2009). This is particularly important for a book that is rooted in studies of discourse and narratives, in that the dominant narrative context is one where Muslims are not only some kind of normative exception to the dominant culture, but one that is an exception at least partially based on security terms. Thus Muslims, and Islam as a body of thought, are constructed as existential threats against the dominant order of things. This takes on a multitude of connotations and forms, whether in terms of the direct physical security threat of terror attacks, or the more abstract and normative epistemological threat to liberal European values. A sociologist may pick up on this logic around group categories and call it racism or marginalisation. Indeed, many of the 'urban' forms of marginalisation so masterfully descried and expressed in the work of Wacquant (2007) in the Parisian suburbs intersect with, define and in turn are defined by the fact that a large portion of the marginalised population that he is discussing are actually French Muslims in one way or another. Here, a far longer standing construction involving French Muslims as physical security threats has been the broader association of men of minority ethnic origin with anti-social behaviour and criminality. Thus, this brief example demonstrates the dynamic and fluid nature of how security threats are constructed.

To avoid this logic this book has to be extremely careful about exactly how it constructs and deploys the terms French Muslim and indeed Muslim in this context of social enquiry. Empirically, homogeneity is far from the reality of French Muslims. It is necessary to be clear from the start that there is a large variation of forms of practices, level of adherence to dogma, and variations between different types of folk (Malešević, 2007) or vernacular (Kapaló, 2013) Islam that originates in Turkey, North Africa, West Africa or the Comoros Islands. Not to digress too much into the study of religions, it should be noted that there is a sociological paradox which Islam, and by extension Muslims, present. While the vast majority of those who came to France from the above Muslim regions are indeed all Muslim, and all Sunni, this observation should not homogenise them. This is because Islam is ostensibly one of the universalist religions, taking an almost republican view that all men and women are equal regardless of colour in their value before God. Islam also presents unified central beliefs (one God, and Mohamed as his prophet) and to some extent a unified set of practices (five daily prayers), but how this is operationalised in daily life in any given context is subject to significant variation. As the scholar Hamza Yousef once said, Islam is like a glass, it takes on the colour of the liquid inside. As such, culture, ethnic identities, local context, pre-Islamic practices and other influences overlap and meld together to create 'local vernacular Islams' with particular flavours and nuances. Thus, this is not different in the diaspora and as such again the use of the term French Muslims is an umbrella which connects both Islam to Frenchness, but importantly an umbrella which seeks to bring together how these many Islams can, and indeed do, connect to the many 'Frenchnesses' present in France. A Muslim of Algerian origin living in Marseille may find it extremely difficult to relate to his relative from Paris, ostensibly of the same faith, ethnic background and indeed republican citizenship. During my research I have witnessed such conflicts play out for a number of reasons. This could be because of their very different experiences of 'Frenchness' between the landlocked grey capital city and the sunny sea-facing Mediterranean port and the conflicting sense of civic pride each has for their respective home town. This could also possibly be due to opposing views on football, as Paris Saint-Germain and Olympique de Marseille fans never see eye to eye. These are just small examples of the cross-cutting divides which contradict notions of a homogenous mass of Muslims with common ideological and religious goals to dominate a declining Christian Europe. Indeed, a lack of Islamic unity has been a common bug bear of jihadists for decades—further evidence of this inability to easily lump together human diversity. Adding to this complexity is the issue of converts to Islam from those of white French background. There are estimated to be between 70,000–110,000 converts to Islam in France from a variety of cultural, religious and socio-economic backgrounds. Again, both the conversion experience, and the particular 'Frenchness' upon which the convert's new faith of Islam grafts, are extremely variable.

This simple discussion introduces a concept that is fundamental to understanding the state of play of the contemporary Muslim population of France—its increasing 'super diversity' (Vertovec, 2007). This term was not introduced to describe the dynamics of Muslim populations, but rather to describe a broader shift in the structure of minority populations in advanced countries of immigration. Simple conceptions of a 'multicul-turalism' of well-defined minority communities that exist in contrast with 'majority' populations are increasingly problematic. For example, the structuring of multiculturalism in the UK in the latter half of the twentieth century relied to a large degree on their being identifiable 'minorities'—mainly those migrants from British ex-colonies such as India, Pakistan and the Caribbean. In France, while such state-defined 'multicultural' characteristics were never created, the dominant, and sim-plistic, ethnic characterisation of French society can be summed up by the 'black, blanc, beur' characterisation that emerged out of the 1998 World Cup win by France's black, white and North African national team.

In both the British and the French case, these structures were simplis-tic and empirically incorrect in their formulation in that they never reflected the reality of society and 'reified' these social categories with a homogeneity that they never possessed. However, the changing patterns of migration at the end of the twentieth century and beginning of the twenty-first century even further rendered these ideas unrepresentative, as large-scale, unskilled labour migration from former colonies was replaced by diverse flows of political refugees, skilled workers and such like. As Vertovec (2007) asserts, this has created a far less structured situ-ation of 'super diversity' which can be applied to the French, and indeed British, Muslim communities. This can be seen in the somewhat of a reversal of the post-colonial labour migration logic in the flow of Algerian refugees of the 1990s Islamist civil war to the UK, settling for example in the Finsbury Park area of North London, and the Pakistani migrants who have set up home and businesses in the Parisian suburb of Sarcelles. Clearly, these flows do not match the post-colonial labour migration flows in terms of magnitude, but they do demonstrate the increasing diversity of Muslim communities in both places. This is a good concep-tual entry point when thinking about why France's Muslims as a simple dichotomy between a white French society and 'problematic' North African communities has never been, and is definitely not, symptomatic of the current state of play. Inward migration from a large number of other countries and regions of the world massively complicates this issue. Indeed, as does the phenomena of conversion to Islam from a wide range of backgrounds, both white French and immigrant, that gives the idea of

French Muslimness a far more diverse and complicated reality than is often given credence in contemporary discussions.

This very basic discussion about the heterogeneity of the French Muslims' community demonstrates that perhaps the most pertinent conceptual observation here is the need to move beyond seeing 'Muslim' as a uniquely religious identity category. This may appear somewhat paradoxical given observations above that the central unifying logic of the term 'Muslim' seems to be found in the adherence to religion based on the scriptures revealed to Mohamed in the Arabian Peninsula nearly 1400 years ago. And in some cases, there is a factual basis to this in that those who are referred to as French Muslims will indeed have some contemporary attachment to, or some antecedent historical connection to, this faith. However, even in saying that, we are beginning to lose the grip on an idea that there is a central category of individuals united around common beliefs—some of those who are covered by the umbrella term French Muslim were not born as such and chose at some point to convert to the religion. Indeed, there are also many for whom the term 'Muslim' has lost any relevance to their daily actions other than the participation in cultural events. Going even further, there are many for whom the term 'Muslim' itself is something they define themselves against as atheists, communists or religious agnostics. Some of these threads will be unpicked when we come to interrogate the data we have on who the French Muslim population are. But it is worth dwelling on what exactly this nascent discussion of the relationship individuals have to religion means conceptually. Clearly, the first important observation goes back to the point that to capture the social reality that we are seeking, we need to move beyond understanding French Muslims simply in religious terms and be open to the possibilities of Muslims having social relevance in numerous ways. Luckily, we are not treading on virgin ground here and there is a large and well-structured sociological literature to draw upon.

A worthwhile starting point can be found in Roy (2004), who argues that 'Muslim' as a category in France, as in the rest of Europe, shares many characteristics with ethnic categories such as 'black' and 'white'. This opens up the possibility for what may seem a self-evidently religious category to actually be constituted by a range of identity characteristics. Indeed, this builds neatly in the Muslim context on Stuart

Hall's observation that 'race is the modality in which class is lived' (Hall, Roberts, Clarke, Jefferson, & Critcher, 1978). Thus, here the category of Muslims is a modality through which a number of class, racial, cultural and gender categories are lived. That is to say, it is a category that can relate as much to inter-subjective, non-religious forms of identification (such as ethnic, national and/or cultural) as it does to any religious affiliation. This is important because the logic of marginalisation vis-à-vis Muslims in France is often seen in simply religious terms, when in fact it draws heavily on notions of class and race (Wacquant, 2007). When Sarkozy sought political capital from the 2005 suburban riots in France, he did not address the disturbance in ways that would become familiar ten years later, as isolated religious communities outside of the French state, as Kepel described them in 2012 (G. Kepel, 2012). Rather, he chose to argue that what was required was the cleaning of the estates with expensive, designer pressure washers (Karcher) to remove the 'racailles'. While it is worth pointing out that he was correctly not addressing a population of rioters who could by any stretch of the imagination be described as 100% Muslim, the choice of term demonstrates the secular, pejorative aspects of French Muslim identity. Here, 'racailles' refers to the poor youth in French cities who wear sportswear and are associated with the French rap subculture. This was not the first time that this term was used to describe a subsection of French youth in such a way. The then equal opportunities minister, Azouz Begag, used the term to describe young people who 'frighten everyone … and ignore traffic lights just as they challenge all other codes of social conduct' (Pulham, 2005) A useful comparison is with the construction of the white British underclass around the term 'chav' (Hayward & Yar, 2006; Tyler, 2008). Here, these terms emerge in the context of reconfiguring the idea of the underclass in increasingly pejorative terms, linking undesirable and vulgar social characteristics with socio-economic statuses.

An important stepping stone from this discussion of the sociological characteristics of the French Muslim population, and indeed something touched on in the Begag quote above, is a sense somehow that Islam, and by extension Muslims, have become a 'threat' to France and as such have become 'securitised'. Begag's discussion above rightly points to this occurring in 'secular' ways towards Muslims long before the Charlie

Hebdo attacks and before politically they were referred to via a religious marker. Indeed, the construction of the Muslim, and in particular the North African Muslim, as a threat is something that goes back much further. Its genesis harks back to the colonial era and worries about Muslims in North and West Africa agitating for independence, even before the bombings by the FLN were a feature of life in French Algeria (Fogarty, 2012). This idea of a 'threat' has been extremely dynamic and has changed dramatically over time—taking on Begag's idea of a criminal underclass in the latter half of twentieth century (Pulham, 2005), before morphing once again into a notion of an Islamist terror threat in the early twenty-first century (Hussey, 2014). This is precisely the kind of dynamism that the Copenhagen School's concept of securitisation (Buzan et al., 1997; Huysmans, 1998; Roe, 2004) so elegantly captures in their affirmation that security is not a simple objective fact, but rather is something which is 'socially constructed'. As previously mentioned, social constructivism has often been vulgarised as a wishy-washy body of postmodern thought which argues for no universal truths and that 'everything is a construct'. This vulgar caricature does not do justice to a body of thought which offers so much more to the social sciences in understanding that, while there are indeed objective facts to the world (for example, people do commit acts of mass violence), it is important also to acknowledge that the meaning ascribed to any objective fact is rendered through, and contested by, relational social processes (i.e. said act of mass violence being labelled as 'terrorism' or the just actions of a sovereign state protecting its territorial integrity). As such, while French Muslims have experienced a period where their 'threat' was constructed through, and understood in terms of, a violent urban underclass as late as the 2005 riots (see inter alia Cesari, 2005; Hargreaves, 2007; Wacquant, 2007), public discourse has shifted to discussions of jihadist terror threats and religiosity, not only class, being the characteristics which render French Muslims a threat.

I would be unfair to single out France here, as this is a far broader trend in developed democracies across Europe. We don't need to cast our minds far back to remember when declaring 'multiculturalism' a failed project seemed de rigueur amongst European leaders, paradoxically and ironically even for the French President Sarkozy, despite France never actually formally embracing multiculturalism. It seems quite farcical to declare a project a failure that one never actually undertook. But this political irony underscores a far more serious point in that Muslim communities and migration have been presented as a source of instability for the best part of a decade, if not longer (Kaya, 2009). This process goes much further than simple recent security concerns brought to the fore by the wave of Islamist terror attacks on Western Europe in the past decade. Rather, there is a much longer-term, more diffuse ideological element to the securitisation of Europe's, and indeed France's, Muslims, pitching them as culturally alien and an existential threat to the Western liberal state and order which must be controlled, regulated and restrained (Cesari, 2013). Coming back to the founding conceptual framing of the Copenhagen School, that security threats are created through 'talking' security—through narratives and discourses (Buzan et al., 1997; Huysmans, 1998)—brings us back to this book's founding methodological statement in that narrative, discourse and elaborating the diversity of domains in which they are created and disseminated in and through is the task to which the substantive chapters of this book turn to.

1.4 The Path from Here: Charting This Journey Through the Social, Political and Cultural Experiences of French Muslims

To echo what has previously been said, a key aim of this book is not only banalise the French Muslim experience through examining a wide range of historical, social and political happenings and structures, but also to examine French Muslims beyond the highly securitised context of recent years that have been dominated by questions of terrorism, security and radicalisation. However, taking a diverse approach sets this book up for failure from the start for those who are seeking an account which contains every last word on the subject of French Muslims. Thus, rather than being *the* final account on this subject, this book seeks to continue to open up debates in the much wider field of sociological enquiry into questions of ethnicity, race, religion and post-colonialism in contemporary France which have been years in the making (see inter alia the masterful work of Hargreaves, 2007, *Multi-Ethnic France*). It is hoped by focusing on French Muslims through the themes of each chapter that greater and broader understandings can be reached about the more general context for post-colonial migrants in France, while also illuminating some of the specific domains in which narratives about Muslims in France are constructed.

This first chapter of this book will seek to tackle one of the most dynamic and notorious facets of the French Muslim experience—the assimilationist stance of the French state. Here, headline-grabbing occurrences, such as the regulation of women's dress and banning of religious symbols, obscure what is in fact a highly complex reality where many republics situate themselves vis-à-vis assimilation in a number of different ways. Even assimilation itself is not per se a unified approach but rather constituted by two key approaches that the state employs towards forms of difference in not recognising religions in the political realm (laïcité) or other markers of identity such as ethnicity or race. This approach emerged from the reality that 'France' as a unified cultural, linguistic or religious entity has never actually existed, but has required constant attempts to socially construct a common identity out of regional cultural and linguistic traditions with very little in common. Weber's (1976) concept of turning peasants into Frenchmen captures this very well. In the contemporary era this approach stems from the commitment of article 1 of the French constitution of 4 October 1958, which states that the republic will 'ensure the equality of all citizens before the law, without distinction of origin, race or religion. It shall respect all beliefs' (Assemblé Nationale, 2018). However, this is only the beginning of the broader discussion on how the state relates to this question of difference for two key reasons. Firstly, one does not have to be a lawyer or public policy expert to notice the vagary of the actual constitutional commitment to not recognise difference. As with all abstract principles, operationalising this in different social, political, economic and historical contexts is not only open to significant and constant interpretation, but actually *requires* interpretation for each context. Secondly, there exists significant evidence of contexts in which the French state has actually worked to institutionalise difference in extremely negative ways, even when having this commitment to equality—an irony was not lost on those in French colonies who were considered 'less human' than their white counterparts, nor the French Jews who were deported under the Vichy regime to the death camps of central Europe. Arguments could and indeed have been made that rather than being examples of the failings of France's assimilationist position, these examples demonstrate deviance from it and also re-enforce the need for an ever-stricter adherence to assimilation. These arguments miss, however, the key point about republican assimilation that unites it with every value-based political system—that it is not a panacea, nor is its meaning fixed or immune to change over time. This is why, to this day, the French courts are busy trying to figure out what is exactly acceptable under assimilation and what is not—highlighted by the recent controversy over the burkini ban, which originated in local manifestations of the many republics and was overturned by one of the central, national, facets of the many republics. This example highlights yet another complexity in this situation—just as there is not one assimilation, there is not one republic which has to interpret and implement it—but rather a somewhat rag-tag collection of civil servants, local politicians, lawyers, judges and all manner of other functionaries which exist in different manifestations of the republic. Thus, both the lofty chamber of the Conseil d'état in the Grand Palais-Royal in grey, rainy Paris, and the more tumble-down Hôtel de Ville on the sun-drenched old port of Marseille, must come up with their own definition of what the daily operationalisation of this political system actually means to them. This prompted the ex-mayor of Marseille Robert Vigouroux to write a book about his experience of governing with the paradoxical mix of 'laïcité + religions' (Vigouroux & Ouaknin, 2005). This also highlights the second key feature of the way that assimilation works in practice in situations of political isolation. Here, actors engage in policy innovation separate both from each other and from the central state. At least in part this is due to the fear of being engaged in a polemic about violating assimilationist dogma which can bring an end to policy innovation. The intrusion of European forms of government (the European Union and the Council of Europe) into the French context also add a further layer of complexity to this situation, because of the political dichotomy created by Europe's insistence on respecting and celebrating ethnic and cultural pluralism and France's assimilationist stance. This is problematic for policy contexts where policy innovators and implementers are required to meld together two very different bureaucratic cultures.

This question of bureaucratic cultures and the recognition of religion sets up well the second chapter of this book, which seeks to account for both the contemporary and historical discourses around the participation of Muslims in the French security services. This is because the army is one of the few branches of the state which has an exception and can provide religious services to troops because of their inability to physically leave the institution to seek independent religious provision. However, this is not where the role of the security services stops in its relations to the question of Muslims in France more generally. France, like much of Western Europe, is littered with the stone and bronze memorials of war. In France, these are poignant reminders of not just the sacrifices made by Muslim troops for the values of France, whether positive liberalism and freedom against the Nazis or the far more negative oppression of the French empire, but they also serve as reminders that the French state has not always been so reluctant to both recognise and valorise the origins of those who serve in its security services. This is important because it has been estimated that in the present day, there are at least numerically ten times more Muslims serving the security needs of the republic than there are jihadis that have joined Islamist groups (Roy, 2015). Thus, it is necessary to analyse both the historical commemoration of Muslim service, in addition to those that seek to do so in the contemporary era. This is where, in the absence of historical monuments to read, other sources such as mainstream and social media (for example, Twitter) can provide important, and all too rare, insights into the contemporary Muslim contribution to the French security services.

The observation about the far larger number of French Muslims who serve the republic than those who serve jihadist groups is the empirical reality which sets up the conceptual backbone of this book's chapter on French Muslims and jihadism. Rather than it being a product of a historically and socially rooted 'war' between France and 'its Arabs' (Hussey,

2014), it is a highly unrepresentative anomaly that is not indicative of broader problems. This deconstructivist stance taken from critical terrorism studies (CTS) offers this book the ability to take a stance in direct opposition to those scholars and media sources that would like to construct grand theories of French jihadism, whether as a product of historical grievances or contemporary socio-economic dysfunctions. Both of these are extremely dangerous narratives about French Muslims because they, perhaps inadvertently, create causal links between socio-economic deprivation and disagreement with the colonial era, and becoming a terrorist. Indeed, there are millions of French Muslims with these opinions that do not commit acts of violence. Empirical studies demonstrate that there is no common thread in the biography of French jihadists which allows us to isolate them. What is important, and for which generalisations can be made, are the banal security failings of the French state which, independent of any 'Muslim' related issues have presided over an influx of military-grade weapons from the Balkans onto the streets of French cities. Another means by which this chapter argues that a greater insight can be gleaned into the French Muslim relationship to jihadist violence is through the analysis of the victims of jihadist terror attacks. It should not be surprising, given the integral social and economic roles that French Muslims play in society, that a significant number of the victims of recent jihadist violence in France have actually been French Muslims. Analysing these victims' biographies provides a rare insight into the banality and integrated nature of the French Muslim condition in a situation where media coverage overwhelmingly focuses on the violent exceptions of French Muslim security threats.

This book then moves on to analyse a key means to understand the discourse created around Muslims in contemporary France in terms of orientalised and exotified gendered roles created in French popular culture. This analysis adds to a lively literature and debate about the ways in which gender forms an important means by which French Muslims politically mobilise, but also constitutes a vital component of what makes policy narratives about the regulation of women's dress plausible. An underexplored aspect of constructions of femininities for French Muslims in the contemporary era are the means by which pornography, a now mainstream part of the French cultural landscape, acts as an orientalist medium which enables one to 'gaze' upon the internal other of the exotic French Muslim women. While the orientalist paintings of the nineteenth century set their feminine subjects in highly ornate harems and hammams, the contemporary internal other is gazed upon in the concrete suburban housing estate. Here, these women are constructed through an intersection of ethnicity and class, demonstrating that the internal other is not simply a 'Muslim', but rather contains significant discursive recourse to class. Masculinities are also relevant in the orientalist constructions of the contemporary French Muslim, in erotic production where French Muslim men seeks to abuse, control and oppress women. However, masculinities play a more important role in the construction of the 'Muslim gangster' in French popular culture. Here, overt religious piety intersects with class and criminality to construct the new oriental man, whose 'savagery' has metamorphosed from the noble warrior of the desert to the ruthless gangster of the suburban housing estate.

The role of gender opens up a wider discussion of their situation vis-à-vis the broader constructions of French national identity. This chapter seeks to sketch out three key paradoxes of contemporary French nationalism that demonstrate the differential treatment French Muslims are subject to, sometimes as part of the broader question of post-colonial minorities, in the re-creation of the French nation at the intersection of culture and politics. Firstly, narratives created about the suburban riots of 2005 sit as problematic in a broader national context where national identity is significantly defined as produced by repeated rebellion against oppressive socio-economic conditions. Secondly, and less overtly political, the involvement of politicians in attempts to regulate and at times even prosecute French rap once again stand in contrast to a broader cultural tradition of not only accepting, but celebrating controversial forms of cultural expression. Finally, ongoing debates about the 'Frenchness' of non-white players in the French national team over the past 20 years demonstrate the ongoing struggles to create a French cultural identity that can include French Muslims, and other post-colonial minorities, as integral parts of the French story.

Bibliography

Assemblé Nationale. (2018). *Welcome to the English Website of the French National Assembly – Assemblée Nationale.* Retrieved August 21, 2018, from http://www2.assemblee-nationale.fr/langues/welcome-to-the-english-website-of-the-french-national-assembly

de Beauvoir, S. (2011). *The Second Sex* (C. Borde & S. Malovany-Chevallier, Trans.) (1st ed.). New York: Vintage.

Begag, A. (2011). *Arithmétique migratoire, Azouz Begag: Il y a 15 à 20 millions de musulmanes en France.* Retrieved January 5, 2018, from https://www.daily-motion.com/video/xiwsnc

Berger, P. L., & Luckman, T. (1966). *The Social Construction of Reality* (Later Reprint ed.). New York: Anchor Books.

Bhaskar, P. R. (2008). *A Realist Theory of Science.* London; New York: Verso.

Bourmeau, S. (2015, January 2). *Scare Tactics: Michel Houellebecq Defends His Controversial New Book.* Retrieved February 7, 2019, from https://www.theparisreview.org/blog/2015/01/02/scare-tactics-michel-houellebecq-on-his-new-book/

Bouvet, L. (2015). *L'insécurité culturelle.* Paris: Fayard.

Brenner, E., & Bensoussan, G. (2015). *Les territoires perdus de la République* (3rd ed., amended and enlarged). Paris: Fayard/Pluriel.

Brown, M. D. (2006). Comparative Analysis of Mainstream Discourses, Media Narratives and Representations of Islam in Britain and France Prior to 9/11. *Journal of Muslim Minority Affairs, 26*(3), 297–312. https://doi.org/10.1080/13602000601141216

Bruckner, P. (2006). *La tyrannie de la pénitence.* Paris: Grasset.

Bruckner, P. (2018). *An Imaginary Racism: Islamophobia and Guilt.* Medford, MA: Polity Press.

Buzan, B., Waever, O., & de Wilde, J. (1997). *Security: A New Framework for Analysis* (UK ed.). Boulder, CO: Lynne Rienner Publishers.

Caldwell, C. (2014). *Une révolution sous nos yeux: Comment l'islam va transformer la France et l'Europe (Poche).* Paris: L'artilleur.

Camiscioli, E. (2009). *Reproducing the French Race: Immigration, Intimacy and Embodiment in the Early Twentieth Century.* Durham, NC: Duke University Press.

Cesari, J. (2005). *Ethnicity, Islam and les Banlieues: Confusing the Issues* [Online]. Brooklyn, NY: Social Science Research Council. Retrieved from http://riotsfrance.ssrc.org/Cesari/

Cesari, J. (2009). *The Securitisation of Islam in Europe*. Vol. 15. CEPS. Retrieved from http://aei.pitt.edu/10763/1/1826.pdf

Cesari, J. (2013). European Conundrum: Integration of Muslims or Securitisation of Islam? *World Review*. Retrieved from https://berkleycenter. georgetown.edu/essays/european-conundrum-integration-of-muslims-or-securitisation-of-islam

Couvelaire, L. (2019, February 12). *Antisémitisme: en France, les différents visages d'une haine antijuive insidieuse et banalisée*. Retrieved from https://www.lemonde.fr/societe/article/2019/02/12/en-france-les-differents-visages-d-une-haine-anti-juive-insidieuse-et-banalisee_5422326_3224.html

Dell'Oro, J. L. (2015). Combien y a-t-il de djihadistes en France et quels sont leurs profils? – *Challenges*. Retrieved October 1, 2018, from https://www.challenges.fr/france/combien-y-a-t-il-de-djihadistes-en-france-et-quels-sont-leurs-profils_45504

Elder-Vass, D. (2013). *The Reality of Social Construction* (Reprint ed.). Cambridge: Cambridge University Press.

Fogarty, R. S. (2012). *Race and War in France: Colonial Subjects in the French Army, 1914–1918*. Baltimore, MD: Johns Hopkins University Press.

France 24,. (2016). Des attentats déjoués "tous les jours" en France et 15 000 personnes radicalisées. Retrieved from https://www.france24.com/fr/20160911-terrorisme-franceattentats-dejoues-tous-jours-15000-personnes-radicalisees-valls

Gelman, S. A. (2003). *The Essential Child: Origins of Essentialism in Everyday Thought*. New York: Oxford University Press.

Gorski, P. S. (2013). What Is Critical Realism? And Why Should You Care? *Contemporary Sociology, 42*(5), 658–670. https://doi.org/10.1177/0094306113499533

Hackett, C. (2017). *5 Facts About the Muslim Population in Europe*. Retrieved October 1, 2018, from http://www.pewresearch.org/fact-tank/2017/11/29/5-facts-about-the-muslim-population-in-europe/

Hacking, I. (2000). *The Social Construction of What?* (Revised ed.). Cambridge, MA: Harvard University Press.

Hall, S., Roberts, B., Clarke, J., Jefferson, T., & Critcher, C. (1978). *Policing the Crisis: Mugging, the State, and Law and Order*. Macmillan. Retrieved from https://www.amazon.co.uk/Policing-Crisis-Mugging-Critical-Studies/dp/0333220617

Hamilton, C. (1998). *Terrific Majesty: The Powers of Shaka Zulu and the Limits of Historical Invention* (1st ed., 3rd ed.). Cambridge, MA: Harvard University Press.

Hargreaves, A. (2007). *Multi-Ethnic France: Immigration, Politics, Culture and Society* (2nd ed.). New York; London: Routledge.

Hayward, K., & Yar, M. (2006). *The 'Chav' Phenomenon: Consumption, Media and the Construction of a New Underclass*. Retrieved February 15, 2018, from http://journals.sagepub.com/doi/abs/10.1177/1741659006061708

Heneghan, T. (2007, November 29). *Why We Don't Call Them 'Muslim Riots' in Paris Suburbs*. Retrieved October 20, 2018, from http://blogs.reuters.com/faithworld/2007/11/29/why-we-dont-call-them-muslim-riots-in-paris-suburbs/

Hobsbawm, E., & Ranger, T. O. (1984). *The Invention of Tradition*. Cambridge: Cambridge University Press.

Houellebecq, M. (2017). *Soumission*. Paris: J'AI LU.

Hussey, A. (2014). *The French Intifada: The Long War Between France and Its Arabs*. London: Granta.

Huysmans, J. (1998). The Question of the Limit: Desecuritization and the Aesthetics of Horror in Political Realism. *Millennium – Journal of International Studies, 27*, 569–589.

Jackson-Preece, J. (2005). *Minority Rights: Between Diversity and Community*. London: Polity.

Jacob, E. (2016). *La population musulmane largement surestimée en France*. Retrieved from http://www.lefigaro.fr/actualite-france/2016/12/14/01016-20161214ARTFIG 00214-la-population-musulmane-largement-surestimee-en-france.php

Kapaló, J. A. (2013). Folk Religion in Discourse and Practice. *Journal of Ethnology and Folkloristics, 7*(1), 3–18.

Kaya, A. (2009). *Islam, Migration and Integration: The Age of Securitization*. Reston, VA: AIAA.

Kepel, G. (2012). *Banlieue de la République*. Paris: Institut Montaigne.

Khosrokhavar, F. (2014). *Radicalisation (fiche technique)*. Les éditions de la maison des sciences de l'home. Retrieved from http://www.editions-msh.fr/livre/?GCOI=27351100399910&fa=details

Kimlicka. (2010). The Rise and Fall of Multiculturalism: New Debates on Inclusion and Accommodation in Diverse Societies. In S. Vertovec & S. Wessendorf (Eds.), *The Multiculturalism Backlash: European Discourses, Policies and Practice*. London: Routledge.

Malešević, S. (2007). *Ernest Gellner and Contemporary Social Thought*. Cambridge, UK: Cambridge University Press. https://doi.org/10.1017/CBO9780511488795

Mamou, Y. (2018). *Le grand abandon: Les élites françaises et l'islamisme*. Paris: L'artilleur.

Max, A. (2017). Plan Anti-Kebab à Marseille reportage dans le centre-ville, entre boboïsation et «repas du pauvre». Retrieved from https://www.20minutes.fr/marseille/2097739-20170702-plan-anti-kebab-marseille-reportage-centre-ville-entre-boboisation-repas-pauvre

Moon, J. (1975). *The Logic of Political Inquiry: A Synthesis of Opposed Perspectives*. Reading, MA: Addison-Wesley.

Pulham, S. (2005, November 8). *Inflammatory Language*. Retrieved February 15, 2018, from http://www.theguardian.com/news/blog/2005/nov/08/inflammatoryla

Roe, P. (2004). Securitization and Minority Rights: Conditions of Desecuritization. *Security Dialogue, 35*, 279–292.

Roy, O. (2004). *Globalised Islam: The Search for a New Ummah*. London: C Hurst & Co Publishers Ltd.

Roy, O. (2015, January 10). *There Are More French Muslims Working for French Security Than for Al Qaeda*. Retrieved September 1, 2018, from https://www.huffingtonpost.com/olivier-roy/paris-attack-muslim-cliches_b_6445582.html

Rumelili, B. (2013). Identity and Desecuritisation: The Pitfalls of Conflating Ontological and Physical Security. *Journal of International Relations and Development, 18*, 52–74.

Tribalat, M. (2017). *Assimilation: la fin du modèle français: Pourquoi l'Islam change la donne*. Paris: L'artilleur.

Tyler, I. (2008). Chav Mum Chav Scum. *Feminist Media Studies, 8*(1), 17–34. https://doi.org/10.1080/14680770701824779

Vertovec, S. (2007). Super-Diversity and Its Implications. *Ethnic and Racial Studies, 30*(6), 1024–1054. https://doi.org/10.1080/01419870701599465

Vigouroux, R., & Ouaknin, J. (2005). *Laïcité + Religions: Marseille Espérance*. Marseille: Transbordeurs.

Wacquant, L. (2007). *Urban Outcasts: A Comparative Sociology of Advanced Marginality*. Retrieved from https://www.amazon.co.uk/Urban-Outcasts-Comparative-Sociology-Marginality/dp/0745631258/ref=sr_1_3?ie=UTF8&qid=1517652872&sr=8-3&keywords=wacquant

Weber, E. (1976). *Peasants into Frenchmen: The Modernization of Rural France, 1870–1914* (1st ed.). Stanford, CA: Stanford University Press.

Zemmour, E. (2009). *Le premier sexe*. Paris: J'AI LU.

Zemmour, E. (2014). *Le Suicide français*. Paris: Albin Michel.

Zemmour, E. (2018). *Destin français*. Paris: Albin Michel.

2

Many Republics, Many Solitudes: Europeanisation, Politics, Islam, Ethnicity and the State in France

2.1 Introducing the Many Republics and Their Dealings with Islam

The national burka ban, the regional burkini bans, halal food provision in schools. It seems that barely a year goes by when French Muslims are not the subject of either a new raft of regulatory law or huge, normative, media polemic about how aspects of their daily lives *should* be structured under the secular republic. However, on closer inspection it becomes clear that a situation that appears relatively simple and straightforward—a secular state dealing with contemporary questions of religion in public life—actually belies a much more complex structural and discursive reality (Cole, 2008; Raymond & Modood, 2007). There is firstly the important nuance that the commitments in the French constitution to the assimilationist ideas of colour- and religion-blind equality, and indeed how these should be operationalised in society, are far more ambiguous and complex than they appear. Additionally, it is all too easy to mistake these questions uniquely national in their scope, being contested and settled only at the national level. However, this is not the case and it is necessary to identify the multiplicity of actors, norms and levels of

© The Author(s) 2019
J. Downing, *French Muslims in Perspective*,
https://doi.org/10.1007/978-3-030-16103-3_2

governance that become involved in shaping this ongoing process for French Muslims and what is at stake for actors at all levels, in addition to identifying how they operate in situations of political solitudes that do not translate into national policy changes.

For the proponents of French secularism, the constant attention lavished on France's largest religious minority is a vital exercise in renewing, re-forming and ensuring the legacy of the very DNA of French political life—the commitment of article 1 of the French constitution of 4 October 1958, which states that the republic will 'ensure the equality of all citizens before the law, without distinction of origin, race or religion. It shall respect all beliefs' (Assemblé Nationale, 2018). This is the key principle for which the French political system is known, valorised and criticised: laïcité—the specific way that the French state separates religion from political life. However, the French republic is far more complex in this regard. In addition to the obvious question of religion under a secular republic, there is also the issue with the formal prohibition of discussion of race and ethnicity, not just at the national and local levels, but also in official government research (INSEE, 2016). Also, there is the lack of conceptual clarity even with the principle of laïcité, whose exact origin and form is far more flexible, subjective and fluid than it first seems. Already, we can see here from the wording of the constitution that there is more to discuss than simply a question of religion under the republic—there is also the question of race and ethnicity. This is critical in discussing the contemporary French Muslim experience because, as has been outlined earlier, the situation for Muslims in France, in common with the rest of Europe, is much more complex than simply a question of religion. Here the social category of Muslims takes on significant class and racial characteristics in its social construction (Wacquant, 2007). However, it still remains extremely complex, from the wording given above, to get from this commitment to radical, 'colour-blind' equality to actual policies and day-to-day operations of a functioning democracy.

This complexity and fluidity are a key reason, in addition to institutional and political racism and Islamophobia, for the recurring explosions of polemical and political attention lavished on how secularism should be operationalised in contemporary France. This is especially prominent in regard to how these principles relate to France's Muslim population. This is where both the casual observer and the trained scholar could be forgiven for marvelling at a situation where children's school meals seem far removed from the lofty ideals of the 1789 French Revolution and the operation of a large, European democracy. Additional wonderment could also be produced by noticing the paradox of France producing a law in 2010 specifically addressing the sartorial preferences of an estimated 1900 women—some 0.003% of the French population who wore the burka—when national unemployment hovered just below 10%. However, such observations, while valid, miss the key dimensions of laïcité, which go far beyond examining a specific law and the complexity of operationalising abstract constitutional principles. Laïcité is symbolically and discursively an extremely powerful symbol in French political and social discourse that lends politicians struggling with complex, systemic and intractable social ills such as unemployment a cloak of dynamism and potency. More diffusely, as demonstrated by controversies around halal school meals, this symbolic power resonates in far more banal, mundane and seemingly apolitical contexts, precisely because the importance of laïcité has transcended the purely legal context and has become a pillar of national identity. It is the aim of this chapter to make this first argument by tying together discussions around laïcité.

The cases above also demonstrate a significant and underexplored trend in the discussions around laïcité in France in the multifaceted nature of the French state and the effect this has on the principle's implementation. The burka was banned by the national French senate in 2010, while the burkini bans emanated from the local administration of Villeneuve-Loubet, and were subsequently overturned by France's highest national court, the Conseil d'État. This demonstrates from a legislative perspective the ways that the different levels of the French state can pull in different directions on any given religious issue, and even the same national level of the French state can contradict itself through the varying opinions of its different institutional bodies with different personnel, logics, and political and legal interests. What we are dealing with here, both in institutional and discursive senses, is a situation of multiple solitudes, multiple republics. What this means in this case is quite clear—the various parts of the French state operationalise the vague principles of assimilation in different ways depending on specific local contingencies—but always alone and without a comprehensive policy overhaul occurring at the national level. Borrowing from the concept of two solitudes, which describes the decades of isolation between the French- and English-speaking cultures of Canada, the idea of solitudes captures well the nuances of the contemporary French republic when confronted with discussing issues of managing both religious and ethnic differences because of this policy operationalisation and innovation occurring in isolation.

While the senate is made up of elected members, possibly keen on enjoying the political capital of a burka ban, the Conseil d'État's members are not subject to popular suffrage, and due to the separation of powers are outside of the central state's control and thus are freer in this case to make rulings based on jurisprudential, rather than political, concerns. This discussion of the purely legal begins to elucidate the multiplicity of ways that the question of religion and state are addressed in France concerning French Muslims. However, if we begin to open up and tease out the even broader, symbolic and discursive meanings and manifestations of this question that, while falling under the rubric of sitting under constitutional and legal principals, are not so obviously related nor specifically governed by them, we begin to see an even greater diversity of ways that different levels of the French state interpret and operationalise concepts of religion and ethnic difference in political life. Adding a further variable into this equation, France is a member of the European Union and the Council of Europe, both transnational bodies of governance that in some cases have judicial and political powers that trump the French state, a third level of power emerges in a formal sense above the French central state which itself sits above the manifestations of local state and power in France. Again, in a more discursive sense, these European institutions are of specific importance because, in addition to being able to make formal laws, they also formulate, advocate for, and enforce 'norms' of governance that are heavily wedded to ideas that plurality and diversity require not only legal protection, but also more diffusely public valorisation and celebration in a discursive and symbolic sense. This picture is very complex, and it is the task of this chapter to empirically and normatively make sense of this massive diversity.

2.2   Conceptualising Assimilation, Laïcité, Religion, Ethnicity and the Republic

As has been already alluded to, the relationship between the French republic and its contemporary Muslim citizens is far more complex than it first seems. Emphasising this complexity is not simply an exercise in academic nuance. Rather, it is fundamental in understanding the situation that Muslims in France face today because the laws, polemics, and indeed broader discursive context are shaped and rendered relevant by a long historical trajectory of exogenous and endogenous developments, shocks and political developments. Questions about Muslims in France are intimately tied to questions about the very nature of the French polity itself. This is because of the specifics of the post-revolutionary states that evolved through many external shocks, including the lingering shadows of collaboration with the Nazis during the Second World War and the brutality of the French overseas empire (Camiscioli, 2009). These two situations are key because they demonstrate how even a state and form of political organisation based overtly on religion and colour-blind equality can actually be cajoled and manipulated shockingly easily into not simply instituting racial hierarchies, as happened during the empire, but also quickly aiding and abetting in the extermination of European Jewry. This demonstrates the ahistorical nature of claims consistently made in French politics that the republican model is incapable of being racist, or indeed 'religion-ist' because of the constitutional commitment to radical equality. However, when thinking about the evolution of the principles of the separation of church and state in France, it is important to remember that this came out of a long evolution. The settlement of 1905 (loi du 9 décembre 1905 concernant la separation des Églises et de l'État) developed out of the progression from 1789 onwards of the move away from the Catholic church having a large role in political life. However, the term laïcité did not specifically appear in a French constitution until the fourth republic in 1946.

Two things become clear here that are important in understanding the dynamic and changing nature of the French policy landscape, which can seem on the surface extremely static. Firstly, the fact that France is on its fifth republic since the revolution of 1789 demonstrates the instability of the French political system. The constitution of 1958 signalled the fifth time the republic required significant redefinition in only 169 years. At this specific point, the unrest in Algeria had resulted in a coup by military officers disgruntled with the prospect of granting Algeria independence. Thus, Charles de Gaulle came out of retirement to act as a uniting figure for France, trading on his credentials and credibility as leader of the French Resistance in the Second World War. Here, he was required to re-craft the political system where he moved power away from the parliament and towards the president. Prior to this, the fourth republic was created after the liberation of France from Nazi occupation, with the third republic coming to an end due to Nazi occupation. Thus, both exogenous and endogenous shocks and crises have required the principles of the 1789 revolution to be re-formed to meet the needs of the times. This highlights a second and more abstract important point about the French state and constitutions, and indeed constitutional principles more generally—their need for operationalisation. Thus, article 1 of the fifth republic's constitution, outlining equality, clearly does not set out the specific nuts and bolts of any given policy platform and could be interpreted in any number of ways, some of which could be very different to the current French policy platform.

Therefore, laïcité does not have a formal legal definition beyond a vague commitment to it being 'of legal effect'. This explains, to a certain extent why over 100 years later the discussion of laïcité still stirs such strong political and legal debate in France, because the principle itself from the very beginning was more a legal 'spirit' than a legal 'letter', and as such it's exact applications in any detail very much depend on the specific interpretations and opinions of politicians, policy makers, lawyers and in a more public, discursive sense, scholars, journalists and commentators. Like all legal and political principles that are open to significant interpretation, such as 'justice', 'freedom' and 'democracy', this inbuilt flexibility enables both an adaptability to the time and circumstances at hand, but also undoubtedly to abuses of the original 'spirit' of the law in the way that this is translated into the 'letters' of any given legal edict. In short, the law is only as good as your lawyer.

A similar process is involved in the refusal by the state to recognise ethnic and racial differences. Again, it is important to note that there is not a specific constitutional commitment written in stone that prohibits the collection of ethnic or religious statistics, nor one that specifically sets out that these categories are a taboo. Rather, the current state of affairs has arisen from a process of jurisprudential reasoning that has adapted and changed to the competing demands of society, policy makers and scholars. These set out to interpret the same provision in article 1 of the French constitution of 4 October 1958, from which contemporary debates about laïcité emerge. Thus, similar ambiguity required the state to rule on exactly what this meant once again, this time in 1978 with an act on 'information technology and freedoms', which itself required updating by a decision of the French Constitutional Council on 15 November 2007. Thus, the principles outlined in the constitution, like all abstract legal and political concepts and/or commitments, require operationalising so that they can actually be put into logical practice under a political system at any given time. This ruling also gives important body to the question of statistics by outlining that official bodies can carry out studies of diversity of origin, discrimination and integration, but that these must be based on 'objective' data, such as a person's name, geographic origin or nationality prior to gaining French citizenship (INSEE, 2016). Here, we can see the genesis of some of the key principles that have come to mark French research and policy on this subject in recent decades, which Doytcheva (2007) refers to as 'territorial affirmative action', due to the concentration on geographical markers rather than those of religion or ethnicity. This has, however, come under significant private ridicule from scholars, policy makers and practitioners during my research, where they acknowledge the absurdities of 'playing the game'—pretending to investigate or solve one issue defined by class or geography when clearly the focus should be on ethnic or religious markers of difference. This has even been expressed as problematic in a funding sense, because these laws do not apply to funding applications for European money, where referencing and agreeing to operate on norms based on ethnic and religious diversity are often key requirements, only to then not be able to operationalise the resulting projects in such ways due to these data laws.

Further adding to this complexity is the provision within the ruling that subjective data, such as that based on 'feelings of belonging' can also be collected and used in resulting studies. This is highly confusing as surely this is the clear way around official banning of the collection of religion and ethnicity statistics by simply asking individuals what their feelings of belonging are. However, it is not that simple, as official bodies must submit plans for surveys on this subject to a regulatory board, the French Data Protection Authority (CNIL), to obtain their authorisation under article 2 of the 1978 act (INSEE, 2016). Thus, a gate-keeping system operates which further complicates questions of statistical collection of dissemination. These two principles come together to characterise France as a country that structures its political system around 'assimilation' rather than the 'multiculturalism' of other diverse democracies such as the UK, Holland and the USA. It is important to pause here for a brief discussion on multiculturalism from a state, politics and policy perspective, because it is a highly multivalent term that has produced varying policy perspectives. On a basic sociological level, multiculturalism can denote the reality of a society constituted of multiple cultural groups, with the groups defined as such either internally by self-definition or outside by society at large (Modood, 2010). Thus, out of diverse societies, multiculturalism as a policy response has 'grown up in contradictory ways in response to reflections and crises to address the question of plural minorities' (Modood, 2010) in Europe and North America. Within this, two key approaches have emerged; the structural inequality model and the socio-cultural model (I. Young, 2009). The structural inequality model focuses on challenging the formal rules of organisations to tackle the enduring structural, socio-economic inequalities that minorities are often afflicted by to greater extents than the majority population (Tilly, 1998). Here, the recognition of minority difference is rooted in the need to identify and tackle this inequality through mechanisms such as the US's 'affirmative action' and the UK's 'equal opportunity' legislation. As such, this approach is rooted in the material concerns of multiculturalism, which are, correctly, vital aspects of how societies seek to foster greater equality for minority communities within the tolerated inequality of capitalist, market-driven economies. These concerns are also rightly highlighted by scholars such as Hargreaves (2007) as central to the French case, where structural economic inequality is a continuing concern for Muslim communities.

The second 'socio-cultural' model of multiculturalism, advocated by scholars such as Kymlicka (1996, 2002) involves a more symbolic accommodation of difference through recognising the validity of norms, practices and cultural expressions of post-migration communities (I. Young, 2009), where it is posited that 'learning about people's culture reduces prejudice' (Modood, 2007). With this model being the ascendant means by which difference has been managed in the advanced capitalist democracies over the past several decades (I. Young, 2009), it is the subject of a wide body of literature. For Taylor (1994), the ability of political systems to enable some form of 'recognition' is not just important for a sense of identity but also for psychological well-being:

> a person or group of people can suffer real damage, real distortion, if the people or society around them mirror back to them a confining or demeaning or contemptible picture of themselves. Non-recognition or misrecognition can inflict harm, can be a form of oppression, imprisoning someone in a false, distorted, and reduced mode of being. (Taylor, 1994)

Thus, Taylor (1994) argues that a 'politics of equal recognition', where everyone is forced to recognise everyone else's equality before the law, is important for the functioning of democracies. Clearly this position, and that of other advocates of multiculturalism, have not been universally accepted, with the elected leaders of France, Germany and the UK at the start of the twenty-first century declaring that multiculturalism is dead. Nor is there a universal consensus of what this equality before the law means—as the French model proposes that it is precisely and only through a politics of 'non-recognition' that equality before the law can be ensured. However, regardless of one's normative position in political philosophy, France remains a paradox of a socially 'de facto multicultural country' (Wihtol de Wenden, 2004), due to its history of mass immigration, that has, as we have seen above, not embraced multicultural policies (Modood, 2007).

It is precisely out of a predicament of diversity that assimilation emerged to hold a religiously, ethic and culturally diverse France together.

Assimilating to a common idea of colour- and religion-blind citizenship is the central ideal upon which membership of the national community is defined, and is the pre-eminent means of incorporating notions of difference into the central idea of French nationhood (Alba, 2005; Bleich, 2011; R. Brubaker, 2001; E. Weber, 1976). Indeed, there is even a sub-discipline of nationalism studies that emerged in the twentieth century that was concerned with constructing, and then contesting, France as the 'ideal type' of a 'civic' national model (Safran, 1991; Todorov & Anzalone, 1989). Here, the logic goes, because the republic is founded on the notion of nationality conferred by jus soli, 'law of the soil', with individuals simply needing to be born on French soil to gain nationality, the republic is the beacon of colour-blind liberté, egalité and fraternité. This was contrasted with the 'ethnic' ideal type of Germany, where nationality was defined more by 'jus sanguinis' or law of blood, meaning that a notion of being part of a Germany ethnicity was the fundamental requirement of being a citizenship of Germany. This ethnic component, so the logic goes, was exclusionary, 'backwards' and 'bad' because of the way, with catastrophic results, it aided in the construction of an ideal of German ethnic unity all too ready to be called upon in the rise of Nazism and its insistence on Arian purity. Zimmer, however, calls this static and deterministic dichotomy into questions by attempting to nuance and enliven a conception of nationhood that considers how the 'overtly' civic can actually be used to construct nationhood in exclusionary terms. Here, 'nationalists create new ideological syntheses from available cultural idioms and resources' (Zimmer, 2003, p. 179). Following this rationale, civic ideas encompass not just a definition of national identity, but specifically a set of ideas and institutions that can be used either to include or exclude, depending upon how they are formulated and applied. So, an idea of secular civic national identity can be and is used to exclude those who are religious in their private life, even though technically there is nothing set out constitutionally to do this. This is why, despite the local state attempting to ban burkinis on beaches, the constitutional court was able to overturn them as being anti-constitutional. The situation gets far more complicated, however, when discussions are centred more on the grey areas between official state statistics and clearly private choices of beachwear. Thus, areas such as the provision of halal or kosher school meals are open to debate—is this about respecting private beliefs and enabling equal access to education for citizens, or does the provision of different meals make the state complicit in recognising religions in the state sphere, or indeed favouring and giving preference to certain religions over others? Regardless of our personal opinions on these issues, it is clear that an ambiguous commitment to 'ensure the equality of all citizens before the law, without distinction of origin, race or religion' (Assemblé Nationale, 2018) does not give us concrete answers.

Coming back to the question of assimilation, it has been conceptualised as being the means by which this policy of the non-recognition of ethnic, religious or cultural exceptions played an important role in incorporating, firstly, France's culturally disparate regions, and then waves of migrants from South and Eastern Europe (Weil, 2008), into a centrally defined French nationhood. However, this in itself has been very dynamic, and has been interrupted by historical and social contingencies. Noiriel (1988) correctly points to how notions of Frenchness, even when defined by the two principles outlined above, have been dynamic and responsive over time in a historical evolution influenced by encounters with other European, and indeed non-European, peoples and cultures. This means by which the national state defines the boundaries of the nation has also been critiqued widely for being unable to redefine the nation in a way to take into account, and indeed integrate, migrations from France's ex-colonies, notably those in North and West Africa (Hargreaves, 2007; Hussey, 2014). Here, the focus on colour-blind legal equality and the separation of church and state has proven ineffective at tackling social, economic and xenophobic forms of exclusion for these arrivals and their descendants. However, going a step further, it has also rightly been argued that these principles work in uneven and exclusionary ways. For example, the enforcement of secularism laws that particularly target Muslim forms of religious expression dovetail with republicanism's lack of ability and willingness to target ethno-religious forms of discrimination in arenas such as the labour market (Hargreaves, 2007).

Adding further complexities to the already muddy picture of vague constitutional principles and their application, there is also a plethora of manifestations of the French state who themselves must define exactly what laïcité means in the given contexts that they operate. Thus, there are not simply vague principles that require interpretation and operationalisation to function, but there are a multitude of different state actors, agencies and departments which are required to do this on an almost daily basis. Thus, what is present here in reality is not a singular republic, but a set of multiple republics. Previous conceptions of this as 'multiple states, multiple republics' (Downing, 2015) that focus on national identity, or 'state dominated pluralism' (Dunn, 1995) which focuses on bureaucratic autonomy, are insufficient in a study on how this impacts French Muslims because neither capture (a) the relations of solitude that local innovations exist in, nor (b) how these solitudes stop policy innovations translating into a change in national norms.

The literature on political and social 'solitudes' (inter alia Oliver, 1999; Rice, 2009), developed in the Quebec context, offers some important insights into how different social, political and economic developments can surprisingly exist in extreme isolation, even in a state like Canada that is renowned for its multicultural settlement and focus on 'recognition' based policy platforms that celebrate not only the diversity of recent migration, but the very diverse nature of the country since its foundation (Taylor, 1994). This idea of political solitudes offers a much-needed means to conceptualise how different manifestations of power and state in France display their republican colours differently and in isolation from each other. This captures the means by which local, national and even international forms of government relate to race and religion in a context where this is not only politically taboo, but technically illegal, yet a political necessity in the twenty-first century. This paradox of an engagement with norms, ideals and kinds of politics that are technically illegal is extremely important to grasp in the highly nuanced ways that it takes place, yet remains taboo and somehow separate from mainstream discourse. No matter how much massaging, interpreting and even contravening of assimilation and laïcité occurs at the local level, it should not be mis-read as some kind of laïcité or republican 'glasnost' where the attachment to these principles is in anyway institutional or rhetorically a thing of the past. Even under Macron, who is far less vocal about questions of national identity, migration and religion than his predecessors such as Nicolas Sarkozy or voices on the fringes of French politics such as Marine

Le Pen, neither he nor the state distance themselves from republican or laïque norms.

Thus, what is occurring here is best captured as a multiple of republics which exist in multiple solitudes. The innovation in policy, norms and politics occurs, yet remains isolated both from the national but also from other local manifestations of change. This idea of political and social solitudes actually comes from a fictional account of life in multilingual, mid-twentieth-century Canada: MacLennan's 1945 novel, *Two Solitudes*. The novel used a notion of two solitudes to discuss the relationship between English- and French-speaking Canada during the early part of the twentieth century, when there was a sense that the two entities existed in a solitude from each other. Here, MacLennan used this concept of a lack of communication between the two Canadas as a metaphor for exploring the issues the main character had in reconciling his English and French-Canadian identities.

However, because of this fictional concept's resonance with the reality of the Canadian context, the concept has found significant purchase in the political sciences. Many scholars have used, adapted and furthered this idea of forms of political, social and economic isolation across a number of Canadian, and importantly, non-Canadian, contexts. These discussions have never strayed far, however, from critical questions of minorities and the need for their accommodation and recognition under even multi-ethnic federal states such as Canada. Oliver (1999) makes this point when, even while making the rallying cry of the need for Quebec to be linguistically and politically strong to survive, it must also must respect its minorities, anglophone and indigenous. This question of indigenous cultures and languages is significant, as they are somewhat the 'Achille's heel' of the Canadian multicultural model, as while Canada venerates itself for not just balancing francophone and anglophone concerns, but also for welcoming and celebrating those from all over the world, its record on caring for, and valorising, the culture, rights and languages of its indigenous populations leaves much to be desired. Rice (2009) picks up on this point to discuss how indigenous languages, otherwise absent from this narrative of two solitudes, fight for existence and recognition in a context dominated by this bilingual rivalry.

It is also important to not simply essentialise this solitude in Canadian social and political life as something that is limited to superficial and sometimes farcical concerns of multilingualism. Rather, these solitudes translate into much 'harder' political concerns. This dichotomy of solitude translates beyond the linguistic into differences in key areas such as opinions about security and defence policy and spending. (Rioux, 2004) highlights that the power of this dichotomy is not simply linguistic, but also translates to difference in politics, finding that the anti-military stance of Quebec shapes Canadian defence policy, seeing that the English-speaking provinces were too quick to support British and US military engagements. This occurs across a number of areas including defence spending and coverage of defence issues. In terms of capturing the dynamism of political and social structures, the times of the 'two solitudes' in the Canadian context were decried as being 'over' in 2005 by the Governor-General Michaëlle Jean. However, this was presented as much as a normative cry for an end to remaining forms of isolation, as much as it was a post facto statement about the state of national dialogue, arguing that Canadians must 'eliminate the spectre of all solitudes', hinting strongly that they still exist (T. Weber, 2005). However, regardless of the current state of intra-group dialogue in Canada, the concept of two solitudes has found wider adoption through discussion on such diverse contexts as the Aceh secessionist movement in Indonesia, where the Indonesian government exists in a situation of two solitudes (Waizenegger & Hyndman, 2010). This example demonstrates the dynamism of situations where political solitudes exists, in that these solitudes required breaking during the response to the Boxing Day tsunami disaster in order to get relief to the shattered towns and villages of Aceh. What this chapter aims to do is to demonstrate that while the situation regarding the treatment of ethnic and religious difference by different parts of the state in France remain more dynamic than it first seems, this dynamism occurs overwhelmingly in positions of political solitude from both the central French state and also from each other. This does not mean that they do not come to the attention of the central government or the public more generally, especially in the form of the regular polemics generated by the issues, but rather that the dynamism does not spread and each separate kind of policy innovation remains isolated in its very specific contexts.

This chapter aims to do this by examining several of these specific contexts to typologies and how this occurs across different settings in which the many republics find themselves.

2.3   The Many Central States and Political Solitudes

So far, this chapter has established the ideational and historical evolution of the combined principles of the non-recognition of both race and religion that come together to give France its particular secular assimilationist state structures. While this chapter will focus on how many republics exist in many solitudes both under and over the national state, it is important also to nuance the actions of the central state and how these also complicate an otherwise overtly simple picture of a coherent republican veneer (Raymond & Modood, 2007). This is critical because it is true that, in a similar vein to the many republics that exist in other levels of governance, the national central state is also not a unitary entity and thus its dealings with French Muslims have also been varied and paradoxical.

Modood (2007) picks up on this theme with the discussion of the establishment of two national bodies by central governments to structure the affairs of two communities—one religiously defined, Muslims, and one racially defined, 'blacks'. In 2003, Nicolas Sarkozy as minister of the interior created the French Council of the Muslim Faith (Conseil Français du Culte Musulman, CFCM) to represent all Muslims to the government in matters of worship and ritual. However, this is actually not as radical as it sounds, as the Protestant, Catholic and Jewish communities in France all have similar bodies which represent their needs to the central government. As Modood (2007) has noted, the creation of this group by the government can also be seen as an effort to 'control' French Muslims—an assertion buttressed by comments about the need to 'stop the Islam of basements and garages'. The establishment of this body, will provide an interesting insight into how the state seeks to deal with Muslims, but it does not represent a massive policy shift. This is not to say, however, that this organisation does indeed represent Muslims or that it is universally accepted or respected, which clearly is not the case. However, this is somewhat a separate, if not critical question. It is sufficient in this context of analysing how the state engages with notions of ethnic and religious difference under the rubric of assimilation, that the state, even in tokenistic and problematic ways, when so suited, is not averse to applying the very difference orientated principles that in other settings it is so against.

The establishment of a second association, this time based on racial identity, also affects Muslims in France because creating a 'black' association in France affects those Muslims in France who are black. This comes in the form of the 2005 founding of the country's first black association, the Representative Council of French Black Associations (Conseil Représentative des Associations Noires de France, CRANF) (Modood, 2007). This is especially interesting given the importance that this association attaches to a platform of anti-discrimination and affirmative action based on racial identity—something that is formally taboo for the French republic. However, again this is not representative of a massive policy shift—and as with the CFCM it is doubtful if the association has large-scale support or impact on significant national issues. Rather, it serves as another example of how the state, when so inclined, will engage with not only religious ideas of difference but also racial ones, once again contravening its own notions of how such groups should assimilate politically in the face of the state individuals politically void of racial and religious characteristics. Thus, we can already see that even in the national, central context, the republic is indeed very fickle and will instrumentally engage with notions of difference if it sees some kind of political and/or social advantages to be gained from doing so. Already then, at the national level the veneer of universalism is beginning to crack, even if ever so slightly.

Following on from this, it is also essential to understand that the central state is not a unitary entity when it engages with notions of difference, in that even at this level of governance in France there are varying institutions, all of which have to define what assimilation means to them, depending on their positionality and particular political interests. This is highly relevant in a discussion which engages with questions of how the

French state interacts with Muslims in different ways, because different parts of the central state have different and contending opinions on how assimilation should be practised on the ground, and what the limits of the ability of the state to regulate religious issues are. This is especially important given that the dominant logic of the central French state has been its numerous bans on public displays of religiosity, often specifically focused on Muslims, and more specifically on Muslim women. These include the 2004 ban on hijabs in schools (among other religious symbols) and the 2010 ban on the niqab or full-face covering. It is also necessary to understand that these particular legal bans are much more nuanced and multifaceted than they appear.

The 2004 hijab ban actually banned a range of Sikh, Jewish and Christian symbols from only public primary and secondary schools, albeit with a clearly pro-Christian bias in the permission to wear 'small crosses'. Additionally, the law also recommended that both the Muslim festival of Eid and the Jewish Yom Kippur should be given as yearly school holidays as the current school calendar has a bias in recognising Christian religious holidays, somewhat paradoxical under a secular republic. Thus, this law sought somehow to give a degree of religious recognition in public life with one hand, while taking a form of public religious expression with the other. It should be noted that these recommendations for the changing of the school holiday calendar were not followed, while the banning on religious symbols was.

Regardless of the discriminatory nature of this law and how it has been applied, it can be seen that the law, at least in spirit if not in application, was seeking to make a much wider contribution to the national discussion of how to structure relations between the state and religious groups in society. This contrasts strongly with the niqab ban, coming as it did from the directly elected senate, which sought specifically to not only target one religious subgroup, Muslim women, but to do so in a way which pushed the regulation of religion out from the political, state field into the public sphere. This is not to diminish the significant support given to the ban by both French Muslim politicians and Islamic scholars, which adds another dimension of nuance to the public discourse overseas, which presented the ban as racist and opposed by French Muslims— clearly there is a far more diverse dynamic at play in France. However, what is important when examining an idea of many republics which relate to Muslims differently here is that such a fringe issue was given such resources and political attention in the French senate at a time when the country faced a multitude of social, economic and political problems. It was estimated at the time that only estimated 1900 women—some 0.003% of the French population—actually wore a full-face veil covering (Erlanger, 2010).

Additionally, it is necessary to understand that another part of the French central state actually intervened on the subject of religious freedom in the public sphere to push the boundaries of secularism the other way—out of public life and back into the political and state sphere. This time the contested political field was that of the beaches of the south of France, where local administrations attempted, with a degree of success at first, to regulate women's swimwear. The first to do this was the world famous resort of Cannes, where the mayor David Lisnard expressed wishes to prohibit 'beachwear ostentatiously showing a religious affiliation while France places of religious significance are the target of terror attacks', to avoid 'trouble to public order' (Dearden, 2016). The second ban, by the commune of Villeneuve-Loubet, did not reference security in its ban, but simple alluded to swimwear needing to be 'respectful to morality and secular principles, and in compliance with hygiene and safety rules' (Dearden, 2016). Importantly here, neither of these bans specifically mentioned 'burkini'—and the woman being told to undress by French police in Nice, whose picture was beamed worldwide, wasn't actually wearing one. However, it was clear that other groups in France that might cover up on the beach—nuns or those wearing wetsuits to stay warm while doing water sports in the cool Mediterranean waters—would be or were party to police enforced restrictions. The bans quickly spread across the south of France, with the ban in Villeneuve-Loubet being upheld by a lower court in Nice (Vinocur, 2016). However, civil society groups took the legal challenge to the state council, which ruled the bans unconstitutional and a 'serious infringement on fundamental freedoms that are the freedom of movement, the freedom of belief and personal freedom' (Vinocur, 2016). Thus, again we can see that the French state relates to issues around Muslims and Islam in France differently, and even at the national level defies attempts to construct a homogenous, unitary entity that acts from a position of conceptual or policy coherence. Rather, the positions of the state, the forms that concepts such as laïcité or the ban on ethnic markers of identity take, are constantly being questioned, re-evaluated and tested. Therefore, even the national level is an example of a situation of 'many republics', which should be remembered as this chapter goes further, beyond the nation into the local and international contexts, to understand how the French state's relationship to Muslims is characterised by a situation of many republics, many solitudes.

2.4   Local Republics, Vulnerability in Solitude: Exploring the Issues with Forming Local Policy Relationships to French Muslims

Now that we have seen that the national manifestations of the many republics can be actually quite fickle and dynamic in their application of notions of ethno-religious difference, as well as their definitions of the legal limits of clothing bans, it is time to turn to the local level of the state. In France, there are a plethora of local forms of governance that have significant autonomy on a number of issues, their own administrations and thus their own political and social interests. The local level is also particularly significant for an analysis of French Muslims because of their uneven spread throughout the hexagon. In line with the general trend across Europe, migrant diversity is concentrated in large urban areas—as the historical nodes of industrial development and the places which suck in labour, skills and those seeking a better life away from poverty or persecution. In the French context, Hargreaves (2007) cites INSEE statistics on the locations of foreign-born populations in France, somewhat of a proxy for measuring where ethnic and religious diversity sits in France. These statistics indicated where large ethnic minority populations reside, and state that 57.5% of them reside in only three regions of France—Île de France, with Paris at its centre, Rhône-Alpes, with Lyon at its centre, and Provence-Alpes-Côte d'Azur, with Marseille at its centre. These three cities alone account for a large amount of the country's diversity, and if one was to drill down on where this diversity is located within these localities, one would likely find that it is even more concentrated on the micro level of particular urban and suburban districts. This means that the particular manifestations of the many republics which exist to serve such diverse populations also have the bureaucratic and administrative autonomy and flexibility to formulate their own particular forms of policy making and implementation.

Following this line of argument, this chapter presents two contrasting examples of how local manifestations of the French state have sought to engage with Muslim populations in two different ways. These both involve an interesting and common means by which local manifestations of the state structure their relations with minority communities, namely through cooperation with local non-governmental organisations (NGOs), under the law of 1901 which regulates non-profit associations which are neither part of the church nor the state. This idea that they are not part of the formal state is one that requires significant nuancing here in a discussion of their relationships to the local state, which will follow in more detail. However, while not de jure part of the French republic, they receive significant financial, material, symbolic and political support from the French state. This adds an important nuance to the discussion of how the French state handles the question of its Muslim populations because, in a similar vein to the creation of the associations for blacks and Muslims at the national level, this move by the local state to support organisations and associations with a specifically Muslim target base is a means by which the state seeks to formulate and deploy policy, political and social responses to the paradox of governing a multicultural society while being hamstrung by the state-approved stance of assimilation. These associations, and their relationships with the local state, exist here in interesting positions of solitude, because they are not technically part of the state, not endorsed by a national funding or policy platform, and sit in a grey area between an assimilationist state and a multicultural society. This means that such associations exist in relationships of close cooperation, if not outright patronage, with local politicians. This makes them, and their work, specifically vulnerable because of these very local and personal ties. The two examples below seek not only to typologise the working relationship of the state with local associations in very different ways, one using overtly religious markers, the other being more nuanced and 'cultural', but it also seeks to typologise the vulnerabilities that ensue from such working relationships of solitude.

The first example is rooted in the local political structures and concerns of Marseille. Here, it has long been argued that the local government follows an 'exceptionalist' political trajectory, being more open to recognising religious difference in politics through policy innovations such as the 'Marseille Espérance' forum that brings local religious leaders into political life (Mitchell, 2011).

Another means by which this multicultural platform was advanced vis-à-vis the city's Muslim population was a public celebration of the Muslim festival of Eid al-Adha through the creation of the public festival 'L'Aïd dans la Cité', which was created and run by the Union of Muslims Families of the Bouches-du-Rhône (UFM13). This association was funded by the regional council of Provence-Alps-Côtes-d'Azur, but was intimately linked to a political relationship of the head of the association, Nasera Benmarnia, and also a socialist politician, Patrik Menucci, who represented an agglomeration of poor, immigrant-rich parts of central Marseille, until his defeat by the far-left candidate Jean-Luc Melanchon in 2017.

L'Aïd dans la Cité was first organised in 2003 with the overt purpose of normalising the presence of Muslims in the city and as such move migrant culture out into the public sphere (Pervis, 2007). However, this festival should not be simply considered a fringe, communal affair, because while clearly it celebrates a particular religious holiday of the Muslim community, the organisers of this event not only invite members of the non-Muslim communities of Marseille but also regularly achieve 30% attendance at these celebrations by non-Muslims (Pervis, 2007). L'Aïd dans la Cité is considered to be a valuable opportunity to meet other members of the local community in a festive context, and it helps counter the more negative images of Muslims that tend to predominate and get the most attention (Geisser & Lorcerie, 2011). Thus, it falls within a notion of 'socio-cultural' multiculturalism that is involved with facilitating a politics of recognition rather than tackling entrenched socio-economic inequalities.

Each year the particular theme of the festival changes and it seeks to explicitly address the question of migrants and their contributions to

France. In 2010, the programme was themed around the idea of a 'Eulogy for the foreigner' (Med'in Marseille, 2010), where the contribution of migrants is directly addressed. Chief organiser and head of the UFM13 Nassera Benmarnia set this programme directly in opposition to the negative depictions of migrants in the French media; 'they [foreigners] are not getting good press at the moment … they are causing lots of problems and annoying the real French people' (quoted in Med'in Marseille, 2010).

However, the situation of political solitude that the association existed in made this event, and indeed its parent organisation, extremely vulnerable to exogenous political shocks, which ultimately killed the association. The parent organisation, the UFM13, collapsed amid allegations of clientelism and corruption (Zemouri, 2013). This centred on funding of €90,000 given to the UFM13 by the cultural commission of the regional council of Bouches-du-Rhône, authorised by then-member Patrick Menucci (Zemouri, 2013). Thus, it was the same close relationship of patronage with the head of the UFM13 that had made the work of the association possible that lead to its decline. This form of solitude away from the structures of the central state, relying on relationships of patronage, made this form of the state relating to the French Muslim population extremely vulnerable. Thus, solitude is intimately linked to precarity. This is especially pertinent because these allegations of irregularities and favouritism resulted in the initiation of a police investigation, which concluded in the finding of no irregularities (Zemouri, 2013). However, even though there was no wrong-doing uncovered, nor formal charges brought, this was enough to end the existence of the UFM13 and thus the existence of L'Aïd dans la Cité.

This example demonstrates how the position of solitude that policy innovations that create many republics exist in ultimately place such pluralities of the republic in positions of extreme precarity. In part, this can be attributed to the specificities of local politics in Marseille, long decried for operating a 'mafieux' system dependent on local connections and networks of patronage and clientelism (Menucci, 2013). This, combined with the urban instability caused by high levels of drug-related crime and a continued lack of tax revenues (Moore, 2001) renders creating sustainable municipal initiatives difficult. As such, the fact that an initiative that has seen annual attendance figures exceed 20,000 (Agence France-Press, 2007) can so easily fold demonstrates how precarious the many republics are because of their position of solitude.

A second example, one where the republic is redefined locally through the recognition of ethno-cultural groups, demonstrates how another relationship of patronage between an association and a local mayor is not only structured differently, but also how its solitude makes its work vulnerable from a different angle. Here, it is the ability of national politics to create a powerful anti-recognition polemic that makes politics existing in situations of local solitude vulnerable. This example exists in the context of the municipal politics of Nanterre in the Hautes-des-Seine department, which is an economically mixed area of suburban Paris, containing both poor high-rise estates and relatively wealthy areas. In this context a local voluntary association Les Oranges has worked on bringing narratives about migrant history, the contribution of migrants to France and the colonial experience of the Algerian community into the public realm. This has received significant support from the local communist mayor, Patrick Jarry, who has served as mayor of Nanterre since 2004. The close relationship between Jarry and the association's president, M'hamed Kaki, has enabled the association to receive significant material support from the local authority, if not direct cash handouts as was the case in Marseille. Here, the local state has made the resources of the municipality accessible to the association. This includes the municipality making an office available for Les Oranges in a municipal building. The municipality also makes facilities available to the group for holding debates and theatrical productions at no cost. This is done in the large municipal arts and culture centre, l'Agora ('maison des initiatives citoyennes', Ville de Nanterre 2013). While it is technically free for the use of citizens for their cultural initiatives, the fact that the municipality would allow a group such as Les Oranges to hold activities in the facility that directly addresses such sensitive subjects in France as immigrant history and cultural identity as a means to create symbolic power, could be argued to demonstrate a significant level of support from the municipality for such activities.

This support also continues with the personal and symbolic support of Jarry. He accompanied Kaki on a trip to Tlemcen in Algeria, a town with which Nanterre is twinned and a town of cultural and religious significance in the Maghreb. This support also extends to the municipal authority giving public support to the work of the association in public domains such as the renaming of geographical landmarks in the city to reflect themes of migrant history. Jarry began this trend by offering very public support for the naming of a new high school in the commune after the French-Algerian sociologist Abdelmalek Sayad, a figure who conducted a large amount of his sociological research in Nanterre, as discussed earlier. With the support of the mayor, Les Oranges started a national campaign to have this school named after the sociologist to redress a massive imbalance in the distribution of figures chosen as names for French high schools—an important national custom that attempts to valorise important figures from French history and culture. To date, there is not a single French high school that is named after a figure from a minority community; rather they are all named after ethnically French figures (Bel Hadi, 2007).

Owing partly to this clear imbalance, Les Oranges generated significant support for the initiative by getting researchers and politicians to sign a petition and to get media coverage for the effort of naming the college. Nikolas Sarkozy, then president of the Conseil Général of the Hautes-de-Seine department, accepted the proposal to name the school after Abdelmalek Sayad. Ultimately, however, the decision was overturned by a vote of the Conseil Général of Hautes-de-Seine.

This was not before the issue stirred up widespread controversy in the French press that arguably inflated the importance of this issue. This polemic is of significance and worthy of attention in addition to the failure of the proposal itself, as Vale (1999) correctly argues that, in the redefining of national identity in the media-dominated contemporary age, the way that gestures and monuments are covered and what they actually are have become increasingly inseparable. In this instance, the attempt to name a high school after Abdelmalek Sayad resulted in a large media polemic where numerous French politicians waded into the fray. For example, Elisabeth Balkini-Smadja argued for the college to be named after Guy Moquet, a young member of the French Resistance who died at the hands of the Nazi occupiers. She argued that any attempt to name the college after an Arab sociologist was an example of the communist mayor of Nanterre attempting to start a polemic around the issue. This demonstrates again the precarious positions of solitude the work of such associations and local manifestations of the republic are, because of their isolation from the national norms of assimilation. Here the polemic referenced the violation of national norms by attempting to bring a minority figure into the naming of a school, which is paradoxical because it is technically in no way a violation of laïcité, the banning of ethno-racial state identities, and thus is not a violation of assimilation. This shows the deeper discursive power that assimilation has in that as a dogma it is even applied by politicians and state actors in ways that go further than the formal state laws. This makes the work of municipalities and associations acting in solitude from the central state difficult because they can never be sure at what point their work will be deemed against the grain of national ideals and thus subject to potentially harmful critique. This shows how, as with the previous example from Marseille, even when no formal laws are broken, the work of municipalities and local associations can be derailed.

However, the work of the municipality and the association did not stop here, and their redefinition of republicanism in solitude was able to weather the polemical storm and still go on to do further work. Again, highlighting the important recognition and cooperation that Les Oranges have secured from the municipal authorities, the mayor of Nanterre held a symbolic inauguration of the college on 23 May 2007, where a plaque was placed on the side of the college to commemorate the life and work of Abdelmalek Sayad. Also, out of this process came the successful initiative to rename a Nanterre street after the sociologist—Rue Abdelmalek Sayad. This continued with the renaming of a street in Nanterre as 'Boulevard du 17 Octobre 1961' in 2011, to commemorate the massacring of Algerian protesters by French authorities. Additionally, the municipality in 2013 named a new primary school after Sayad, after backing was given to the proposal by the mayor, with unanimous backing gained from the municipal council.

2.5 Europeanising Solitudes: Transnational Norms and Their Conflict and Complementarity with Many Republics

Another key way that many republics are manifested in situations of political solitude is through the intervention of international forms of governance which shape the way that assimilation can be practised. This again is not a formal, national, de jure change, as the national position of the French state has brought France into significant conflict with European norms of pluralism and the respecting of minority rights. This dovetails with the broader observations on Europeanisation (see inter alia Bulmer & Radaelli, 2004; Hooghe, 1996; Knill, 2001; Richardson, 2006), that the implementation of this EU programme has resulted in paradoxical and undesirable outcomes and a general ineffectiveness. Rather, this is again a de facto shift at the local level where local policy entrepreneurs initiate local shifts so that they can bypass the central state and interact with European governance and funding for the benefit of their local contexts. Because of France's national assimilationist stance, it has neither signed nor ratified the Council of Europe's Framework Convention for the Protection of National Minorities (FCNM) (Carrera, Guild, Vosyliūtė, & Bard, 2017). The FCNM was designed to respect the rights of national minorities, specifically focusing on combatting discrimination, promoting equality and to preserve and develop the culture and identity of minorities (Carrera et al., 2017). Additionally, France signed but did not ratify an earlier minority protection instrument of the CoE in 1992, the European Charter for the Regional or Minority Languages (ECRML) (CoE, 2018). As such, France stands out as a significant anomaly in the European context as a state which refuses to even acknowledge and protect the languages and cultures of national minorities, such as the Bretons, Provençals and the Basques. This is particularly pertinent because these measures do not even seek to include provisions for the protection of the languages and cultures of 'new' minorities, such as the French Muslims that this book addresses. Thus, these measures, aimed at categories of 'existing', white, mainly Christian, national groups have proved far less contentious for European states to endorse than those aimed at 'new' minorities, such as post-migration Muslims groups, who are constructed as a much more contentious issue in contemporary politics.

This is all well and good for the practices of the national state, as while normatively objectionable, the central sovereign state has significant, if not total, autonomy to choose which policy platform it deems most fit for the society over which it governs. However, the position of assimilation creates significant problems at the local level for policy makers and practitioners because to access the programmes and funding of European levels of governance, such as the EU and the CoE, implementation of these principles of plurality and diversity act as 'gate-keepers'. As such, if projects do not only recognise, but even valorise, celebrate and place at centre stage, post-migration diversity, then funding will not be forthcoming. This has significant possible ramifications for local contexts. Marseille was awarded the 2013 European Capital of Culture title, which led to significant funds pouring into the city for regeneration and the upgrading of cultural infrastructure. Lyon, a city which was also bidding for the same title, was refused it, at least in part, due to a poor grasp of notions of plurality and diversity.

Therefore, local levels of governance have to work to de facto subvert assimilation in positions of solitude to enable them to engage with, and access, European funding. This intervention of European norms into the local sphere creates new manifestations of republicanism at the local level, but which once again find themselves in a position of solitude vis-à-vis the national state because of their need to subvert dominant norms of assimilation to align themselves with European norms of plurality. This chapter demonstrates this with recourse to two specific examples—one of a large-scale project, the Intercultural Cities Programme (ICP) in Lyon, and a smaller-scale project focusing on enterprise development in the suburbs of Paris. These two different scales of activity, and indeed the fact that they engage with two different European forms of government, the CoE and the EU, demonstrate different issues with the need to act in solitude to engage with pluralistic norms to engage with the socio-cultural and socio-economic issues that French Muslims face.

The ICP emerged out of the 2008 European Year of Interculturalism proposed by Jan Figel, European commissioner for Education, Training, Culture and Youth (Wood, 2004). It was conceived to 'promote awareness of the ways in which intercultural dialogue can help create strong and cohesive communities in an increasingly culturally diverse Europe' (Wood, 2004, p. 12). The inclusion of Lyon in the ICP is an important example of the subversion of assimilation in a position of solitude, because Lyon is not only one of France's largest cities, but along with Marseille and the Paris metropolitan area, the Lyon metropolitan area has one of the largest concentrations of French Muslims in the country (Hargreaves,

2007). The CoE's ICP is important because it sets out, in line with the European norms of pluralism outlined above, to 'combat discrimination and racism, and actively promote constructive interaction between individuals and groups of different backgrounds, cultures and generations' (Wood, 2010). Even in its local incarnation, these are not goals compatible with the French state, because they necessitate recognising group differences.

The participation in the ICP represents an opportunity for Lyon to harness European resources and expertise to formulate and apply difference-based policies in local policy. This has not been a smooth process, however, as the encroachment of European norms of pluralism into a local state dominated by assimilation has been difficult because of administrative inertia. This produced a conflict between existing administrative assimilationist inertia and the pluralist notions embedded in the ICP (Pascual, Courouble, & Bonniel, 2009). This is in line with broader observations about other efforts to Europeanise governance which often comes into conflict, and is stymied by, existing administrative inertias (Bulmer & Radaelli, 2004; Knill, 2001). It was precisely the mainstreaming of the idea of interculturalism, which would necessitate not only recognising group difference but also promoting a dialogue between them, which caused concerns about the political sensitivity of these issues (Pascual et al., 2009). However, the membership of the ICP was not completely de-railed by these issues and Lyon still produced important intercultural policies for French Muslims, with the CoE making a positive assessment of the city's ongoing commitment to interculturalism from local policy makers (Council of Europe, 2008).

These measures included some which aimed to deal with the sociocultural forms of marginalisation and discrimination that the assimilationist French state is unable to deal with due to its inability to acknowledge group difference. The creation of the annual 'our cultures of the city' (Nos Cultures de la Ville) days brought together experts and policy makers from the city council to discuss how to approach cultural diversity and make it part of the sustainable development of the city (Ville de Lyon, 2012). In the 2011 edition, there was a discussion held on 'the richness of the other: the construction of our identities' (Ville de Lyon, 2011), where the programme included a discussion of the construction of France and the reality of the multiple identities that people have in French society. The involvement of official government bodies and local government representatives in such an exercise is remarkable in a country where such discussions are prohibited at the state level, beyond measures that aim to increase assimilation, such as the Sarkozy government's creation of a ministry for 'national identity'. This difference between the local and the national context again demonstrates how these innovations exist in a vacuum of solitude.

The ICP has also brought new forms of cultural policy and encounter to Lyon, which is important for French Muslims because of the inclusion of specifically religious markers of local history and culture onto the municipal agenda. This is not to say that Muslims only consume, are interested in, or are represented by cultural activities which are overtly labelled 'Muslim', which would be a highly paternalist and empirically incorrect assumption. However, it is significant that a category to which the central state, and politics more generally, is hostile is brought into the public sphere through the intervention of European governance, because it further demonstrates the existence of many republics. Cultural policy is a key policy for Lyon, which spends around 20% of its municipal budget on culture (Gnedovsky, 2009), but also at the national level because of the ongoing questions about cultural policy in France and as part of France's quest to redefine its identity and self-image in an era where insecurities about globalisation and diversity bring into question notions of assimilationist, colour-blind national homogeneity (Poirrier, 2013). As such, the central state has articulated significant ambitions to bring high culture to the masses with direct government policy intervention (Ahearne, 2002; Poirrier, 2013) through ideas of democratising culture (Martin, 2013; Poirrier, 2013). The observation that the democratisation of culture in France has largely failed (Martin, 2013) is important here, because efforts to widen the activities of mainstream cultural institutions to take account of new audiences and cultural forms in France have largely failed and have been abandoned (Poirrier, 2013). This is at least partly due to rolling out a notion of appropriate culture that has been criticised for being overly directive, bourgeois (Ahearne, 2002) and not reaching out to minorities and subcultures (Council of Europe, 2008). Here, this tallies with a CoE audit which criticised Lyon for having 'little cultural activity that has taken place outside of established activities for the majority ethnic middle classes, such as opera and theatre', with 'very little outreach of urban sub-cultures or to new audience groups' (Council of Europe, 2008, p. 3).

The ICP seeks to intervene here through the creation of a Charter of Cultural Cooperation (Charte de Coopération Culturelle) that ties the city's largest 22 cultural organisations into playing a key role in fostering interculturalism, not just in an artistic sense but also as a means to enhance inter-communal dialogue in the city. This has even extended to bringing religion overtly into this equation through one of the signatory cultural institutions, the Musées Gadagne, working with an inter-religious dialogue group from a diverse and poor suburb of Lyon. Here, the Abrahamic Group of La Duchère (GAD), active in Lyon since 1982, emerged in the poor suburb out of a lack of provision for religious spaces resulted in the Protestant community renting part of their building to the Muslim community on religious holidays, and then to the Jewish community to hold a Talmudic school up until the local synagogue was created and the Muslim community created their own prayer facilities. This resulted in the creation of inter-faith meetings and discussions monthly from 1986, and from 2002, the group facilitated visits to religious buildings to further inter-communal dialogue and understanding (Centre Resource Prospective du Grand Lyon, 2012). As part of this process they issued mutual declarations on key events, such as the recent killings in Toulouse by an Islamist extremist. Here, they issued an inter-religious declaration whereby they reaffirmed their belief in the importance of dialogue, especially between religions, as a means to get to know each other (Abrahamic Group of La Duchère, 2012).

However, despite undertaking these activities over several decades, the organisation did not have a relationship with municipal authorities owing to the French state's strict laïcité rules. This has changed under the Charter of Cultural Cooperation, which committed the city's large cultural institutions to the 'valorisation of diversity and increased visibility of minorities' and 'inter-culturality to introduce new arrivals' (Ville de Lyon, 2012). Here, the GAD was consulted on possible cultural projects it would be interested in initiating and being associated with. This has facilitated a relationship with municipal authorities by giving the association's activities a cultural dimension. The result has been an event dedicated to 'the religious minorities of Lyon from the Middle Ages to the present' (Musées Gadagne, 2013), that demonstrated how Lyon has received and accommodated various religious minorities during its history. This event was held in the historic Musées Gadagne, a site in Lyon that contains three different museums, including the official museum of Lyon. The event included discussions of the Armenian Christian, Jewish and Muslim presence in the city, with a session discussion of how a 'Lyonnais Islam' has been represented over the decades by community associations such as the Rhône-Alpes Council for the Muslim Faith (Musées Gadagne, 2013). While public discussion about religion and exhibitions about it do not transcend laïcité or assimilation per se, being outside of the state, it is an important observation that through the ICP the state has become involved in facilitating these. In a sense, this is the inverse of the process identified above with the burkini ban, where the local state sought to push laïcité out of the state and into the public realm of beaches, with here the ICP pushing laïcité and assimilation back further and forcing the state to recognise and work with forms of difference. Here, however, this still exists in a position of solitude, which was not lost on the GAD, who when interviewed expressed concerns that this situation of solitude meant that they found it difficult to transcend their context and extend their work to wider audiences. Thus, the effect of the intrusion of European norms into the French assimilationist context is limited to very specific local context where it exists in solitude, away from a national policy shift.

European governance also gets involved in far more covert ways in the area of minority policy by funding projects that are specifically targeted at impoverished minority communities run by existing NGOs through the supplying of funding for specific projects. This occurs through the various ways that European forms of funding such as the European Social Fund enable NGOs to apply for funding in addition to that which would be offered by the French government. An example of such a successful bid for funding demonstrates the way that European forms of funding enable such NGOs to plug some of the service gaps which are evident in the impoverished areas where Muslims are concentrated in the suburbs of large French cities. Here, in a similar vein to insightful discussion about 'territorial affirmative action', where the French state targets impoverished minorities not through ethnic or religious identity categories, but rather through defining geographical areas where they live, European funding enables this to occur through local-level NGOs.

The network of management consulting of the Paris/Île de France region (BGE PaRIF) is an example of one such organisation. This organisation specifically works to give advice and training to small-scale, local enterprises who are thinking of setting up in the Parisian region or who have set up in the region. This is particularly important for French Muslims because discrimination against migrant minorities in the labour market is rife in France, and self-employment and opening your own business is one way by which minorities can side-step discrimination in the labour market (Hargreaves, 2007). Their remit means that BGE PaRIF work not only in some of the poorest areas of the Parisian region, but these areas are also where much of the Muslim population of the region is concentrated, such as in the departments of Seine Saint Denis and Hauts-des-Sein. Under the conditions of significant economic deprivation present in the region, entrepreneurship is an important means by which those of Muslim origin who are excluded from formal employment can engage in economic activity of their own making. This particular NGO takes expertise and advice directly to poor areas via an advice bus, which was donated by the French car maker Peugeot. EU funding, however, paid for the two advisers who staffed the bus and offered start-up and self-employment advice for free to anyone that required it.

The representative of BGE PaRIF who was interviewed for this research identified that the majority of their clients in these areas that the EU funding enabled them to reach were of migrant and/or minority origin. They also expressed that it would be impossible to pitch such a project to funders in France in terms of who they were working with, as it would have to follow the rules on colour-blind forms of equality that would mean they would have to pitch the project as something that was dealing with more general economic deprivation than deprivation concentrated in particular minority communities. Additionally, they highlighted that accessing such European funding is not a panacea and presents specific problems for small organisations like themselves. The main problems emerge because of the administrative load such EU funding requires to meet its auditing and concurrence requirements—for example, any project costs for buying a physical object required three quotes to be obtained, and a case made for whichever quote was chosen. It was highlighted that this was highly impractical for the small purchases that the workers may have required in the field, and so this meant that some expenses were not reimbursed. Additionally, there were also concerns expressed about the temporary nature of EU funding for fixed-term projects, which meant that it was hard to ensure the longevity or legacy of projects. Thus, even with the backing of a large international funder, outside of the political constraints of the French republic and its requirements to not focus on particular identity groups, such projects suffer from similar fragility to some of the local NGOs previously discussed, who relied on local government funding and material support that was at least somewhat dependent on the support of local politicians. It was highlighted that another concern that makes such funding unreliable is the significant barriers to entry which exist for small NGOs when it comes to EU funding, in that the costs involved in the complicated administrative processes of both applying for funding (which may or may not be successful) and administering the grant itself deters many small NGOs from applying for such funding. While the EU funding does not rely on such close connections, it still remains a precarious means by which NGOs can side-step the concerns of the French state to help French Muslims, and is one which can incur its own administrative costs. Thus, policy innovation from such NGOs sits once again in a situation of precarious solitude, because of its reliance on precarious external funding which it may or may not be able to access again in the future, and the costs of applying for and administering such funding may act as a gate-keeper to such organisations and to future funding bids.

2.6   Conclusions on Many Republics and Many Solitudes

This chapter set out to examine the nature of how the republic relates to French Muslims from the perspective of a social and political state. This sought to go beyond the concept of the republic as a unitary, unchanging and secular state that has remained unchanged and static since the rights of man came out of the 1789 revolution that swept aside the absolutist monarchy and installed a republican government. Rather, history tells a very different story that does not require much digging to find—most notably in the fact that the French republic has been a highly unstable political system that is already on its fifth incarnation. This is also true when one understands how the state seeks to deploy its principles of state secularism, laïcité, and a ban on the collection of ethnic statistics, both of which come from the constitutional commitment to 'ensure the equality of all citizens before the law, without distinction of origin, race or religion. It shall respect all beliefs' (Assemblé Nationale, 2018). What exists here is also a much more complex reality where the operationalisation of these vague and diverse principles can lead to many different state-sanctioned outcomes. Previous conceptions that see this partially at the national level (Raymond & Modood, 2007) miss how this occurs across different aspects of the French state. Even when the local is taken into consideration as territorial affirmative action (Doytcheva, 2007), bureaucratic pluralism (Dunn, 1995) or 'multiple states, multiple republics' (Downing, 2015), they still fail to capture the complex relations that exist between these levels of governance and the national level of the republic. Here, because policy innovations are overwhelmingly occurring in complete isolation from each other, this chapter set out to use the idea of political solitudes (inter alia Oliver, 1999; Rice, 2009), developed in the Quebec context, because it offered important insights into how different social, political and economic developments can surprisingly exist in extreme isolation, even in a state like Canada that is renowned for its multicultural settlement and focus on 'recognition' based policies.

On a more macro level, this more nuanced understanding of many republics existing in situations of many solitudes seeks to challenge and nuance grander ideas in the political field that saw France as the archetype of the civic nation (Safran, 1991; Todorov & Anzalone, 1989). Clearly, this book is not unique here, as much of this work has been done already (a particularly insightful example can be found in Zimmer, 2003). However, much of this previous work ignores other breaks in colour-blind republicanism, such as the persecution of Jews during the Second World War and the racial hierarchies which were created under the

French empire (Camiscioli, 2009). These have been extremely well documented by those interested in state and political history, but have been rarely brought into analysis of the republic from the perspective of examining the issues around the operationalisation of laïcité and equality more broadly, where these ideational ruptures demonstrate the historical fragility of these ideas, both inside the French state and in French society more broadly—something which is not visible when simply analysing state structures and their evolution over time.

However, the analysis of state bodies does offer some important insights in the contemporary era into how the republic continues to change, morph and bend depending on the contingencies of the time and the more general fickle tastes of successive governments. The creation of France's first national Muslim and Black associations has been argued by some to be evidence that an assimilation is giving ground to multiculturalism in some sense at the national level (Modood, 2007). However, these analyses miss the machinations and differences in the application of assimilation at the national level, which is even more complex than the creation of these two associations belies. Indeed, various incarnations of the French state operate with significant autonomy at the national level and even come into conflict with other parts of the republic and overturn local interpretations of laïcité in rare instances where different facets of the republic intrude into each other's solitudes. The national council of state overturning the regional 'burkini bans' is an example of this, where it ruled that these bans were unconstitutional and thus pushed assimilation back from the beaches and into the state realm where constitutionally it is said to belong.

Examining the local level has uncovered even more complexities in the various solitudes of facets of the republic's attempt to interpret the political norms of assimilation to enhance, complement and buttress the interests of local activists, politicians and populations. However, operating in solitude is indeed extremely risky and exposes local policy innovations to a high degree of vulnerability. Indeed, the clientelist relationship between the UFM13 and a socialist politician, and the resulting unfounded allegations of corruption, resulted in the retrenchment of the L'Aïd dans la Cité festival. This was not only unique in France as a public commemoration of Eid, but also unique because it was funded by the local state. It was not even issues around violating secularism and assimilation that sunk this initiative, rather the murky nature of local politics in the Bouches-du-Rhône. However, this does not mean that allegations of violating assimilation do not arise, and are not dangerous at the local level. Les Oranges in Nanterre, operating with significant material and political support from the local mayor is an example where even polemical, public allegations of violating assimilation can result in local solitudes running into trouble. Indeed, the polemic that ensued about the naming of a high school after a French-Algerian sociologist did not even target the association or the local government for an actual violation of assimilation at the state level. Rather, they were attacked simply for exporting public 'communitarianism'. This not only technically does not fall under the remit of the constitutional provisions, which are supposed to leave the public sphere to the public, but it also remains unclear as to how renaming a high school after a Frenchmen is communitarian simply because he has Algerian origins. Here, one can gain an insight into how some seek to promote selective renditions of assimilation that can be applied to those of migrant origin, while not seeking to apply them to the naming of high schools after French figures with other ethnic origins.

Adding to this complexity is the creation of political solitudes through the intervention of European forms of government into the political field of French politics. Here, France is, and has been, at odds with European ideas of pluralism for quite some time—having not fully implemented European legislation on minority rights. This conflict extends into more immediate daily practices of statehood when local parts of the French state or local NGOs access European funding as a means to engage local minority and migrant communities, a number of whom are French Muslims. This can take extremely diverse forms, both in terms of the institutional set-ups involved and in the scale of European spending. Two varying examples in this chapter demonstrated that the involvement of the EU in this field is no panacea and does not enable such policies or the principles to exit forms of political solitude, but rather entraps them in new ones. The joining of the ICP by Lyon is a good example of how this works on a large scale, where the city joined a CoE programme whose basic principle is to not only to recognise different cultures, but also to celebrate and valorise cultural diversity. Lyon experienced significant issues with these norms clashing with the local administrative culture of the French state, where such ideas are alien. This did not stop the state, through its cultural institutions, reaching out to local NGOs that do inter-religious work to host exhibitions about the multi-religious nature of Lyon. However, the NGO staff who took part in this work expressed their frustration at how limited such work has been, even under such a flagship programme, and how the political solitude of the project has meant they have not been able to transcend their local audience and spread their work further. Paradoxically at the European level, a far smaller project analysed for this chapter experienced very similar problems, in that the direct intervention of funding from a European form of governance has not been the panacea that has enabled them to transcend their narrow context of action. While EU funding enabled BGE PaRIF to employ two enterprise advisers to give minority communities advice on setting up businesses as a way around unemployment, the precarity of such funding and the significant administrative burden incurred in applying for, and even in getting, such funding significantly limited the ability of this form of policy innovation to transcend the political solitude of the local.

Thus, it is important to strike a balance when analysing the way that the republic relates to its Muslim population. This is because there is a clear need to nuance ideas of the ideal type 'civic' republic that does not deal with notions of religious of ethnic difference, while at the same time acknowledging the issues faced by deviation from the assimilationist norm, regardless of what level they occur at and where the funding for them comes from. This is important because while there are indeed many republics that treat notions of ethnic and religious difference in many ways, as has been established here, they do so overwhelmingly in positions of political solitude where innovation, change and deviation from assimilation remain constrained and trapped in their immediate political situations, dominated by these immediate concerns and limits. This is a vital notion to bear in mind because the national outlook—whether it is state-led assimilation, or more general and diffuse forms of national identity construction that remain hostile to including those from minority backgrounds, French Muslims among them—remains central to the French Muslim story. This precarious balance between the multicultural nature of the French population and the official assimilationist stance of the state is nowhere more important nor more remarkable than in the arena of security—where state security forces have found very interesting and important ways to both accommodate, and also exclude, their Muslim staff over the centuries that Muslims have served the security needs of the republic. It is to this subject that this book now turns.

Bibliography

Abrahamic Group of La Duchère. (2012). *Inter-Religious Declaration of the Abrahamic Group of La Duchère* [Online]. Retrieved from http://www.christianismesocial.org/Declaration-du-Groupe.html

Agence France-Press. (2007). *L'Aïd dans la Cité, un festival qui monte, qui monte à Marseille.* Retrieved from http://www.tv5.org/TV5Site/cinema/afp_article.php

Ahearne, J. (Ed.). (2002). *French Cultural Policy Debates: A Reader*. London: Routledge.

Alba, R. (2005). Bright vs. Blurred Boundaries: Second-Generation Assimilation and Exclusion in France, Germany, and the United States. *Ethnic and Racial Studies, 28*(1), 20–49.

Assemblé Nationale. (2018). *Welcome to the English Website of the French National Assembly – Assemblée Nationale.* Retrieved August 21, 2018, from http://www2.assemblee-nationale.fr/langues/welcome-to-the-english-website-of-the-french-national-assembly

Bel Hadi, F. (2007). *Un Collège Abdelmalek Sayad, pour le symbole, Libération* [Online]. Retrieved from http://www.liberation.fr/societe/010118809-un-college-abdelmalek-sayad-pour-le-symbole

Bleich, E. (2011). Social Research and 'Race' Policy Framing in Britain and France. *The British Journal of Politics & International Relations, 13*(1), 59–74. https://doi.org/10.1111/j.1467-856X.2010.00439.x

Brubaker, R. (2001). The Return of Assimilation? Changing Perspectives on Immigration and Its Sequels in France, Germany, and the United States. *Ethnic and Racial Studies, 24*(4), 531–548.

Bulmer, S., & Radaelli, C. (2004). *The Europeanisation of National Policy?* Queens Papers on Europeanisation (p0042). Belfast, UK: Queens University Belfast.

Camiscioli, E. (2009). *Reproducing the French Race: Immigration, Intimacy and Embodiment in the Early Twentieth Century*. Durham, NC: Duke University Press.

Carrera, S., Guild, E., Vosyliūtė, L., & Bard, P. (2017). *Towards a Comprehensive EU Protection System for Minorities*, p. 182. European Parliament.

Centre Resource Prospective du Grand Lyon. (2012). *Groupe Abraham de La Duchère*. Retrieved from http://www.millenaire3.com/Affichage-de-la-ressou rce.122+M51a10fb25bd.0.html

CoE. (2018). *The European Charter for Regional or Minority Languages Is the European Convention for the Protection and Promotion of Languages Used by Traditional Minorities*. Retrieved August 28, 2018, from https://www.coe. int/en/web/european-charter-regional-or-minority-languages/home

Cole, A. (2008). *Governing and Governance in France*. Cambridge, UK: Cambridge University Press.

Council of Europe. (2008). *Intercultural Cities Joint Action of the Council of Europe and the European Commission Lyon, France 2008*. Retrieved from https://rm.coe.int/1680482a84

Dearden, L. (2016). *Why France Is in Uproar over the Burkini – and Why It Matters*. Retrieved August 26, 2018, from http://www.independent.co.uk/ news/world/europe/burkini-ban-why-is-france-arresting-muslim-women-for-wearing-full-body-swimwear-and-why-are-people-a7207971.html

Downing, J. (2015). Understanding the (Re) Definition of Nationhood in French Cities: A Case of Multiple States and Multiple Republics. *Studies in Ethnicity and Nationalism, 15*(2), 336–351.

Doytcheva, M. (2007). *Une discrimination positive à la Française? Ethnicité et territoire dans les politiques de la ville*. Paris: Broché.

Dunn, J. (1995). The French Highway Lobby: A Case Study in State-Society Relations and Policymaking. *Comparative Politics, 27*, 3–275.

Erlanger, S. (2010, July 13). Parliament Moves France Closer to a Ban on Facial Veils. *The New York Times*. Retrieved from https://www.nytimes. com/2010/07/14/world/europe/14burqa.html

Geisser, V., & Lorcerie, F. (2011). *Rapport Les Marseillais Musulmans*. New York: Open Society Foundation.

Gnedovsky, M. (2009). *Intercultural Cities Program Report on the Visit to Lyon, France*. Council of Europe. Retrieved from http://www.coe.int/t/dg4/cul-tureheritage/culture/cities/GnedovskyICCLyonReport_en.pdf

Hargreaves, A. (2007). *Multi-Ethnic France: Immigration, Politics, Culture and Society* (2nd ed.). New York; London: Routledge.

Hooghe, L. (Ed.). (1996). *Cohesion Policy and European Integration: Building Multi-Level Governance*. Oxford, UK: Oxford University Press.

Hussey, A. (2014). *The French Intifada: The Long War Between France and Its Arabs*. London: Granta.

INSEE. (2016). *Ethnic-Based Statistics | Insee*. Retrieved August 21, 2018, from https://www.insee.fr/en/information/2388586

Knill, C. (2001). *The Europeanisation of National Administrations: Patterns of Institutional Change and Persistence*. Cambridge, UK: Cambridge University Press.

Kymlicka, W. (1996). *Multicultural Citizenship*. Oxford: Oxford University Press.

Kymlicka, W. (2002). *'Multiculturalism' in Contemporary Political Philosophy: An Introduction* (2nd ed.). Oxford: Oxford University Press.

Martin, L. (2013). La démocratisation de la culture en France: une ambition obsolète? In M. Poirrier (Ed.). Retrieved from http://tristan.u-bourgogne.fr/CGC/publications/democratiser_culture/Democratiser_culture.html

Med'in Marseille. (2010). *L'Aïd dans La Cité: Une Fête Pour Tous*. Retrieved from http://www.med-in-marseille.info/L-Aid-dans-la-Cite-une-fete-pour.html

Menucci, P. (2013). *Nous Les Marseillais*. Paris: Pygmalion.

Mitchell, K. (2011). Marseille's Not for Burning: Comparative Networks of Integration and Exclusion in Two French Cities. *Annals of the Association of American Geographers, 101*(2), 404–423.

Modood, T. (2007). *Multiculturalism: A Civic Idea*. London: Polity Press.

Modood, T. (2010). *Still Not Easy Being British: Struggles for a Multicultural Citizenship*. Stoke-on-Trent: Trentham Books.

Moore, D. (2001). *Ethnicité et Politique de la ville en France et en Grande-Bretagne*. Paris: Editions L'Harmattan.

Musées Gadagne. (2013). *Les Minoritiés Religieuses à Lyon de Moyen Age à Nos Jours* [Online]. Retrieved from http://www.gadagne.musees.lyon.fr/index.php/histoire_fr/Histoire/Programmation/Conferences-colloques/Histoire-de-Lyon/Histoire-des-eglises-a-Lyon

Noiriel, G. (1988). *Le Creuset français: Histoire de l'immigration XIXe-XXe Siècles*. Paris: Seuil.

Oliver, P. (1999). Canada's Two Solitudes: Constitutional and International Law in Reference re Secession of Quebec. *International Journal on Minority and Group Rights, 6*(1), 65–95. https://doi.org/10.1163/15718119920907640

Pascual, J., Courouble, E., & Bonniel, J. (2009). *Interculturalism in the Cultural Policies of European Cities*. Retrieved from http://www.coe.int/t/dg4/culture-heritage/culture/cities/CULTURAL.policy_en.pdf

Pervis, A. (2007). *Marseille's Ethnic Bouillabaisse: Some View Europe's Most Diverse City as a Laboratory of the Continent's Future*. Smithsonian Magazine.

Poirrier, P. (Ed.). (2013). *La Politique culturelle en débat: Anthologie 1955–2012*. Paris: Comité d'histoire du Ministère de la culture/La Documentation française.

Raymond, G., & Modood, T. (2007). *The Construction of Minority Identities in France and Britain*. London: Palgrave.

Rice, K. (2009). *Must There Be Two Solitudes? Language Activists and Linguists Working Together*. J. Reyhner & L Lockard (eds.), Indigenous Language Revitalization: Encouragement, Guidance, and Lessons Learned, pp. 37–59. Flagstaff, AZ: Northern Arizona University. http://jan.ucc.nau.edu/~jar/ILR/ILR-4.pdf

Richardson, E. (2006). *Hiphop Literacies*. Retrieved from https://www.amazon.co.uk/Hiphop-Literacies-Elaine-Richardson/dp/0415329272

Rioux, J.-S. (2004). Two Solitudes: Quebecers' Attitudes Regarding Canadian Security and Defence Policy. *Journal of Military and Strategic Studies, 7*(3). Retrieved from https://jmss.org/jmss/index.php/jmss/article/view/143

Safran, W. (1991). State, Nation, National Identity, and Citizenship: France as a Test Case. *International Political Science Review/Revue Internationale de Science Politique, 12*(3), 219–238.

Taylor, C. (1994). *Multiculturalism: Examining the Politics of Recognition*. Princeton, NJ: Princeton University Press.

Tilly, C. (1998). *Durable Inequality*. Berkeley, CA: University of California Press.

Todorov, T., & Anzalone, J. (1989). Nation and Nationalism: The French Variant. *Salmagundi, 84*, 138–153.

Vale, L. (1999). Mediated Monuments and National Identity. *The Journal of Architecture, 4*(4), 391–408.

Ville de Lyon. (2011). *'Our Cultures in the City' Days Program* [Online]. Retrieved from http://www.polville.lyon.fr/polville/sections/fr/les_thematiques/culture/les_journees_nos_cu/

Ville de Lyon. (2012). *Charte de Coopération Culturelle* [Online]. Retrieved from http://www.polville.lyon.fr/static/polville/contenu/Culture/CHARTE%20%203.pdf

Vinocur, N. (2016). *French Court Strikes Down Burkini Ban*. Retrieved August 26, 2018, from https://www.politico.eu/article/french-court-strikes-down-burkini-ban/

Wacquant, L. (2007). *Urban Outcasts: A Comparative Sociology of Advanced Marginality*. Retrieved from https://www.amazon.co.uk/Urban-Outcasts-Comparative-Sociology-Marginality/dp/0745631258/ref=sr_1_3?ie=UTF8&qid=1517652872&sr=8-3&keywords=wacquant

Waizenegger, A., & Hyndman, J. (2010). Two Solitudes: Post-tsunami and Post-conflict Aceh. *Disasters, 34*(3), 787–808. https://doi.org/10.1111/j.1467-7717.2010.01169.x

Weber, E. (1976). *Peasants into Frenchmen: The Modernization of Rural France, 1870–1914* (1st ed.). Stanford, CA: Stanford University Press.

Weber, T. (2005). *Time of Two Solitudes Has Passed: Jean*. Retrieved from https://www.theglobeandmail.com/news/national/time-of-two-solitudes-has-passed-jean/article20426310/

Weil, P. (2008). *How to Be French: Nationality in the Making Since 1789* (C. Porter, Trans.). Durham, NC: Duke University Press.

Wihtol de Wenden, C. (2004). Multiculturalism in France. In *The Governance of Multiculturalism*. Palgrave. Retrieved from http://spire.sciencespo.fr/hdl:/2441/46mbanhapncmp6s99itam92a8/resources/contentserver.asp-1.pdf

Wood, P. (2004). *The Intercultural City: A Reader*. London: Comedia.

Wood, P. (2010). *Intercultural Cities: Towards a Model for Intercultural Integration: Insights from the Intercultural Cities Programme, Joint Action of the Council of Europe and the European Commission*. Strasbourg: Council of Europe.

Young, I. (2009). Structural Injustice and the Politics of Difference. In T. Christiano & J. Christman (Eds.), *Contemporary Debates in Political Philosophy*. Oxford: Blackwell.

Zemouri, A. (2013). *Marseille: soupçon de favoritisme sur la suppléante de Patrick Menucci*. Retrieved from http://www.lepoint.fr/societe/marseille-soupcon-de-favoritisme-sur-la-suppleante-de-patrick-menucci-27-09-2013-1735968_23.php

Zimmer, O. (2003). Boundary Mechanisms and Symbolic Resources: Towards a Process-Oriented Approach to National Identity. *Nations and Nationalism, 9*(2), 173–193. https://doi.org/10.1111/1469-8219.00081

3

Liberating France from Fascism and Upholding Civil Liberties: French Muslims Soldiering and Policing for the Republic

3.1 Introducing Muslims and the French Security Services

On 29 August 1944, the southern port city of Marseille was officially liberated from Nazi occupation. The city had been a key point during the occupation of France for dissidents, artists, Jews, communists and others who were despised by the Nazi regime and its French collaborators to flee to safety in North Africa, the USA and the UK. This role of the city as the point of exit to freedom was even immortalised in the 1942 film *Casablanca*. Interestingly, for a city whose history and present are synonymous with ethnic and religious diversity, the liberation of the city was no different, which gives us an insight into exactly who were the soldiers that brought freedom back to the home of the declaration of the rights of man after a brutal fascist occupation. While the French Resistance in the city and the French troops of the North African regiments played an important role in the liberation of Marseille, a large part was also played by a wide range of Muslim troops, drawn from across North Africa. This shines a light on the vital role played by these troops, who are rarely described as Muslims soldiers.

© The Author(s) 2019
J. Downing, *French Muslims in Perspective*,
https://doi.org/10.1007/978-3-030-16103-3_3

This is an interesting discursive pattern that continues today—with Muslim soldiers in the contemporary French army not discussed as such, while the terrorists who carry out attacks on French soil are freely described as Islamists. Thus, it seems that Muslims are located squarely on one side of the security equation (Roy, 2015). Indeed, the role of French Muslims in securing the republic in the present goes further than simply the army—with French Muslims serving in all facets of the security services, including the police. It has been argued that the number of Muslims serving in the contemporary security apparatus of the French state dwarfs those who have committed terror attacks or travelled to join the so-called Islamic state group in Syria and Iraq (Roy, 2015). However, in a similar vein to their roles in the army being 'colour blind', they are treated simply as soldiers or police officers by the state, absent from ethnic or religious affiliations, and this presents a discursive imbalance in the narratives about French Muslims. Terrorists are labelled 'Islamists' whose cries of Allah Akbar (God is great) are heard during terror attacks, or their dubious claims of allegiance to transnational Islamist networks are broadcast by the media, while a far larger number of Muslim soldiers and police officers remain silent. Thus, narratives about Muslims in the security forces emerge as the 'exceptions', with the 'real' Muslims being those who are terrorists (Roy, 2015). This is clearly not aided by the information asymmetry that the lack of statistics in republican France poses.

As with all domains in France, no statistics exists for the number of Muslim soldiers or police in the French security services. However, there are ways by which social scientists can get an insight into the role played by Muslims in the French army, and importantly what roles they continue to play in the French army. It is necessary to examine both the historical and the contemporary Muslim experience in France for a number of reasons. While the historically and contemporary important role played by Muslim soldiers in the French army renders the army a useful place for the examination of the French Muslim experience, this is far from the only reason to dedicate some time to understanding Muslims in the French army. This is because the army holds a particularly paradoxical position vis-à-vis French Muslims—the military represents an important republican paradox as both a key means by which Muslims have experienced greater integration and recognition than has been afforded them in society, yet at the same time still being subjected to forms of prejudice and discrimination.

This chapter aims to make this argument about the paradoxical role of the French army by bringing together both historical and contemporary instances, debates and social manifestations of the Muslim presence in the French army. This chapter does not aim to be, nor would it be possible for it to be, an exhaustive account of the historical presence of Muslims in the French security forces, and nor should it be, as many insightful chapters, volumes and monographs have been produced on the subject (see inter alia Fogarty, 2012; Ginio, 2017; Settoul, 2015). Rather, this chapter aims to further this argument about the paradoxical role of the French security forces through selected examples that relate to Muslims in the French army. It seeks to bring together the historical and the contemporary in a discussion of the vital role that French Muslims have played, and continue to play, in the armed forces of the republic. The first approach to this will be through setting the Muslim involvement in the French army in historical context, before moving on to an analysis of some of the monuments to Muslims soldiers in the French army that exist in mainland France. To gain a more contemporary insight into the role of French Muslims in the army, this chapter will examine the French Muslims who are employed in the state security forces that have been victims of recent jihadi violence in France. This enables us not only to gain insight into who some of these contemporary Muslims soldiers and police officers are, but also how they are covered in a discursive sense in not only the traditional media outlets such as newspapers, but also through the creation of social media campaigns.

3.2 Liberating France from the Nazis and Upholding the Empire: Conceptualising and Historicising the Muslim Presence in the French Security Services

A book about French Muslims would be incomplete without a discussion of the role of French Muslims in the security forces of the republic. This is something that, while interesting in the contemporary era due to ongo-

ing debates about secularism and the role of Islam in France more generally, has much longer historical roots. Both in France's attempts to
colonise Africa and Asia, and in wars in locations as far flung as Mexico
and Crimea, troops of Muslims origin played significant roles in the ability of France to project its power overseas and at home. However, this is
not the entire story, and such a discussion should not be simply located
in *what was*. This is quite simply because French Muslims playing a key
role in the security of the republic is also *what is* in the sense that French
Muslims maintain a key role in securing the republic and fighting for the
freedoms and liberties which they are so often accused of subverting and
fighting against. Thus, rather than being a deeply situated historiography
of the origin and role of Muslim troops in the various incarnations of the
French army over the past several hundred years, this chapter keeps with
this book's broader methodological statement of engaging with the
broader narrative discussions around Muslims in the French army. Thus,
this chapter will not set out to provide an exhaustive account of particular
events, but will rather look inductively at sites of narrative production
and social relations that structure the relations between Muslim soldiers
in their diversity and the French armed forces. Important in this are also
the legacies left in concrete and stone across France that seek to commemorate and continue to draw attention to this role of Muslims in the
French armed forces.

The French security forces have a long history of being extremely multicultural in their make-up. The first recruitment of non-white troops
into the French army occurred in seventeenth-century India. The use of
North African troops rapidly accelerated in the nineteenth century, with
the North African soldiers having a special place in the French army—
they did not serve in the colonial army, but rather in the French African
Army (Armée d'Afrique), which was a branch of the metropolitan French
army garrisoned in Morocco, Algeria and Tunisia (Fogarty, 2012).
Muslim Algerian troops began fighting for the French during the earliest
days of the conquest of Algeria in 1830, then fighting in other colonies,
Crimea, Italy and even in mainland France during the Franco-Prussian
War of 1870 (Fogarty, 2012). Not all Muslims were so keen to serve in
the French army, with those from West Africa more difficult to recruit
due to a mix of not wanting to compromise religious values during mili-

tary service, and also due to a dislike of egalitarian military service, meaning those from the upper- and middle classes serving alongside those from lower-class backgrounds (Fogarty, 2012). However, from the beginning the service of Muslims in the French army represented a paradox under the strict racial and religious hierarchies of the French empire. This is because the military order, while not totally meritocratic or egalitarian, was far more egalitarian than these strict hierarchies of the colonial order (Bougarel, Branche, & Drieu, 2017). Not only did Muslim troops serve alongside French troops and officers, they also often had their first experiences of the colonial metropole during their time serving in France, where they would mix with the local populace. This was particularly interesting because relations between those of Muslim origin and the white French were much different in metropolitan France than they were in the colonies. North African soldiers were generally welcomed in France, with some exceptions, but there were generally far better relations between Europeans and North Africans in metropolitan France than in Algeria itself (Bougarel et al., 2017). Thus, away from the daily requirements of upholding a de-humanising colonial order, where hierarchies were the dominant organising force of social relations, differences softened and Muslims soldiers experienced social relations with their non-Muslim French peers that would have been shocking in light of the encounters in the colonies (Bougarel et al., 2017).

This does not mean, however, that the army itself was not the subject of creating other forms of racial and cultural hierarchies within the ranks of its Muslim soldiers. This was true both of the construction of the black Muslim troops from West Africa as strong and reliable, and for the North African Muslim troops noted for their 'oriental' penchant for exaggerating (Fogarty, 2012). This trend also continued with troops from the Maghreb. Here, it was seen that even within a culturally similar geographical area the ability of troops to fight varied widely—with Moroccans being seen as warriors, Algerians as men, and Tunisian male troops as 'women'(Fogarty, 2012), which led to the question as to whether Tunisians were fit to go to war at all (Fogarty, 2012).

During their deployments, Muslims soldiers remained remarkably loyal to serving France, even when serving in other Muslim territories. This was even after senior French officers articulated serious concerns about the possible loyalties of French Muslim troops for a number of complex reasons. Because of its supposed opposition to the enlightenment and 'civilisation', Islam was seen as the most suspicious of the religions of the colonised in the French armed forces (Ginio, 2017). This was a particularly complex issue for the French to deal with because of the situations that Muslim soldiers were put in to either fight other Muslims, or allies of Muslim states. An example of this occurred when the Ottomans and Germans in the First World War had called for Muslim soldiers to fight 'holy war' against France and its allies (Ginio, 2017). This was considered extremely worrisome, as at the time the Ottoman Khalif was seen as the highest authority in Sunni Islam, with the Ottoman Empire having nominal control, but significant influence, over Algiers and Tunis prior to French control. However, it soon became obvious that these worries were unfounded when the troops did not mutiny against the French and remained loyal in fighting the Germans. This has been explained in terms of the cultural nuances between Muslims—'the Muslims of North Africa have nothing in common with the Turks but their religion' (Meynier & Vidal-Naquet, 1981, p. 269, cited in Fogarty, 2012).

This was not the only situation that put the loyalty of Muslims soldiers in question when fighting other Muslims. One of the key uses of Muslim troops under the empire was to police, patrol and pacify other colonised territories, some of these Muslim. The reasons for this were multiple—the idea that Muslim troops were more adapted to local conditions, cheaper to employ but importantly that their deaths during colonial misadventures were far less politically contentious than those of French troops (Fogarty, 2012). This French practice of using colonial troops from one colony to pacify and secure another meant that Muslim troops from one region were moved to another to police the country (Ginio, 2017). In particular, the use of Muslim Senegalese troops in Algeria provoked concern that the respect the African Muslims had for Arabic and Islamic civilisation undermined not only their loyalty to the French army but also the reverence they were expected to have for all things European (Ginio, 2017). These concerns were again proved to be unfounded, and the service of such troops was vital in enabling white French troops to stay in metropolitan France to guard against what was seen as the most serious security threat of the time—Germany (Fogarty, 2012). However, when these troops proved to be insufficient in both world wars to thwart German aggression it was colonial troops, a large number of them Muslim, who were called upon to at first aid France in its hour of need during the First World War, and then to actually work to liberate mainland France and fight white French collaborationist forces to free France from fascist occupation. For example, during the First World War some 500,000 out of the 8 million total troops mobilised for the French forces were from the colonies. While not all of these were Muslims, they undoubtedly made up a large proportion of this number.

These encounters in service to France both in the colonies and in the metropole would expose Muslim troops in novel and often life-threatening ways to the complex issues of republican universalism existing alongside racial and religious differences of the colonial subjects. While in many ways they had seen this in the colonies, it was shed a new light and complicated by the sacrifices these troops made for France as dedicated citizens, but recognition of these sacrifices were not forthcoming from the republic in granting them civil parity with their white French counterparts (Ginio, 2017).

This experience of service was significant in shaping notions of independence from France. Not only had the colonial Muslims troops who had fought for France served the republic and then been denied recognition as equal citizens, travelling to France and witnessing its vulnerability to attack and conquest were important in undermining the view that France was the invincible colonial overlord. Also, the French army was a key vehicle of progress that gave non-Europeans an opportunity for self-development in ways that the colonial hierarchies did not allow in other domains. This sometimes worked in paradoxical ways, with Muslim figures who supported the French and fought for them then turning against the imperial power. Thus, these experiences of servitude in the army would sometimes indirectly stir a patriotism and yearning for the homeland that would lead to the resistance to French rule in Algeria (Bougarel et al., 2017). For example, Khaled Abd-el-Kadir, the grandson of the anti-French figure Emir Abd-el-Kadir, served in the French forces and his presence was regarded as demonstrating the legitimacy of fighting for the French, even though his grandfather had been the key figure in resisting the original French conquest of the country.

However, this does not mean that Muslim service in the French army was universally accepted and unproblematic. In the scrabble for independence, those Muslims who served on the side of the French rapidly found themselves on the wrong side of history as independence progressed, especially where it took its most violent and dramatic form in Algeria. This shows the complexity of the Algerian war of independence—while the freedom fighters at the time liked to call it anti-colonial war, the experience of the Harkis demonstrate the uncomfortable reality that it also showed properties of a civil conflict which didn't simply pit the Algerians against European settled colonialists but also squarely against other Algerians (Hamoumou, 1990).

This meant that the Harkis, those Muslim Algerians who served with the French army, suddenly found themselves persona non grata in Algeria, despite promises to protect them as part of the Evian accords which ended French rule in Algeria (Ageron, 2000). This persecution included extremely violent torture and killing of Harkis and even sometimes their entire families (Ageron, 2000). This is pertinent because of the plurality of reasons through which Muslim Algerians would serve in the French auxiliary forces during the Algerian war—they often did so for economic reasons rather than a deep-seated loyalty to the idea of French occupation (Moser, 2014). This was further complicated by many Harkis either being veterans of previous wars, such as the Second World War, or from families or groups who had a history of providing service to the French army (Horne, 2006). Thus, clearly a lot of those who found themselves on the side of the French did so through a mix of many reasons. Indeed, it should also be considered that the possibility of France actually granting independence to Algeria when the war broke out in 1954 seemed extremely unlikely. Algeria was not simply a French colony but an actually department of France, and it also contained a large European settler population and provided significant economic benefits to metropolitan France. There is also something of a class element to the persecution of those Harkis who suffered after the French left Algeria, because many of those who took power as part of the new independent government had also fought for the French at different times, but often in more senior roles, and were not the subject of reprisal killings (Moser, 2014). Perhaps most tragically, while over 2 million European settlers moved to France at the end of French rule in Algeria (the 'pieds noirs' or black feet, so called because they wore black boots), the French government of the time attempted to block a similar move for Harkis, leaving them to face brutal treatment in Algeria (Ageron, 2000). Additionally, those that managed to get to France were often blocked from integrating into society, and put in internment camps outside of major cities mainly in the south of France (Kader Hamadi, 2006). It took a long time for the Harkis to gain national recognition, with the government of Jacques Chirac offering them national recognition only in 2003 through the creation of a Harkis national day (Ministére des armées, 2013). Even when fighting for France against fellow Algerians, therefore, the Harkis could not fully transcend the hierarchies of the empire, and received significantly different treatment from the state compared to the returning European settlers.

There is another important aspect of Muslim service in the French army that still has implications today. This is the way that, even in their early colonial era with its strict racial and religious hierarchies, the French army was more amenable to Islamic practices than other state institutions. This adds to earlier observations that war and the military order were more egalitarian than the colonial order, because this logic was furthered by the way that the French army was able to adapt and incorporate Islam in ways that today seem so contradictory and impossible for the French central state (Bougarel et al., 2017). This is an early example of the 'multiple states, multiple republics' (Downing, 2015) logic at work, where no organ of the French state has a monopoly on defining what laïcité means, with each having surprising autonomy in defining exactly what the central guiding ideology of the state on religious matters means in any given context. Indeed, this has been argued to have gone so far as to have actually increased and encouraged the conversion of West African soldiers from traditional animist beliefs to Islam (Ginio, 2017). This was argued to be due to the favourable view of West African Islam and the accommodation of Islamic burial and religious practice in the French army during these colonial times (Ginio, 2017).

This practice did not stop in colonial times but rather continues in the contemporary French army. In 2015, after the Charlie Hebdo attack, the French government launched Operation Sentinel, which saw groups of French troops deployed on patrol on the streets of French cities to bolster local police forces against possible terror attacks. Anyone that has been in France and witnessed these patrols may have noticed the ethnic diversity of these patrolling soldiers, which gives a rare glimpse into the diversity of an army in a state which does not collect ethnic or religious statistics in mainstream society, let alone the army. But ethnically diverse the French army is, with many from non-white backgrounds choosing the army as a route of social progress in the face of significant discrimination in the labour market (Wihtol de Wenden, 2010). This is clearly not simply a Muslim issue in a country where youth unemployment among all ethnic groups, including working-class whites, is persistently high and a significant social problem. However, it does mean that, like their forefathers under the colonial order, a significant number of French Muslims have chosen the army as an avenue of socio-economic and individual progress when other avenues are possibly closed to them because of their socio-economic, ethnic and/or religious backgrounds (Wihtol de Wenden, 2010).

This presence of French Muslims in the French army came to the attention of the media in 2009 when it emerged that French Muslim soldiers had refused to serve for the French army in Afghanistan, citing an unwillingness to fight fellow Muslims (Merchet, 2009). However, these are extremely rare cases, totalling only four to five a year, or 0.01% of the engaged French forces (Merchet, 2009). This fringe phenomenon belies the far more significant findings of sociological enquiry, which demonstrate that French Muslims in the army are actually extremely well integrated and loyal. Bertossi and Wihtol de Wenden (2007) found that not only did Muslim soldiers in the army feel French first and foremost and were strongly committed to republican values of liberty and equality, they also saw the army as an important means by which to traverse the endemic discrimination in French society. Additionally, the French military benefits from a clause in the 1905 law that separated church and state in that it falls into a category of government entities, including hospitals, universities and schools, which allows religious practices to be tolerated and the costs covered by the state (Settoul, 2015). While clearly this freedom in schools and universities is constantly the subject of debate about its exact definition, similar questions have not been applied to the army, which enjoys significant autonomy in common with many other government institutions. This enabled the military to create its first Muslim chaplaincy in 2006 (Settoul, 2015). This does not mean that the army is free from problems of discrimination based on religious or ethnic lines (Bertossi & Wihtol de Wenden, 2007). The creation of the Muslim chaplaincy was actually comparatively late as the army already had this provision for Catholic, Protestant and Jewish soldiers—and until 2006, Muslim soldiers in the French army actually existed in a state of non-provision which violated the constitutional provisions of religious practice outlined above.

However, it is not just in the army that French Muslims serve the security needs of the republic. They also constitute an important, yet again statistically hidden, contingent of French police forces across the country. Roy (2015) argues that there are more Muslims serving in the French army and police forces than who fight for Al-Qaida or the Islamic state. He also correctly highlights a greater discursive problem in examining the Muslim presence in the security forces in France. This is the issue with narratives about Muslims in the security forces as the 'exceptions' with the 'real' Muslims being those who are terrorists (Roy, 2015). This is clearly not aided by the information asymmetry that the lack of statistics in republican France poses. While terrorists of many different stripes of Muslim origin are represented as such freely in the media—regardless of their actual guilt in an event, or simply being of 'suspicion' of planning a terror attack—the lack of statistics or details about Muslims in the French army or police render them discursively invisible.

Even from the perspective of organised scholarship, there is a significant dearth of research on Muslims in police forces across Europe, with Sharp (2013) being a notable exception due to his work on the experiences of Muslim police officers. Rather, literature on Muslims and the police follows a pattern which mainly deals with discussions around 'policing' Muslim communities in an age where they have become constructed as a significant security threat (Chakraborti, 2013). This dearth continues historically, there is very little written about Muslims and the French police, apart from some important work done on the Paris special unit which existed to police the Algerian community in the city from 1944 to 1958 (Blanchard, 2004). Even in terms of journalism, very little is published in newspapers about Muslim police officers in France, bar exceptional stories, such as that concerning the French Muslim who was on the terror watch list who successfully applied to the police, and was eventually accepted to become a full police officer (Chieze, 2017). Thus, this is where the victimhood of officers killed in the line of duty provides a rare insight into not only who police officers of Muslim origin are in France, but also how they are discursively constructed.

3.3   Paradoxes in Stone and Bronze: War Memorials and Historical Commemoration of Muslims in the French Army

It is no surprise in a country with such a long history of Muslim soldiers serving in its armed forces that there exist significant amounts of memorials to military campaigns in which Muslims played a central role. However, in keeping with the paradoxes of the military as both a key means by which Muslims have experienced greater integration and recognition than has been afforded them in society, yet at the same time still being subjected to forms of prejudice and discrimination, monuments have a chequered history of commemorating, or not, the Muslim contribution to the French military. This is pertinent because war memorials have been correctly identified as important for the creation of political memory and understandings of nationalism (see inter alia Evans & Lunn, 1997; Hagopian, 2009; Johnson, 1995; Kattago, 2009; Mosse, 1991; Winter, 1998; J. E. Young, 1993).

Monuments are important sites at which the imagined community of the nation are constructed (Johnson, 1995). They are extremely diverse in terms of location, meaning, form, iconography and gendering (Johnson, 1995), and important in the ways a range of local, national, and contending cultural politics and positions have been articulated (Johnson, 1995). The meaning, shape and political position of war memorials are highly contentious (Hagopian, 2009). Thus, it is extremely difficult to balance the inevitable contending and competing understandings of what war, sacrifice and the nation mean to diverse veterans groups, politicians and society more generally (Hagopian, 2009). Attention to this process in the Vietnam War is necessary here because of the neo-colonial nature of the conflict, the somewhat unclear purpose of a war that was fought overseas where the integrity and survival of the state was not immediately in danger, and where the state commemorating the war actually lost the war (Hagopian, 2009). These concerns, which render the conflict all the more contentious, generate even more problems when it comes to how to commemorate them. France's colonial wars have much in common with mass conscription being used to wage a war overseas that was unpopular at home and ultimately resulted in the unexpected defeat of one of the era's most powerful colonial powers. Commemoration involving Muslims fighting for France is a complicated affair. This, to a certain degree, is the result of the Algerian War of Independence, and the chaos which ensued, being a national military embarrassment.

Memorials have been correctly critiqued for being far from neutral entities and like all post facto renderings of history are imbued with the hues of not just nationalism, but of the political, social and cultural concerns, trends and issues of the times (J. E. Young, 1993). Within this, however, is the observation of the centrality of death and sacrifice for the nation in war memorials. Winter highlights the importance of death and sacrifice as shaping the politics and more importantly imagination of the postwar era (Winter, 1998). This takes memory and monuments away strictly from a selection of stone and bronze to include cinema and public culture. But this is not static either—death in service of the nation is a vital feature not just in the creation of war memorials, but also in the shaping of postwar culture, politics and memory (Mosse, 1991).

The dynamism of monuments is also something that is deeply significant to their study and understanding (Mayo, 1988). Monuments change over time and the specifics of the present have powerful forces to render the meaning of monuments to the past very differently (Evans & Lunn, 1997). Thus, monuments 'go to sleep' and can 'wake up', given new social and political developments (Kattago, 2009). This has been well covered in the dramatic sense when a political context changes and a monument is moved, for example, creating resistance and protest (Kattago, 2009).

However, somewhat neglected in this literature is how war memorials to foreign troops are rendered meaningful in light of contemporary debates on multiculturalism and the role of minorities in modern diverse societies. This is important because of the understandings gained from the 'banal' nature of national identity construction (Billig, 1995). National identity is not something that is simply constructed consciously through the state sphere and national politics but is something that is very much constructed in the daily interaction of individuals with symbols, narratives, objects and rituals. Historical war memorials are somewhat paradoxical, because at one time they were part of the state's attempt to create and disseminate conscious constructions of what the nation, and indeed sacrifice in its name, meant politically. However, as time goes on, and they become 'banalised' parts of the daily landscape, they become part of the symbolic repertoire of the banal daily experience. As such, their meaning changes over time depending on the broader context in which they find themselves.

Therefore, narratives to the historical contribution of a contentious minority in the present takes on a different meaning. In the same way that contemporary developments in contexts such as post-Soviet states render memorials to Soviet troops different contemporary meaning (Kattago, 2009), monuments to Muslim soldiers in the French army are key points in the redefinition of what it means to be French in the contemporary era. France, like many other countries around the world, is not short on war memorials or physical tributes to soldiers in its towns and cities—especially concerning the activities of colonial soldiers in the First World War, there are many tributes to them across France (Aldrich, 2005). Alongside the inauguration of the Paris Mosque as a reward for colonial soldiers' service in the First World War, it seems that at this point in history France did not have the reservations about the commemoration of Muslim soldiers in the French army that it has currently. At times, monuments have been extremely late to be constructed for Muslim troops, monuments have been repatriated from North Africa where the Muslim Harkis were left to be persecuted, or given centre stage in cities. Here, there are examples of interesting, multifaceted ways in which these monuments contribute not just to the commemoration of Muslim soldiers' actions in events from over 50 years ago, but also as an important means by which the Muslim contribution to the creation, persistence and defence of France occurs in the public realm. This is significant in a state context that frowns upon public expression of religion or ethnicity, and especially interesting given the overwhelming attention paid to Muslims in the public sphere as threats to the republic.

This first stop that this chapter makes is to examine a monument to war in France, which includes a commemoration of Muslims troops from the First World War. This demonstrates the paradoxes of commemoration around the end of the colonial empires in North Africa which live on in contemporary France to this day. On the independence of North Africa, the French military undertook what has been described as the largest repatriation of monuments in history (Aldrich, 2005). In the wake of independence, and at great expense to the French military, in particular the navy, an entire host of plaques, statues and sculptures were retrieved from North Africa and relocated to bases, towns and cities in metropolitan France (Aldrich, 2005). These have been termed 'monuments in exile', because like the few lucky Harkis that managed to escape post-independence North Africa, they could not return home and were marooned in metropolitan France, away from their original setting.

This is rendered all the more paradoxical because while the repatriation of Harkis was blocked by the French government of the time, these monuments were prioritised above human beings. It has already been established that the denial of repatriation to the Harkis is a particularly dark moment among many dark moments under the French empire (Ageron, 2000; Moser, 2014). However, to fully understand the paradox of this event in light of the commemoration of war in France, it is necessary to analyse the repatriation programme that was granted to war memorials. An example of such a monument is the Monument aux Morts d'Oran now located in Lyon. This is a particularly interesting case because of the changing nature of its location in Lyon. After repatriation from Oran in Algeria, it was inaugurated in the neighbourhood of La Duchère during its construction when it was conceptualised as a new, modernist, desirable suburb of the city. However, like many high-rise estates constructed at this time it has since fallen into disrepair and marginalisation from the city, resulting in it being one of the sites of the sporadic social unrest common in such areas of French cities. As such, today it exists in a marginalised location, away from the historical centre of the city.

The Monument aux Morts d'Oran also has a context that renders this placement even more significant. The monument was inaugurated in May 1927 to commemorate the 12,000 residents of Oran who died during the First World War, and was originally called the Monument of Victory and erected in Oran in French Algeria. It was over 12 metres high, and consisted of an imposing stone plinth, on top of which was the representation of three symbolic soldiers. It contained an inscribed dedication to 'The Department of Oran and its children who died for the fatherland—1914–1918'. It was also inscribed with the names of famous battles at which the residents died: Charleroi, Marne, Aisne, Flandre, Artois, Lorraine, Somme, Champagne, Verdun, Argonne, Dardanelles, Orient. At the back of the monument, facing the sea, is the inscription 'Souvenez-vous (Remember)'. It also contains the numbers of the dead from each arrondissement of Oran: 3208; Sidi-Bel-Abbès: 1217; Mostaganem: 3439; Tlemcen: 1136; Mascara: 2257; Sud-Oranais: 1252.

It occupied a prestigious location in a central square of Oran, next to the sea front. In 1956, the city of Oran was twinned with Lyon in France, shortly after which the French occupation of Algeria ended in 1962. At the time in Lyon, the large housing complex of La Duchère was still being built, and the mayor of Lyon, Louis Pradel, recognising the needs of the influx of uprooted people from Algeria, who at the time mainly consisted of European settlers (pied noirs), gave half of the homes in the estate to them.

He also wished to create a memorial space to commemorate their contributions to France, at which time attention fell on the war memorial in Oran. The municipal council mobilised a team to organise and negotiate for the repatriation of the statue, with Napoleon Bullukian, a Lyonnais Armenian philanthropist, funding the entire cost of the exercise. In 1967, negotiations with the Algerian authorities were successful and the monument was cut from its eight-metre-high base in Oran in December, and left for Marseille. The statue was inaugurated in July 1968 in a ceremony attended by many returnees from Algeria, where Mr Fenech, president of the National Federation of Returnees gave the following, insightful speech: 'It reminds our land of Oran and the struggle of two generations of his son to live in France. It will be the Shrine where returnees, who have lost their graves, will evoke the memory of their dead' (La Région Auvergne-Rhône-Alpes, 2007). Several plaques were also added to the monument: a tribute to the 'Army of Africa' and a tribute to the battles fought on the 'Rhine and Danube', with the following inscription added in gold letters: 'In memory of their native land, from the city of Lyon to the children of North Africa that it has received'. This specifically brings French Muslims into the frame in this renewed setting of commemoration, because the Army of Africa contained significant numbers of French Muslims who fought for France during the First World War.

However, this act is rendered somewhat hypocritical when compared with the treatment of the Harkis left in Algeria. While it was possible to fund the negotiations and transportation of a large piece of stone from Oran to Lyon, it was not possible for the French authorities to negotiate or even accept the return of those Algerian Muslims who had fought in Algeria for the pacification of the country for French interests. They were deliberately blocked from returning to France by the policy of the de Gaulle government of the time, unlike Algerian Jews or European settlers who were given French nationality and welcomed back to metropolitan France. Despite guarantees by the Algerian authorities that no reprisals would be taken against them, it is estimated that between 30,000 and 150,000 Harkis and their dependants were killed after independence in extremely brutal circumstances (Horne, 2006).

Another facet of history that would render this effort to commemorate foreign service in the French army in a different manner than originally intended was the fate of La Duchère itself. When the statue was installed, the development had barely been finished, and the installation of the statue in a neighbourhood that was largely used to house returning settlers and those that fought for France, may have been regarded with some optimism as something to commemorate these communities' efforts for France. But unfortunately, by the 1990s this was a case par excellence of French urban decay and the well documented failures of the postwar building boom and its concentration on constructing high-rise, high-density housing on the isolated outskirts of French cities. Accordingly, this great effort to commemorate this contribution to France eventually came to stand at the centre of a run-down, stigmatised and highly problematic area of Lyon, site of regular urban disturbances. Also, the area, like many of those built during the 1960s, would come to house migrants from the Maghreb who came to France as migrant workers, who may not have seen the memorial for those who fought to maintain the harsh colonial regime in the middle of their housing estate as something that would have aided in their inclusiveness in the narrative of France. This placement in La Duchère symbolises the paradoxical nature of the commemoration of conflict across changing geographical, social and political contexts and demonstrates the dynamism of monuments, even when they may seem to 'sleep' (Kattago, 2009) in a situation of passive 'exile' (Almato, 1979). The changing local and national conditions are important in the changing nature of their meaning and significance. However, this does not mean that the national memorial is not important in the commemoration of Muslims in France's wars.

The creation by the French government in 2002 of a national memorial to those who died in its colonial wars in North Africa is an interesting monument to analyse when discussing the commemoration of French Muslims in French military history. The national scale is important, not least because of the way that national politics is the field within which contending notions of the meaning of death, conflict and the sacrifices made by those who died are playing out (Hagopian, 2009). Thus, the ongoing debates about the role of Muslims in republican life render the national memorial an important scale at which to examine the way that Muslim soldiers are commemorated in France. In particular, the fact that it is the national level that imposes policies of non-recognition on French society adds a further level of complexity to commemorations that are made on ethnic or religious grounds, as the republic is extremely hostile to enshrining such ideas in both public politics and also to the (re)construction of the French nation more broadly.

It should be noted that there remains no united national memorial to the service of Muslim soldiers in the French army. This is not something that is just specific to France, as many ex-colonial powers have been reluctant, and late, to acknowledge the role of those who served them from their former colonies. For example, a memorial to the African and Caribbean soldiers who served Britain during the world wars was not unveiled until 2017, despite over two million African and Caribbean soldiers serving Britain during these two conflicts (BBC, 2017). This does not mean, however, that there was no physical recognition given to the Muslims that gave their lives in service of France. Indeed, the Grand Mosque of Paris, located in the Latin Quarter with its beautiful Moorish design, was built to commemorate the lives of the Muslim soldiers who died fighting for France during the First World War (Davidson, 2009). Interestingly, the mosque would go on to become a central force, if a contentious one, in the Muslim presence in France which continues to the present day. The mosque even played an important role in saving Jews during the Nazi occupation of France (Katz, 2012). However, the mosque itself is not a war memorial per se, and has far larger public functions than simply being a commemoration of the Muslims who died, and continue to serve and die, for France. Given the massive contributions of Muslim soldiers during the liberation of France during the Second World War, and indeed in the defence of French control in Algeria, the creation of the mosque to commemorate those who died during the First World War misses these great sacrifices made in later years.

The closest that France comes is the national memorial inaugurated in 2002, that memorialises the Algerian war and combatants from Morocco and Tunisia (Mémorial national de la guerre d'Algérie et des combats du Maroc et de la Tunisie). The complexities of this monument and its relation to Muslims because of the complicated nature of the events that it commemorates should be pointed out. In line with observations about memorialisation on the national level (Hagopian, 2009), memorialisation is never a simple process, especially when it comes to wars that were fought for colonial preservation or expansion that were extremely controversial. Indeed, there remains little as controversial in France as the legacy, shame and human rights abuses committed in Algeria. As such, scholars have named it a forgotten war—a 'war with no name' (Cohen, 2002). It has been the significant focus for post-colonial activities to attempt to bring some of the events of the Algerian war out into the public realm (Downing, 2016). Thus, France has been quite late in tackling its colonial legacy. This should be borne in mind when examining this monument to those who died in the wars in North Africa. It should also be noted that this monument has an extremely limited remit overall, and is even more limited when it comes to commemorating Muslim soldiers.

The monument is located in central Paris, in the shadow of the Eiffel Tower. It does have significant implications for French Muslims because a large number of Algerian Muslims also served in the French army during the colonial era in Algeria (the Harkis) and fought to keep that territory part of France (Ageron, 2000; Moser, 2014). On independence these troops faced the choice of leaving for France or staying and potentially being executed for their collaboration with France. It is partially these troops who are commemorated here, alongside their non-Muslim counterparts that died in the independence struggles of France's North African colonies.

The memorial itself consists of three columns, 5.85 metres high, at the centre of which are electronic screens, which correspond to the colours of the French flag. Each screen shows a different aspect of information. The first column continuously displays the full names of the 23,000 soldiers and Harkis who died for France in North Africa. The second column displays messages recalling the period of the Algerian war and the memory of those who disappeared after the ceasefire. On 26 March 2010, the French government decided to add the names of civilian victims of the massacre of pro-independence demonstrators at the rue d'Isly, Algiers, on 26 March 1962. The third column includes an interactive screen at its foot where visitors can search for and view the names of a particular soldier. The ground near the monument bears the following inscription: 'In memory of the fighters who died for France during the war in Algeria and battles in Morocco and Tunisia, and all members of the auxiliary forces, killed after the cease-fire in Algeria, many of which have not been identified'. There is also a plaque with the following message: 'The Nation commemorates the disappeared persons and the civilian victims of massacres and abuses committed during the war in Algeria and after March 19, 1962 in violation of the Evian agreements, as well as civilian victims of the fighting in Morocco and Tunisia, in tribute to the soldiers who died for France in North Africa'.

This is significant because it addresses the sacrifices of those Harkis who not only died during the war but those who were subsequently denied entry to France after the war and were killed in revenge killings by fellow Algerians. Adding to the importance of this gesture is its location in a prime area of central Paris. The situation of monuments is important in rendering them meaning and prominence in the national narrative (Johnson, 1995). The Quai Branly location of this monument puts it very much at the centre of Paris, near to sites of national importance such as the Eiffel Tower, Les Invalides and the École Militaire. This places the commemoration of these events, at least physically, at the centre of French national life, and the life of the city of Paris. Thus, a monument at least partially dedicated to the deaths of Muslims for France has a central location and has not been hidden away in obscurity.

However, this does not mean that the monument itself is unproblematic for other reasons when it concerns the question of commemorating French Muslims and their efforts fighting for France. There is firstly the issue of chronology; the establishment of the monument in 2002 demonstrates how long it has taken for France to begin to offer commemoration to these groups. This means that the memorial was constructed some 40 years after the main influx of immigrants from the Maghreb at the end of the French empires, allowing 40 years during which their history was not commemorated in any way in the national capital of France.

This time lag is arguably important for several reasons. Firstly, a significant number of those that came to France from North Africa on the independence of France's ex-colonies did not do so voluntarily, but were forced to flee owing to their collaboration with the French forces and civil administration in North Africa, most notably Algeria. As has been mentioned, even on their return to France they were interned in 'temporary' camps and denied national recognition of their roles fighting for the interests of France overseas (Kader Hamadi, 2006). On the granting of the ex-colony's independence, this community was faced with the choice of leaving North Africa or staying and risking death at the hands of those who had fought for independence, and indeed many that stayed behind or who were impeded in their exit were killed in extremely brutal circumstances (Horne, 2006). While this monument does include the names of some civilians who were killed during the war, it does little to confront the brutality of French occupation and the large numbers of Muslim Algerians that died, both civilians and pro-independence combatants, during the war of independence. This remains work that is not being done by the French state, but rather by activist groups, such as Les Oranges in the Parisian suburb of Nanterre (Downing, 2016).

Understanding the complexities of the colonial encounter and the commemoration of war becomes even more complicated when examining the monuments which, unlike the Harkis who were left to be murdered in Algeria, were actually repatriated by the French military as part of the colonial withdrawal.

We have seen that in both Paris and Lyon the commemoration of Muslims in the French military remains a paradoxical and problematic process in France, which is dealing with its colonial history rather late. An important example of an opportunity to commemorate Muslim contribution in Marseille exists in the Monument of the Dead of the Armies of the Orient and Distant Lands (Monument aux Morts de l'Armée d'Orient et des Terres Lointaines). The monument's geographical placement is key (Johnson, 1995), having pride of place on the important corniche road of the city, one of the city's main thoroughfares, running alongside the beach and fairly affluent neighbourhoods. In 1921, the French government gave authorisation to Marseille for a national monument to commemorate victims of the French army who died overseas during the First World War (Monumentum.fr, 2018). A competition for the design was launched after the colonial exposition of 1922, with Gaston Castel being chosen out of 17 contestants. With the sculptor Antoine Sartorio, they proposed a monument in the shape of a door on the coastal road facing out to sea, to remind that Marseille has the position as the 'Porte de l'Orient' and also so that it can be seen from a long distance by ships entering the city's port. Inaugurated in April 1927, the monument forms a large arch, with a crescent and star at its centre, and its underside decorated with stylised palms. It is flanked on either side by characters of soldiers on foot, in memory of the army and air force, while two female figures with large wings stand on pedestals, representing the heroism of these troops. At the centre of the arch stands a statue of Victory, represented in a female form, with arms outstretched to the sky. On the side, the names and dates of the major campaigns of the war are inscribed. This monument has arguably played an important part of the commemoration of the role of outsiders in the city.

This monument very prominently gives recognition to the important function played by those from outside the city in not only defending the city, but also defending the French nation during the First World War.

However, this monument again demonstrates an interesting phenomenon in that the meaning of monuments can change dramatically over time, given the contextual changes that occur around them. We have already seen that the monument to the dead of Oran in the La Duchère neighbourhood of Lyon has suffered from the progress of history, with the deterioration of the area around it from a new promising neighbourhood to a decaying suburb that sees recurring social violence. However, the placement of this monument in Marseille in effect works in the opposite direction, because the location has maintained prominence as the city around it has socially changed in the years since it was built, welcoming as it has large numbers of North African migrants not just into Marseille to settle there, but also as the point of entry into France more generally. It is probable that very few of those involved with its commissioning or inauguration in 1927 could have foreseen that it would see the loss of the French empire from which those troops came and then the mass movement of people from these ex-colonies to the city as refugees or to seek employment or political asylum. Additionally, this monument has been adopted by contemporary French Muslims as a symbol of the city and has been used on a French rap album cover. The rap group 3ème Oeil, consisting of two Marseillais Muslim artists originally from the Comoro Islands, chose this monument for the cover of their 1999 album 'Hier, Aujourd'hui, Demain', which sold over 160,000 copies in France.

3.4 Insights into Contemporary Muslim's Contributions: Conceptualising Victimhood

Bringing this analysis from the historical to the contemporary, we now turn our attention to the recent Muslim victims of jihadi terror attacks who worked for the security services. The narratives created by these forms of victimhood not only influence the way that contemporary Muslim identities in France are constructed and created, but also how recent terror attacks in France can be labelled. Thus, the fact that Muslims have died in the service of the French security services at the hands of Islamist terrorists not only brings attention to their work, which is much needed (Roy, 2015), but also makes a dichotomy of the Muslim terrorist who kills Europeans in a 'clash of civilisations' (Huntingdon, 1993) hard to maintain.

The asymmetry of information on ethnic and religious backgrounds in France continues into this domain. It is impossible to get statistics or detailed information on the religious or ethnic background of French soldiers. As already stated, this is due to the national laws which, in the name of the second amendment of the constitution, guarantee equality and forbid the collection of statistics on the ethnic or religious backgrounds of French citizens. This clearly presents an obstacle to scholars who are interested in exploring the roles, origins and social status of Muslim soldiers in the French army. A notable exception to this was the ground-breaking work of Bertossi and Wihtol de Wenden (2007), who were the first sociologists to gain access to the French army to conduct research into the experience of soldiers within the institution itself. Here, they uncovered a situation where French Muslims not only saw the army as a vehicle for socio-economic improvement in a society which discriminated against them, but also that the soldiers saw themselves as French first and above all and were very committed to Republican ideals (Bertossi & Wihtol de Wenden, 2007).

As mentioned earlier, the numbers of Muslims serving in the contemporary security apparatus of the French state dwarfs those who have committed terror attacks or travelled to join the so-called Islamic state group in Syria and Iraq (Roy, 2015). However, it is impossible to formally substantiate this statistically, because the statistics do not exist. This means that paradoxically the colour-blind nature of the French police and army, where those serving are treated simply as French soldiers or police officers by the state, presents a discursive imbalance in the narratives about French Muslims, where terrorists are labelled 'Islamists', whose dubious claims of allegiance to transnational Islamist networks such as Al-Qaida or ISIS are broadcast by the media, while a far larger number of Muslim soldiers and police officers remain silent. Thus, narratives about Muslims in the security forces emerge as the 'exceptions', with the 'real' Muslims being those who are terrorists (Roy, 2015). This is clearly not aided by the information asymmetry that the lack of statistics in republican France poses. However, there is one instance where insights into the nature of the Muslim presence in the French security services can be had. This is also something that demonstrates how discursively these individuals are created, through the death in service of French security personnel and the resulting commemoration of their deaths and backgrounds. Such victimhood allows scholars to gain a rare insight into the ethnic mix of the French army. This is because when soldiers die, it is one of the few times that details of their names, family origins and religions are released to the public.

Victimhood has important sociological and political implications and is far from a value-neutral process, especially in the case of victimhood during terror episodes (McGowan, 2016). The critical literature on terrorism (Critical Terrorism Studies, CTS) pays scant attention to notions of victimhood, even when elite discourses on terror events pay significant attention to the victims (McGowan, 2016). Transitional justice literature helps here, because it deals with both the category of victim and also how hierarchies of victimhood are created and reproduced (Christie, 1986; Lawther, 2014). Drawing on notions of the 'ideal victim' from criminology (Christie, 1986), it is possible to understand that there can also be an 'ideal victim' of violence, who is passive, uncomplicated and vulnerable, the 'epitome of pure good and pure innocence' (Lawther, 2014). This is rarely the empirical reality in any conflict situation, where perpetrators of violence can also be victims and vice-versa. This is particularly the situation with the cases handled here, as they are all working in the service of the security apparatus of the state. This means that, unlike civilian victims of terror attacks, these are individuals who are overtly employed by the state for a coercive purpose. Thus, regardless of efforts by politicians to construct them as state heroes, which they may indeed be, they still bear arms and go to war. Victimhood is also constructed along lines of racial and geographical hierarchies, where Western victims of terror are generally afforded more attention, their lives constructed as more important than the lives lost to conflict and terror in the global south (Herring, 2008). We are dealing with nuance here as while they are westerners in the sense of their passport, citizenship and even place of birth, they have origins in the global south. Thus, following from Roy's (2015) insightful observation that Muslims who serve in the security services in France are constructed as anomalies versus the more usual idea of the Muslim terrorist, the fact that these victims died in the service of the French state at the hands of Islamists does something to nuance the dominant distinction which follows the erroneous 'clash of civilisations' paradigm of Islam versus the West (Huntingdon, 1993). Issues arise here when it comes to agency and representation, because ideally victims should have the agency to take on the designation of victim, or indeed to reject it (Lawther, 2014). This is a chance to exercise agency that clearly those who die don't get to take. This also applies to the representation of these victims as 'Muslim' victims, as they have not chosen this label, nor to be posthumously constructed as representation of the French Muslim community. Here, the problematic of the 'good' and 'bad' Muslim dichotomy becomes apparent (Maira, 2009; Mamdani, 2008; Sirin & Fine, 2007). This is because the representations of those Muslim victims of terror could re-enforce ideas that there are 'good' Muslims that need either defending from, or who should be actively fighting against, 'bad' Muslims (Maira, 2009; Mamdani, 2008). This distinction was used to justify the War on Terror in the post-9/11 era, where 'good' Muslims needed help to defeat the 'bad' Muslims in their societies through a civil war, thus justifying interventions such as the invasion of Afghanistan to unseat the Taliban (Mamdani, 2008). Not all French Muslims can, or indeed should, serve in the security services. As such, as with the firefighters that died in 9/11, who were constructed as heroes in death (Rothenbuhler, 2002; Simpson, 2006), one has to be careful when analysing victimhood not to create hierarchies of victims of ideal-type 'heroes' who died in the line of duty and those who do not die in the service of the state.

Victims and the ways that they are commemorated are important sites of 'vernacular' memory about terror events (Haskins, 2007; Jarvis, 2011). They offer opportunities to broaden the understanding of how these events are constructed beyond 'official' state accounts (Jarvis, 2011). Online commemorations of the spontaneous Ground Zero memorials to 9/11 demonstrate the tendency to attempt to codify victimhood into permanent or semi-permanent online memorials (Haskins, 2007), such as those created by *Le Monde* to the victims of French terror attacks (*Le Monde*, 2015). Thus, in a similar vein to the war memorials covered above, whether created electronically or in bronze and stone, the act is never neutral and neither is the memorial itself, being shaped by the concerns of those that have the power to 'author' memorials and those that pay for their construction. Absent from this literature, however, is the way that the democratisation of the online sphere, through the proliferation of user-created, content-driven social media platforms, enables commemoration and vernacular memory to be created online by 'lay' actors. The key case, that received the most coverage on social media, was that of the death in service of Ahmed Merabet, a French Muslim police officer who died during the Charlie Hebdo attack, which spawned the #jesuisahmed Twitter campaign.

3.5 Insights into Contemporary Muslim Contributions to French Security: Muslim Victimhood in the Army and Police Forces

Examining the victimhood of French Muslims from the security services offers insights into the ways in which vernacular memory about French Muslims are created in the contemporary era, but also demonstrates the ongoing issues of the commemoration of the dead and the definition of victimhood more broadly. Examining this from the perspective of looking at Muslims as a sociological group adds a level of complexity, because of the ways in which even positive coverage of these victims can inadvertently re-enforce the good/bad Muslim dichotomy. Indeed, the first Muslim victims of the recent jihadi violence to receive media attention were those killed in 2012 by Mohammed Merah, before he went on to attack a Jewish school.

These first victims were actually French servicemen. Merah killed three soldiers and injured one, all of which were of immigrant origin—the survivor was of Guadeloupian extraction and the three who died included one Moroccan Muslim, one Algerian Muslim and one mixed Berber French who was Catholic. The first victim, Imad ibn Ziaten, was of Moroccan origin and his family buried him in Morocco following the attack. His mother, Latifa, went on to create a foundation of inter-religious dialogue and wrote a book chronicling the aftermath of the death of her son (Ibn Ziaten, 2014). The second, Mohamed Legouad, of

Algerian origin, grew up on a poor housing estate in the suburbs of Lyon, and was chronicled in the French newspaper *L'Express* in a comparative biographical piece with his killer, Merah (Caeux, Haget, Saubaber, & Thiolay, 2012). Under the title 'They were called Mohamed … Two young Frenchmen', the newspaper compared the striking similar biographical profiles of the two French Muslims, including the fact that Merah had attempted to join the French army but had been refused entry. Additionally, the asymmetry of press coverage and public interest in the two men was not lost on the newspaper, who commented that 'France doesn't forget Mohamed Merah, when they should remember Mohamed Legouad' (Caeux et al., 2012). As such, without saying it overtly, the newspaper is shining a light on the diversity of French Muslims and attempting, albeit in a limited way, to address the imbalance that Roy (2015) highlights on the coverage of Muslims in the French security service versus those who commit acts of terror. However, the commemoration of Abel Chennouf, who was a Catholic of partial North African Berber origin, is important to cover briefly because it demonstrates the difficulties of commemoration in the public sphere. His home village, Manduel in the Gard department, installed a memorial to him which included his photo. It was reported in 2017 that the memorial had been vandalised (La Dépêche, 2017). This demonstrates the lack of ability of the origin creators of such memorials to victimhood to control who they are related to and how they are interpreted as time passes. All three taken together also demonstrate the different ways Muslim victims of French terror attacks who serve in the security services are covered from a narrative perspective.

However, the coverage of the Muslim police officer who died during the Charlie Hebdo attacks, Ahmed Merabet, offers not only deeper empirical insights into how Muslim victims are constructed, but also theoretical insights because of the importance of the #jesuisahmed social media campaign in creating and disseminating narratives about Ahmed and his victimhood. Ahmed is constructed on Twitter here as a hero—the 'ideal victim' who dies for a noble cause. This is in line with media constructions of the three soldiers murdered by Mohammed Merah in 2012 who also are constructed in terms of dying in service to the state. Indeed, social media, with these narratives created democratically from below, does not have the editorial constraints of 'traditional' forms of media, nor do they have the space to tell a nuanced story about Ahmed and his victimhood, with 140 characters and possibly an image. Here, the narratives focus on Ahmed as a defender of the nation. This demonstrates that while France de jure incorporates its Muslims into the nation on an individual, colour- and religion-blind basis, social norms do not always follow suit. Widespread discrimination in society and far-right political rhetoric about the incompatibility of Islamic and French values have de facto called this republican settlement into question (Alba, 2005; Eroukhmanoff, 2015). This is significant specifically in the context of terror events for two key reasons. Firstly, depicting Ahmed as not only part of the nation but also a defender of it, nuances Muslim group identity and makes it harder to pit the idea of French Muslims against either the idea of the French nation or the French republic. Following on from this, the construction of Ahmed as defender of the nation changes the way that a terror event can be labelled and constructed, making the dichotomy of Muslim terrorist and European victim difficult to sustain. However, this analysis should not be taken as an unproblematic endorsement of these narratives. The situation of Ahmed as a police officer, which enables him to be constructed in such a way, may also work to further enforce the 'good' and 'bad' Muslim dichotomy so dominant in discourses since the launching of the War on Terror post-9/11 (Maira, 2009; Mamdani, 2008).

A key component of the substantive content of narratives created about Ahmed on Twitter situate Muslims as defenders of the nation and of national values. This is a nuanced and complex process which situates Muslims both as defenders of free speech and of the French nation. This has important implications for ongoing debates in CTS, because it shows how narratives about Muslim victims make it difficult to view terror attacks as simply attacks by 'Muslim' terrorists on 'Europeans'. Here, a Muslim dying in the line of police duty demonstrates that Muslims exist on both sides of the dichotomy. There are several ways in which specific tweets situate Ahmed as a defender of free speech.

This situation of Muslims as defenders of free speech accounts for the largest single block of tweets connected with #jesuisahmed. This can be seen in a translation of a tweet where an individual comments that 'Charlie Hebdo did caricatures of Muslims and the man who tried to defend them was one'. Here, Ahmed plays an important role, given that as a Muslim he is situated as a defender of the nation and its values. This presents an opportunity to nuance Muslim identities in France because it sits in stark contrast to the claims of politicians on the right and Islamist organisations themselves that Islam, and thus Muslims, are the antithesis to national belonging and liberal values (Woodhead, 2009).

Ahmed's victimhood also was constructed through the creation and circulation of memes that gave a graphical dimension to representations of not only his victimhood but also what his victimhood means. One in particular nuanced the relationship between Muslims and liberal values in Europe. This tweet, and indeed those like it, which constitute the second largest single block of total coded tweets at 31%, situates Ahmed as a police officer but also as a member of the French state. This represents an important process of blurring because it directly relates a Muslim to the secular republic, not simply as living peacefully under it but taking an active role as the coercive arm of the state and indeed dying in the state's service. This brings the previous historical observations about the historic roles of Muslims serving in the French security forces into the contemporary era (see inter alia Alba, 2005; Bougarel, Branche, & Drieu, 2017). This demonstrates the memorialisation of these Muslims is a constant process where forms of vernacular memory are created depending on current developments, and where memorialisation is constantly morphing and responding to the concerns of the times. It also reconstructs the dichotomy of illiberal Muslims versus liberal Europeans, because it shows in a stark and dramatic way that Muslims are indeed compatible with liberal, modern, European democratic value systems (Alba, 2005). Thus, the death of a Muslim in the service of the state is an important reminder that compatibility between Islam and European political systems is the overwhelming norm and not the exception or indeed even an impossibility.

A further tweet, representative of a broader trend, constructs Ahmed as a defender of free speech. Here, this tweet directly references Ahmed and his colleague as French, both having died for the French nation, its liberty and diversity. Much has been written on the diversity and heterogeneity of the French national project both internally (see inter alia Weber, 1976) and vis-à-vis post-migration communities (Downing, 2015; Hargreaves, 2007). As such, diversity is not a new phenomenon in France but is again an important fact that requires constant and consistent re-construction, especially when the banning of the compilation of statistics, and laïcité, make discussions of diversity de jure illegal in some cases, and de facto off limits in others. This is important in the face of constant questions both about the place of minorities, and more specifically Muslims, in the national project and their assumed 'problems' of integration. Here, this tweet and those like it (accounting for 4% of total tweets on the subject) are important ways in which Muslims are constructed as parts of the French national project.

However, this is not something that is unproblematic because of the exceptional nature of Ahmed in his role as a French police officer. Paradoxically, situating Ahmed in his role in law enforcement as being exceptionally 'good' could further enforce the distinctions made between 'good' and 'bad' Muslims. Mamdani (2008) correctly identifies the danger of this logic coming out of the War on Terror, whereby 'good' Muslims were pitted against 'bad' Muslims. A similar logic is also put in force by the valorising of a Muslim death in the service of the French republic, because not all Muslims are in such a discursive position in their daily lives to be heroes for free speech and thus could never live up to being this 'good' or so 'ideal' as a victim (Lawther, 2014). Thus, Muslims that cannot live up to this benchmark could risk at best being labelled part of the 'silent majority', who do not do enough to condemn and fight terror, or at worst part of the 'bad' Muslims that require suspicion, regulation and even coercive control.

3.6 Historical and Contemporary Conclusion on French Muslims in the French Security Services

This chapter has aimed to highlight the contributions that French Muslims have made both historically and contemporarily to the security and defence of the French nation and the ideals of the republic. This has not been a straightforward task, with this requiring the bringing together of highly complex, both historically and contemporary, forms of commemoration. It has been equally important to understand not just the circumstances around the Muslims that served and continue to serve in the French security services, but also how the meanings, contexts and indeed location of such commemorations have changed over time. Following on from the discussions around the nature of the French state and how it relates to French Muslims, the domain of the Muslim contribution to French security has been somewhat hamstrung by the state's lack of statistics and refusal to acknowledge the ethnic or religious make-up of society, and by extension, the armed forces. This means that those serving the republic's security needs who are Muslims, both in the army and the police, are not officially discussed as Muslims, while the terrorists who carry out attacks on French soil are freely described as Islamists (Roy, 2015). Indeed, the role of French Muslims in securing the republic in the present goes further. This is all the more pertinent an observation given that this asymmetry of information means that it is little known that the number of Muslims serving in the contemporary security apparatus of the French state dwarfs those who have committed terror attacks or travelled to join the so-called Islamic state group in Syria and Iraq (Roy, 2015).

This does not mean, however, that the army in particular does not recognise or adapt to the needs of its Muslim soldiers. The army, like many other facets of the republic, has significant autonomy to define its relations with religious groups. In keeping with the observations of the previous chapter concerning the way that different parts of the republic relate to French Muslims in different ways, the army is no exception, and is one of the 'many republics' which formulate its own policy responses to French Muslims.

Many of the historical sites of commemoration to Muslim troops that exist in France, particularly those erected in the wake of the Muslim contribution to the effort in the First World War, also demonstrate that at times France has not been so hostile to publicly acknowledging religious and ethnic differences. This is somewhat paradoxical, given that the racial hierarchies of the colonies constructed those African Muslims that served the republic as less equal and therefore less free than Europeans, while their service received significant attention in the works of bronze and stone that were created in France and its overseas colonies. Again, this process of historical commemoration has been beset with paradoxes and tragedy. This has been well highlighted by the lateness of commemoration and recognition of those Muslim Harkis who fought for France, even after their mass exclusion from repatriation to the metropole. The trajectory of the monument to the dead of Oran, erected in Oran and then moved to a suburb of Lyon, puts this episode into an even more sinister light because of the significant resources that France spent repatriating lifeless monuments after leaving behind those who served its interests to die in revenge killings. However, this does not mean that historical war memorials do not have contemporary relevance, nor that they are not important symbols which have been appropriated by French Muslims. The monument to the dead of the Orient on the corniche of Marseille demonstrates this by being included on the cover of an album of a Muslim French rap group as a key symbol of their home city.

The presence of Muslims in the security services in France means that alongside their French counterparts of other religious and ethnic background, die in the service of the Republic and it's ideals. These deaths are important because they are one of the few instances where it is possible to get insight into the nature of the contemporary Muslim presence in the French security services and how they are constructed from a narrative perspective. This is because these are some of the few moments where the colour blindness of the republic slips, and the names, origins and personal details of those serving the republic are released. This itself does not come without its own problems, with comparisons between those who serve the republic and those who commit terror attacks risking re-enforcing a good/bad Muslim dichotomy. This is because those who serve risk easily being constructed as ideal victims, with whom Muslims that are not so overt in their displays of devotion to France can be compared in a negative light, even though it is not possible for every Muslim to serve their home country in the same way. This is a process that can be seen to continue in the social media campaign that emerged under the #jesuisahmed hashtag to commemorate the police officer Ahmed Merabet, who died during the Charlie Hebdo attacks. It is interesting that these 'bottom-up' creations of vernacular memory go so far in tying Ahmed and his service to the French nation, and upholding liberal ideals of free speech. Creating such narratives about Muslims is significant as it sets a counter narrative to those in mainstream politics that so often depict French Muslims as some kind of problem that needs control and regulation. However, once again the posthumous construction of Ahmed in this way risks the creation of the ideal victim—a 'good' Muslim against whom other Muslims can be measured. These discussions of terror and victimhood, however, have far larger relevance to contemporary French politics, and indeed to a discussion of French Muslims, because of the wave of jihadist attacks in France that began with Mohammed Merah in 2012 and reached its crescendo with the horrific Paris attacks on 13 November 2015. Understanding French jihadism, and indeed the discursive constructions around it, is the task to which this book now turns in its chapter on French jihadism.

Bibliography

Ageron, C.-R. (2000). Le 'Drame des harkis': Mémoire ou histoire? *Vingtième Siècle. Revue d'histoire, 68*, 3–15. https://doi.org/10.2307/3772174

Alba, R. (2005). Bright vs. Blurred Boundaries: Second-Generation Assimilation and Exclusion in France, Germany, and the United States. *Ethnic and Racial Studies, 28*(1), 20–49.

Aldrich, R. (2005). *Vestiges of Colonial Empire in France*. Retrieved from http://www.palgrave.com/us/book/9781403933706

Almato, A. (1979). *Monuments en exil*. Editions l'Atlantrope. Retrieved from https://www.amazon.fr/Monuments-en-exil-Amato-Alain/dp/2864420066

BBC. (2017). African-Caribbean War Memorial Opened. *BBC News*. Retrieved from https://www.bbc.com/news/uk-england-london-40372063

Bertossi, C., & Wihtol de Wenden, C. W. D. (2007). *Les couleurs du drapeau*. Paris: Robert Laffont.

Billig, M. (1995). *Banal Nationalism*. London: Sage.

Blanchard, E. (2004). La dissolution des Brigades nord-africaines de la Préfecture de police: la fin d'une police d'exception pour les Algériens de Paris (1944–1958)? *Bulletin de l'IHTP, 83*, 70–82.

Bougarel, X., Branche, R., & Drieu, C. (2017). *Combatants of Muslim Origin in European Armies in the Twentieth Century: Far From Jihad*. London: Bloomsbury Publishing.

Caeux, P., Haget, H., Saubaber, D., & Thiolay, B. (2012). *Ils s'appelaient Mohamed… Deux jeunesses françaises*. Retrieved September 4, 2018, from https://www.lexpress.fr/actualite/societe/ils-s-appelaient-mohamed-deux-jeunesses-francaises_1098162.html

Chakraborti, N. (2013, June 17). *Policing Muslim Communities*. https://doi.org/10.4324/9781843926504-10

Chieze, G. (2017). *Police: un ancien fiché S est devenu gardien de la paix*. Retrieved September 1, 2018, from https://www.rtl.fr/actu/debats-societe/police-un-ancien-fiche-s-est-devenu-gardien-de-la-paix-7790220004

Christie, N. (1986). The Ideal Victim. In *From Crime Policy to Victim Policy* (pp. 17–30). London: Palgrave Macmillan. https://doi.org/10.1007/978-1-349-08305-3_2

Cohen, W. B. (2002). The Algerian War, the French State and Official Memory. *Historical Reflections/Réflexions Historiques, 28*(2), 219–239.

Davidson, N. (2009). La mosquée de Paris. Construire l'islam français et l'islam en France, 1926–1947. *Revue des mondes musulmans et de la Méditerranée, 125*, 197–215. https://doi.org/10.4000/remmm.6246

Downing, J. (2015). Understanding the (Re) Definition of Nationhood in French Cities: A Case of Multiple States and Multiple Republics. *Studies in Ethnicity and Nationalism, 15*(2), 336–351.

Downing, J. (2016). Fighting Cultural Marginalisation with Symbolic Power in a Parisian Banlieue: Post-colonial Culture and the Voluntary Association Les Oranges. *International Journal of Sociology and Social Policy, 36*(7/8), 516–530.

Eroukhmanoff. (2015). The Remote Securitisation of Islam in the US Post-9/11: Euphemisation, Metaphors and the "Logic of Expected Consequences" in Counter-Radicalisation Discourse. *Critical Studies on Terrorism, 8*, 246–265.

Evans, M., & Lunn, K. (1997). *War and Memory in the Twentieth Century*. Berg Publishers. Retrieved from https://researchportal.port.ac.uk/portal/en/publications/war-and-memory-in-the-twentieth-century(67f47f22-7690-43ae-9517-8981a7e00b17).html

Fogarty, R. S. (2012). *Race and War in France: Colonial Subjects in the French Army, 1914–1918*. Baltimore, MD: Johns Hopkins University Press.

Ginio, R. (2017). *The French Army and Its African Soldiers: The Years of Decolonization*. Lincoln: University of Nebraska Press.

Hagopian, P. (2009). *The Vietnam War in American Memory: Veterans, Memorials, and the Politics of Healing*. Amherst: University of Massachusetts Press.

Hamoumou, M. (1990). Les harkis, un trou de mémoire franco-algérien. *Esprit (1940–), 161*(5), 25–45.

Hargreaves, A. (2007). *Multi-Ethnic France: Immigration, Politics, Culture and Society* (2nd ed.). New York; London: Routledge.

Haskins, E. (2007). Between Archive and Participation: Public Memory in a Digital Age. *Rhetoric Society Quarterly, 37*(4), 401–422. https://doi.org/10.1080/02773940601086794

Herring, E. (2008). Critical Terrorism Studies: An Activist Scholar Perspective. *Critical Studies on Terrorism, 1*(2), 197–211. https://doi.org/10.1080/17539150802187507

Horne, A. (2006). *A Savage War of Peace: Algeria 1954–1962.* New York: NYRB Classics.

Huntingdon, S. (1993, Summer). The Clash of Civilisations? *Foreign Affairs, 72*(3), 22–49.

Ibn Ziaten, L. (2014). *Mort pour la France – Mohamed Merah a tué mon fils.* Paris: J'ai lu témoignage. Retrieved from https://www.amazon.fr/Mort-pour-France-Latifa-Ziaten/dp/2290076007

Jarvis, L. (2011). 9/11 Digitally Remastered? Internet Archives, Vernacular Memories and WhereWereYou.org. *Journal of American Studies, 45*(4), 793–814. https://doi.org/10.1017/S002187581100096X

Johnson, N. (1995). Cast in Stone: Monuments, Geography, and Nationalism, Environment and Planning D. *Society and Space, 13*(1), 51.

Kader Hamadi, A. (2006). Mémoire des lieux: les 'camps' ouverts aux 'harkis' dans le sud de la France (Places of Memory: 'Camps' of 'Harkis' in the South of France). *Bulletin de l'Association de Géographes Français, 83*(1), 105–120. https://doi.org/10.3406/bagf.2006.2497

Kattago, S. (2009). War Memorials and the Politics of Memory: The Soviet War Memorial in Tallinn. *Constellations, 16*(1), 150–166. https://doi.org/10.1111/j.1467-8675.2009.00525.x

Katz, E. (2012). Did the Paris Mosque Save Jews? A Mystery and Its Memory. *The Jewish Quarterly Review, 102*(2), 256–287.

La Dépêche. (2017). *Profanation de la stèle d'Abel Chennouf: 'J'ai chialé comme un môme', raconte son père.* Retrieved September 4, 2018, from https://www.ladepeche.fr/article/2017/12/08/2700620-profanation-stele-abel-chennouf-ai-chiale-comme-mome-raconte-pere.html

La Région Auvergne-Rhône-Alpes. (2007). Monument aux morts d'Oran online at https://patrimoine.auvergnerhonealpes.fr/dossier/monument-aux-morts-d-oran/2f0a2558-1574-498b-ac0dc61012cbc8aa

Lawther, C. (2014). The Construction and Politicisation of Victimhood. In *Victims of Terrorism: A Comparative and Interdisciplinary Study.* London: Routledge.

Le Monde. (2015). *Le mémorial du 'Monde' aux victimes des attentats du 13-Novembre.* Retrieved from http://www.lemonde.fr/attaques-a-paris/visuel/2015/11/25/enmemoire_4817200_4809495.html

Maira, S. (2009). 'Good' and 'Bad' Muslim Citizens: Feminists, Terrorists, and U. S. Orientalisms. *Feminist Studies, 35*(3), 631–656.

Mamdani, M. (2008). Good Muslim, Bad Muslim: A Political Perspective on Culture and Terrorism. *American Anthropologist, 104*(3), 766–775. https://doi.org/10.1525/aa.2002.104.3.766

Mayo, J. M. (1988). War Memorials as Political Memory. *Geographical Review, 78*(1), 62–75. https://doi.org/10.2307/214306

McGowan, W. (2016). Critical Terrorism Studies, Victimisation, and Policy Relevance: Compromising Politics or Challenging Hegemony? *Critical Studies on Terrorism, 9*(1), 12–32. https://doi.org/10.1080/17539153.2016.1147772

Merchet, J.-D. (2009). *Exclusif: l'armée reconnait que quelques soldats musulmans refusent de partir en Afghanistan.* Retrieved September 1, 2018, from http://secretdefense.blogs.liberation.fr/2009/01/14/exclusif-larme/

Meynier, G., & Vidal-Naquet, P. (1981). *L'Algérie révélée: La guerre de 1914–1918 et le premier quart du XXe siècle.* Geneva: Librairie Droz.

Ministère des armées. (2013). *25 septembre: 'Journée nationale d'hommage aux harkis et autres membres des formations supplétives'.* Retrieved November 12, 2018, from https://www.defense.gouv.fr/actualites/memoire-et-culture/25-septembre-journee-nationale-d-hommage-aux-harkis-et-autres-membres-des-formations-suppletives3

Moser, K. (2014). *A Practical Guide to French Harki Literature.* Lanham: Lexington Books.

Mosse, G. L. (1991). *Fallen Soldiers: Reshaping the Memory of the World Wars.* New York: Oxford University Press.

Monumentum.fr. (2018). 'Monument aux héros de l'armée d'Orient et des terres lointaines, square Lieutenant-Danjaume à Marseille'. Retrieved from https://monumentum.fr/monument-aux-herosarmee-orient-des-terres-lointaines-square-lieutenant-danjaume-pa13000057.html

Rothenbuhler, Eric W. (2002). Chapter 17: Ground Zero, the Firemen, and the Symbolics of Touch on 9-11 and After. In Eric W. Rothenbuhler & Mihai Coman (Eds.), *Media Anthropology.* London: Sage.

Roy, O. (2015, January 10). *There Are More French Muslims Working for French Security Than for Al Qaeda.* Retrieved September 1, 2018, from https://www.huffingtonpost.com/olivier-roy/paris-attack-muslim-cliches_b_6445582.html

Settoul, E. (2015). 'You're in the French Army Now!' Institutionalising Islam in the Republic's Army. *Religion, State and Society, 43*(1), 73–84. https://doi.org/10.1080/09637494.2015.1022400

Sharp, D. (2013). Policing After Macpherson: Some Experiences of Muslim Police Officers. In B. Salek (Ed.), *Islam, Crime and Criminal Justice.* https://doi.org/10.4324/9781843924586-10

Simpson, D. (2006). *9/11: The Culture of Commemoration*. Chicago: University of Chicago Press.

Sirin, S. R., & Fine, M. (2007). Hyphenated Selves: Muslim American Youth Negotiating Identities on the Fault Lines of Global Conflict. *Applied Developmental Science, 11*(3), 151–163. https://doi.org/10.1080/10888690701454658

Weber, E. (1976). *Peasants into Frenchmen: The Modernization of Rural France, 1870–1914* (1st ed.). Stanford, CA: Stanford University Press.

Wihtol de Wenden, C. (2010). L'armée française face à la diversité: une réflexion sur la citoyenneté. *Migrations Société, 131*, 201–214. https://doi.org/10.3917/migra.131.0201

Winter, J. (1998). *Sites of Memory, Sites of Mourning: The Great War in European Cultural History*. Cambridge: Cambridge University Press.

Woodhead, L. (2009). The Muslim Veil Controversy and European Values. Research Portal | Lancaster University. *Swedish Missiological Themes, 97*(1), 17.

Young, J. E. (1993). *The Texture of Memory: Holocaust Memorials and Meaning*. London: Yale University Press.

4

Confronting Orientalism, Colonialism and Determinism: Deconstructing Contemporary French Jihadism

4.1 Introducing Orientalism and Contemporary French Jihadism

In March 2012, Mohammed Merah went on a killing spree in Toulouse and Montauban. Merah, born in Toulouse of Algerian parents, was from a dysfunctional and xenophobic family. While his actions, which he nominally claimed under the banner of an Islamist movement, were extremely serious, no one could have surmised that this would be the beginning of a wave of spectacularly gruesome, effective, often well organised but mainly unrelated terror attacks that would claim hundreds of lives. Here, quite overtly, the discursive backlash focused on French Muslims, bringing an already highly securitised community even further under the spotlight (Cesari, 2013a; Hussey, 2014). This was something that was engineered by the French Muslim terrorists themselves, who in their public declarations of allegiance with foreign groups openly pitted their notion of being a 'Muslim' against French society. However, this obscured the sociological reality that not only did Islamist terrorism have very little support among French Muslims, but also that many French Muslims died during acts of violence committed overtly in the name of their religion.

© The Author(s) 2019
J. Downing, *French Muslims in Perspective*,
https://doi.org/10.1007/978-3-030-16103-3_4

While touched by Islamist unrest in Algeria in the 1990s and Al-Qaida activity in the 2000s, France had remained mostly untouched by mass casualty attacks, while having Europe's largest Muslim population (Hackett, 2017). However, culminating in the Charlie Hebdo, 13 November and Nice attacks, the country with the continent's largest Muslim population was thrust under the spotlight. Politicians, scholars and policy makers alike suddenly found themselves under this spotlight, where answers were demanded about a large range of themes relating to the role of French Muslims in jihadism touching French soil. There were two key questions, one causal and one institutional. Firstly, there has been a huge amount of attention lavished on ascertaining causal links as to exactly how and why these attacks could take place, regardless of them being in the main unrelated. As such, the hunt quickly began for the 'magic formula' for what turns a normal French Muslim into a terrorist capable of committing very public acts of mass murder.

This causal question unfortunately opened up a Pandora's box of answers seeking to create Franco-centric grand theories for French jihadism. Their assumptions were highly problematic, not just because of their empirical inaccuracy, but also because of the way in which they deployed essentialist notions in the construction of French Muslims. These drew heavily on latent orientalism and intellectual ineptitude that tried to explain a fringe social phenomena with recourse to far wider social and historical forces (Burgot, 2016; Hussey, 2014; Kepel, 2017; Kepel & Jardin, 2017). France here is not alone—not only does it share general social and historical problems with other European states with large post-migration Muslim populations, but it also shares the same problematic approaches to discussing Islamist terrorism that often situates terror perpetuated by someone who acts under an Islamist banner as part of the wider 'clash of civilisations' (Huntingdon, 1993) between an aggressive Islam and a secular, liberal Europe. Thus, France's colonial skeletons were brought out of the closet and dusted off and given causal primacy as the reason for France's recent jihad phenomenon (Burgot, 2016; Hussey, 2014). Yes, France shares issues around a bloody colonial history in the Islamic world and contemporary intervention in the region with European countries such as the UK. Both the UK and France were party to the Sykes-Picot agreement which laid the foundations of the current Israel–Palestine conflict. Additionally, France fought a bloody war against independence forces in Algeria, which France incorporated not as an overseas colony but a department of metropolitan France itself, which included torture and mass killings both in urban and rural areas—facts well known and understood by French Muslims, but facts of history that are yet to be publicly acknowledged and dealt with in a broader sense. However, it remains unclear how these historical facts act to push young men and women from a range of backgrounds in France to commit themselves to jihad. For example, (Hussey, 2014) argues that the current wave of French Muslims involved in jihadist movements are part of a 'French intifada' with roots in the anti-colonial struggle that represents a coherent, continuous and uninterrupted historical arc from the FLN's mobilisation in the Kasbah of Algiers to the white and black converts who took up the call to travel to Syria to fight to create a utopian caliphate. This is highly problematic scholarship, based in part on 'research' he conducts on participants outside bars in the Maghreb. In one example, outside the 'the bars and semi-brothels in rue Ibn Kadloun and rue Oum Khaltoum' in Tunis, Hussey talks to Omar (Hussey, 2014, p. 349). While not identifying as a Salafist or radical, Omar is quoted as saying 'I can't get to France. There's nothing else here now. Why not fight for God?' (Hussey, 2014, p. 350). This kind of assertion does not question radicalisation, nor account for why a large number of those in Tunisia who left to fight in Iraq and Syria were actually very well educated and socially mobile. These causal explanations are presented as taking primacy over the meticulous scholarship on French Muslims which demonstrates that they overwhelmingly identify as French first, and want desperately to be part of the contemporary social incarnation of the historical colonial oppressor.

The second key causal argument goes that France's recent social, economic and political failures create a French Muslim, black and Arab underclass, poorly educated and ripe for the picking by crafty jihadist ideologues (Hussey, 2014). Again, in terms of social facts, it is true that the low-skilled jobs that sucked in Muslim migrant labour after the Second World War have gone—replaced in global nodes such as London and Paris by high-skilled service jobs, and in those places that are less connected to the global system, have been replaced by nothing but unemployment and residual social welfare handouts. Additionally, even at the nodes of the new knowledge capitalism, such as Paris, discrimination, poor schools and social decay have shut out many French Muslims from the knowledge economy, leaving them to suffer the same fate as their compatriots in capitalist peripheries, either facing lives of low wages, poor working conditions and welfare handouts, or employment in the highly developed, sophisticated, well organised and hugely lucrative drugs trade. This explanation focuses on the romanticised figure of 'soldiers of Allah' pushed out of French society by economic marginalisation and social discrimination (Kepel, 2017). This, however, has significant colonialist and paternalist overtures—while under conditions of social marginalisation or economic difficulties, the rational white man seeks betterment or accepts his lot, the irrational Muslim, whether black, white or Arab takes these same conditions as a cue to commit mass murder to seek his salvation in the afterlife. This also does not stack up with the sociological reality that many of those who have radicalised in France, in common with other European countries, are actually highly educated and hardly fit the figure of the marginalised Muslim existing on the periphery of society. This diversity of social backgrounds of French Muslims involved in jihad undermines simple sociological explanations for what remains an extremely fringe phenomenon.

Finally, another aspect of recent French jihadism that does not receive enough attention in the scholarship on the subject is the large proportion of casualties of terror attacks in France who are actually Muslims. Taken together with the observations from the previous chapter, that more Muslims serve in the French security forces than fight for jihadi groups (Kepel, 2017), this again demonstrates the complexity of the French Muslim relationship to jihadism. Importantly, insights gained into French Muslim's lives through the publicisation of victimhood powerfully demonstrate the complexity and banality of the sociological, economic and religious composition of French Muslims. Roy (2015) highlights the media coverage paradox from a security perspective, that Muslims who work for the security services do not receive as much attention as those that commit terror attacks. This is an observation that can be extended to French Muslims more broadly in that the political economy of the news media necessitates focusing on violent anomalies and not the more banal aspects of everyday lives. Thus, the media coverage of French Muslims is overwhelmingly exceptionalist and focuses on those engaged in extremist behaviour. The publicisation of terror victims is an important counterweight to this and brings out important nuances about the lives of French Muslims, in addition to complicating our understanding of the jihadi phenomenon.

4.2   Conceptual Approaches to Deconstructing Orientalism in French Security Studies: Critical Terrorism Studies and Securitisation

In making an argument that the current scholarship on French jihadism is overly orientalist in its position, and overly concerned with problem solving in providing causal explanations, this opens up a broader discussion on how the study of terrorism needs to be conducted in the contemporary era. This is a particularly important macro point when it comes to the study of French Muslims because this book's broader social-constructivist approach will enable both the unpicking of problematic causal explanations in addition to the broader nuancing of French Muslimness through the examination of Muslim victimhood.

Here, the deconstructivist approach of CTS offers particular insights into both the processes of how terrorism studies has been conducted, but also normatively how it should be conducted. CTS emerged out of a well thought out critique of the empirical, conceptual and ontological weaknesses of conventional terrorism studies (R. Jackson, 2007a, 2007b; R. Jackson, Gunning, & Breen Smyth, 2007). In particular, Burnett and Whyte (2005) present an important summary of many of the key arguments which evolve from this agenda and highlight key concerns around issues of terror 'experts' who know little about the contexts in which they operate, have never met nor researched terrorists and are closely involved with state security approaches to terror from a 'problem-solving' perspective (Jackson, 2007). Indeed, Jackson's (2007) observations that the emergence of the widespread term 'Islamic terrorism' owes much to the assumptions that underpinned the orientalist scholarship on Islam and the Middle East that blossomed from the nineteenth century onwards, captures well the intellectual and conceptual issues in contemporary terror events.

A key means by which CTS seeks to fight back against such intellectual follies is to adopt an overtly social-constructivist stance vis-à-vis terror events (Gunning & Jackson, 2011; Jackson, 2007). A key nuance of this approach is not to negate the empirically irrefutable violence involved in terror events—as not to obfuscate the objective deaths, suffering and horror of mass killings, but rather as a means to understand that the meanings rendered to such events are not objective. As such, when it comes to knowledge creation about terror events, one is not dealing with ideologically neutral knowledge on an ideologically neutral subject (Burnett & Whyte, 2005), but rather one is embroiled in deeply political and ideological ground and as creators of knowledge, and scholars need to be aware of this. This is not to say, however, that the creation of good scholarship on terror is at all a simple and straightforward task. Sagemen (2014) makes a very pertinent observation in this regard, that academics often suffer from an information deficit about terror events, where intelligence agencies do not want to share information with them. This is, however, only part of the story of such methodological and data issues. Many terrorists die in the conduct of violence, and thus are not available for post facto interviews about their motivations, ideological rationale or connection to transnational networks. A good example of this was Mohamed Lahouaiej-Bouhlel, whose path to committing the Bastille Day attack which killed 86 in Nice remains unclear, owing to him dying during the attack. However, there are increasingly biographical studies and interviews with jihadists published in reports in France, but these do not get the attention, acclaim or press coverage of the orientalist takes on terrorism studies. In short, orientalism and essentialism offer simple and accessible explanations for terror, which as we will see in this chapter are disproved by examining closely the evidence we have that paints a far more nuanced picture.

This is particularly problematic given the already 'securitised' status of French Muslims, which further essentialism only serves to buttress. This opens up a broader discussion, however, that requires conceptual explanation as to how security threats are constructed, which gives significant insight into why French jihadism would have been constructed in the ways that it has, for example as a product of a colonial legacy or domestic political failings. In understanding the deconstruction and nuancing of group identity in a security context, it is necessary to consult the Copenhagen School's concept of securitisation (Buzan, Waever, & de Wilde, 1997; Huysmans, 1998; Roe, 2004). Here, security threats are not objective truths, rather they are socially constructed as such via discursive 'speech acts' that render narratives about security plausible and salient, and thus possible to be then subjected to emergency politics (M. C. Williams, 2003). The Copenhagen School's key normative aim is to undo this process of 'securitisation' through 'desecuritisation' and deconstruction of security threats (Booth, 2007; Huysmans, 1998; Roe, 2004). One of the key ways in which they prescribe this is through the deconstruction of group identities to give individual faces to security threats (Coskun, 2011; Hansen, 2011; Rumelili, 2013)—exactly the kind of humanisation of Muslim terror victims which is created through the data analysed here.

This is especially important given the context in which this study situates itself, where how Islam and Muslims are securitised in France has direct consequences for the ways in which jihadism is conceptualised. Prior to the recent explosion of terror attacks on French soil, French Muslims had been the subject of significant discursive construction as existential threats both to France's secular political order but also to its liberal social habits. This is not important per se because it explains why French Muslims commit terror attacks as some commentators would have it (Burgot, 2016; Hussey, 2014; Kepel, 2017), but it is important to understand the context out of which scholarship is produced and what dominant ideas shape the context in which Muslims are discussed. The securitisation of Islam in Europe is well covered in the literature (Cesari, 2013a, 2013b; Eroukhmanoff, 2015; Mavelli, 2013). Of particular importance to this study is the observation that the securitisation of Islam in Europe is present in both speech and rhetoric, specifically the link between Islam and political violence (Cesari, 2013a; Eroukhmanoff, 2015). It is at this nexus between Muslims and political violence that is the most important place to situate a discussion of the desecuritisation of Muslims in terms of the speech acts and narratives generated about their position vis-à-vis such phenomena, and in France, where Islam has been set up as a counterpoint and antithesis to the liberal, democratic republican values upon which the French polity is founded (Cesari, 2013b). This has not been a unified process, but rather has taken on numerous forms across time and space—especially in the French context. As such, the position of French Muslims is consistently undercut by elite public narratives that persistently frame French Muslims as 'incomplete citizens' (Fredette, 2014). Discussions of these dynamics of Muslim diasporas have received attention in some very specific ways in the literature. Hamel (2002) examines the role of the politicisation and mediatisation of the Muslim headscarf (hijab) as one of the defining features of debates about the position of Muslims under the secular republic. Here, is the observation again about the essentialising rhetoric explicit in such coverage—Muslims are Muslims when publicly religious and, as also highlighted by Croucher (2008), present a problem to a secular republic and society and thus require control and regulation, often in very reactive, ad-hoc and erratic ways (Samers, 2003). It is worth noting that this occurs in the face of repeated large-scale studies that demonstrate without any doubt that France is a place where the vast majority of Muslims are trying hard to fit in, rather than the commonly repeated mantra that they are intent on 'opting out' and existing, often portrayed in hostile terms, outside of society (Giry, 2006). Thus, it is no surprise if these are the dominant conceptions and narratives that dictate how French Muslims are constructed, that they bleed over into the problematic theoretical explanations of the causes for French jihadism. It is to this question that this chapter now turns, in employing a CTS approach to deconstruct and rebut these explanations. Thus, it is necessary to deconstruct the narratives around both the causes of jihadism and also those Muslims who have fallen victim to it, so as to be able to demonstrate that this securitised rhetoric is unfounded and highly problematic.

4.3   A Question of Misplaced Causality: Deconstructing the Grand Theories of French Jihad

A key tenet of CTS is to employ a deconstructivist approach to terror events and the explanations that are given for individuals who become involved in terrorism. The causal explanations given have far reaching consequences for the concepts of French Muslims themselves in much broader ways than the explanations overtly acknowledge. In demonstrating these broader problems, it is necessary to question overarching 'grand theory' type explanations that assert universal truths as causes of jihadism. This has, however, not been done to the explanations given for the recent jihadist violence in the French case. Instead, what has emerged have been extremely Franco-centric grand theories that seek to root French jihad in both the colonial and historical legacy of France as a colonial power and in the contemporary political and social failings of the French state to both politically accommodate Islam and also to socio-economically enfranchise large parts of its Muslim population. While these explanations may seem logical and discursively coherent, as both a troubled colonial history and significant social and political problems do exist, this chapter argues that they fail the deconstructive and causal tests required by both the CTS literature and the standards of rigorous and robust social science methodologies more broadly. Such a deconstruction must be rooted in the social, religious and economic contexts of French Muslims.

Arguably one of the reasons that such grand theories have become so popular, and even to the general public plausible, is that these are often the language of both the jihadists and the broader movements such as Al-Qaida or ISIS. In the opinion of such groups, it is the duty of Muslims worldwide to fight against the Western domination of the international system, and the moral decadence of domestic political systems whose morality does not conform to their particular extreme world views.

Addressing the question of jihadism in France in recent years requires questioning both the extent of the problem and also the explanations commonly used to account for jihadism in France. To do this we need to examine the numbers of French Muslims who are engaged in jihadist activity. This runs into a significant difficulty in France when we contrast the numbers of French jihadists to the size of the French Muslim population. This is because nobody, the French government included, actually can accurately say how many Muslims are in France. As we have seen, this is because of the specifics of the French system, where the collection of ethnic or religious statistics about the population are forbidden by law (Hargreaves, 2007). As such, the French census does not ask questions about religion or ethnicity. This means that anyone interested in the subject has to rely on estimates that are calculated via indirect forms of estimation. For example, the Pew Research Centre estimated the French Muslim population to be 5.72 million in 2016, 8.8% of the population (Hackett, 2017). However, as mentioned earlier, this cannot be proven or disproven by any official source, the number is thus open to all kinds of contestation and uncertainty from those both on the left and right of French politics. In the past decade both Azouz Begag, researcher at the CNRS, and the far-right 'National Front' political party both argued that a more accurate estimate of the Muslim population in France was between 15 and 20 million, or between 22% and 30% of the French population of 66.9 million (Begag, 2011; Jacob, 2016) Additionally, the French population is uncertain about numbers according to a poll that showed a tendency to overestimate the Muslim population at around 31% of the population, so around 20.74 million Muslims (Jacob, 2016).

Muslim as a category in France, as in the rest of Europe, shares many characteristics with ethnic categories such as 'black' and 'white' (Begag, 2011; Jacob, 2016). That is to say that it is a category that can relate as much to inter-subjective, non-religious forms of identification (such as ethnic, national and/or cultural), if not more than it refers to an individual who believes in and practises a religion. Even within those who identify as Muslims and do practise, there is a large variation of forms of practice, level of adherence to dogma, and variations between different types of folk Islam that originate in North Africa, West Africa or the Comoro Islands. Additionally, there are estimated to be between 70,000–110,000 converts to Islam in France from a variety of cultural, religious and socio-economic backgrounds. Already, the complexity of this socio-cultural and doctrinal patchwork should set alarm bells ringing vis-à-vis simplistic causal explanations that lack nuance.

As there is significant uncertainty around the number of Muslims in general in France, there is also significant variation in the numbers of possible radical Muslims in France and also by extension the number of possible violent jihadists in France. This uncertainty is born out of somewhat different reasons to the general doubts about the Muslim population, because as CTS literature states (Sagemen, 2014), it is extremely difficult to gather data about jihadists due to their clandestine nature. Making estimates about how many violent radicals, as opposed to peaceful ultra-conservative Muslims, is even more difficult as this involves predicting violence prior to the act, thus bringing a problematic pre-crime approach to the study of terrorism, where individuals are deemed future terrorists without significant criminal evidence or charges (McCulloch & Pickering, 2009). These difficulties do not stop politicians and scholars making estimates about the numbers in France. Manual Vals, when he was prime minister, estimated that there were 15,000 individuals being monitored in France for radicalisation, yet only 1400 are currently under judicial prosecution for terror offences. However, as the issues with the terminology are numerous, and Vals also did not give further details on these numbers, they mean very little. Samir Amghar, researcher at the University Libre de Bruxelles, estimates that there are between 20,000 and 30,000 'ultra-orthodox' Muslims in France, less than 1% of the practising Muslim population (cited in Dell'Oro, 2015). This figure of ultra-orthodox does not suggest that these 20,000–30,000 French Muslims are in any way violent or likely to commit acts of jihad. Thus, the number of jihadists in France, even if it was put as Vals states at 15,000, is less than 1% of the French Muslim population. This corroborates with Khosrokhavar's (2014) findings that radicalisation is an 'ultra-minority' phenomenon that remains at the fringes.

Thus, the overarching 'grand theories' of radicalisation begin to look extremely lacking. That is, methodologically explaining French jihadism using these grand theories centres on explaining statistical anomalies, less than 1% of the French Muslim population become jihadists, with recourse to phenomena that affect much larger parts of the Muslim, and indeed non-Muslim French population and does not generate the same results of mass murder. Hussey's (2014) contention that the current wave of jihadism has a coherent and cogent link with a problematic colonial past in Muslim countries thus causally fails to explain why the rest of those over 5 million Muslims are not answering the call of jihad. Additionally, Kepel's (2017) arguments that the current wave of jihadists has its roots in France's recent political intolerance of Islam on the left and right, and inability to deal with socio-economic segregation, is again causally naïve and has not been subjected to the deconstruction asserted by CTS. In short, if these rather general and overarching social grievances are to be evaluated for their causal primacy, then surely the counter factual question of how the explanation does not also tell us why the vast majority of Muslims affected by similar issues in France are not also involved in radical jihadist movements should be asked. For example, in an interview given to security forces after being stopped travelling to Syria, Chérif Kouachi expressed an incoherent world vision, and claimed that he was actually thankful to be stopped and thus unable to carry out jihad (Chrisafis, 2015). Therefore, the overarching, Franco-centric world view that it is a combination of political failings and historical indignities that cause individuals to take up arms does not only fail to explain those who do not commit jihad but also those who actually do.

The damage done by these kinds of explanations is not simply caused by bad social science methods which produce inaccurate causal relationships and thus poor policy responses, they also serve to securitise French Muslims even more. If one is to take on face value the possibility that French Muslims can be turned into mass murderers through things that they have no control over, such as colonial history or dysfunctional national politics, then it means that every French Muslim is a potential jihadist and thus should be under suspicion. This has two key issues. Firstly, it effectively leads to the 'pre-crime' (McCulloch & Pickering, 2009) approach being applied to French Muslims, whereby they are immediately under suspicion of being jihadists simply by dint of being Muslim, however nominally. This is a worrying process that was highlighted by both Amnesty International (2016) and Human Rights Watch (2016), who both identified France's state of emergency as focusing specifically on Muslim communities and placing individuals under house arrest or detention for sometimes nebulous connections to individuals accused of being radicals. Here, law enforcement caught up in their net individuals whose lives were disrupted and who never had a formal charge bought against them for any terror or related offences. The damage here is arguably also done at a broader and more discursive level within society. If we are to take the assumptions of the Copenhagen School's concept of securitisation, security threats are not objective realities but rather are constructed as such through discourse emanating from actors endowed with authority (Buzan et al., 1997; Huysmans, 1998). The broader popularity and mainstreamisation of these explanations acts in a similar way to the 'pre-crime' approach of law enforcement (McCulloch & Pickering, 2009), because it casts its explanatory net very wide and pulls in extremely large numbers of the French Muslim population. Taking a speculative guess that even 30% of the French Muslim population don't agree with France's colonial past and have disagreements with the dysfunctions of French politics, exactly as many of their non-Muslim counterparts do, we are talking about 1.7 million French Muslims under suspicion for the crimes of only several thousand. This is clearly not good enough from an explanatory perspective and would struggle to gain such mainstream acceptance or credibility in many other areas of the social or natural sciences. Thus, here we have prime examples of the empirical, conceptual and ontological weaknesses and a focus on problem solving that the CTS literature highlights so clearly as key problems with conventional terrorism studies (Gunning & Jackson, 2011; Jackson, 2007; Jarvis, 2011).

4.4 Nuancing and Identifying the Soldier of Allah: The Diversity of the French Jihad

We have therefore seen so far that the grand, Franco-centric theories of French jihad do little to advance our understanding of the characteristics of this phenomenon or tell us who these actual jihadists are, no matter how fringe a phenomenon French jihadism actually is. This is where a key feature of CTS becomes extremely important in furthering this endeavour. CTS, in addition to being deconstructivist, aims to also free itself from the problem-solving focus of traditional terrorism studies. This is a problem with the current attempts globally to understand who jihadists are, because of the focus on trying to present causal mechanisms for radicalisation and thus solutions to 'radicalisation'. There are many problems with this—notably both with defining the dominant terms such as 'radicalism' and 'extremism', and perhaps more importantly an inability for scholars to give definitive answers as to how radicalisation takes place (Khosrokhavar, 2014; Schmid, 2013). This flies in the face of the dominant assumptions by those who believe radicalisation occurs due to Salafist readings of the Koran and the Sunnah (Kepel & Jardin, 2017), or colonial history and ongoing Western domination of the Third World (Burgot, 2016). It is not simply that jihadism in France is the result of an overspill from the Algerian civil war in the 1990s—while some can trace their lineage back to this conflict and the resulting upheaval, others do not (Caillet & Puchot, 2017). This is even a key problem with the grand theories—in focusing on politics or history they attempt to provide explanations that affect all jihadists but also importantly for which there are at least real-world solutions that could, so the argument goes, be rectified and thus solve the jihadist problem. For example, if only France would deal with its colonial past and stop intervening in the Muslim world, and would fix its dysfunctional domestic politics, then jihadism would surely evaporate.

Rather, it seems that on examination of the evidence available, jihadism in France as a fringe social movement is not to do with Islam per se but shares much more in common with other forms of radicalisations and political violence, seen with the far right and ultra-nationalists (Roy, 2017). This ties up with broader observations that the conceptual distinction between 'religious' terrorism and other forms of terror and violence is difficult to sustain, as they share so many commonalities in terms of the lack of previous religious practice or knowledge, and the perplexing diversity of motivations and social backgrounds of those committing violence (Gunning & Jackson, 2011). As such, when delving into exactly who French jihadists are, it is clear that the stunning variation in socio-economic backgrounds, previous activities and even paths towards radicalisation paint a far more complex and nuanced picture. Thus, freeing ourselves from this problem-solving focus enables an understanding of this diversity and of the phenomenon more broadly. What stands out from studies which seek to understand the backgrounds and motivations of French jihadists is their diversity of socio-economic backgrounds, with many coming from middle-class backgrounds (Bouzar, Caupenne, & Valsan, 2014). What is also striking is the diversity of opinions and motivations that emerge from the few first-hand accounts of French jihadists that are found in specific studies (Crettiez, Sèze, Ainine, & Lindemann, 2017). The strength of this particular account comes from its comparative design, which examines jihadists in tandem with those in France drawn to secular, nationalist causes such as Basque and Corsican separatismj. This research design does much to escape the essentialist and particularist assumptions about jihadism being a religious backlash against a secular society. Indeed, these motivations do emerge in some of the testimonials of the jihadists themselves, but in somewhat paradoxical and unexpected ways. Both Paul and Abdel are cited as turning to radicalism after early lives in which they did not experience discrimination or poverty, and were not raised in particularly religious households—Paul is a convert to Islam and Abdel is the child of non-practising Muslim parents (Crettiez et al., 2017). In fact, Abdel went as far as to enrol in a cinema school.

This points to a broader trend that confounds many of the assumptions of the securitisation of Islam in France that overtly religious and practising Muslims are an existential threat to society, as many of those involved in jihadist activity discover religion in their late teens or early twenties in a very decontextualised and diffuse way that also does not add credence to the idea that there is a problem with French mosques producing radicalisation. Rather, these processes are very much individualised and thus present significant difficulties to those who wish to apply the 'problem-solving' approach to radicalisation and jihadism that seeks early warning systems for its detection and prevention, whether these are religious organisations or intelligence and security services who seek to anticipate and contain jihadists. Thus, there is no 'silver bullet' for the issues of radicalisation or how those radicalised then go on to commit violence. This does not mean that contextual factors are irrelevant to a discussion of recent French jihadism. However, they are not the causal factors of jihad, rather contexts which lend themselves to certain kinds of violence occurring. It is to making this argument that the final section of this chapter turns in examining the institutional and banal contexts of insecurity that have enabled French jihadism to take such deadly and efficient turns.

4.5   Enabling Jihad to Be So Effective in France: Institutional and Banal Security Problems

Given their essentialist and orientalist foundations, the theories of French jihad that see it as the result of abstract and immediate historical and political grievances fail to examine the broader social and institutional context in which jihadism sits. This is essential because these facets of the French security environment are not only outside direct control of French Muslims (as they are for French non-Muslims), but also receive far less discursive attention when examining the phenomenon of French jihadism than the paternalist explanations discussed above. This is not surprising conceptually, as discussing the less romantic security failings affecting France do little to buttress a grand 'clash of civilisations' narrative, but rather bring the discussion back to more worldly features of the security landscape. However, even when such contextual factors are brought into the picture, their causal roles are significantly over-egged. Senni (2016), in an opinion piece, makes the case that it is the fault of the lack of social mobility present in the suburbs that is the key 'push' factor towards jihadism. It is impossible, however, to address these questions of banal security problems without discussing the vectors of broader insecurity so often brought into discussions about terror in France—the poor suburbs of French cities, the banlieues. Much has been written on the daily grind of poor housing, poor education and high crime in these areas over the past three decades, much of it very good sociological work providing nuanced accounts of the ethnically and socially diverse inhabitants of these areas, fighting dominant stereotypes that these areas are populated by threatening, tracksuit-wearing, drug-dealing young men (Wacquant, 2007). Indeed, the first wave of 'securitisation' directed at post-migration communities in France referenced the class and race deferential between these individuals and French society and did not see religious differences as such a key 'problem'. However, around the early 2010s, scholarship began to take a worrying orientalist turn (perhaps the most well known is Kepel's (2012) *Banlieue de la République*) and began to put a threatening assessment of an 'Islam' that was bit by bit dominating and taking over the politics and social relations of these areas. This has reached a worrying crescendo in light of recent attacks in France, where these areas have been widely labelled in the press as the heartlands from which jihadists rise and attack the French state (Hussey, 2014).

However, Zappi (2015) is correct to question these narratives, arguing that the jihadist has become the new 'scarecrow' of the suburbs. Thus, it is not pursuing the economic and social problems of the suburbs that cause jihadism—as we have already seen, the backgrounds of those who have sought to depart France to fight in Syria and Iraq for ISIS are from staggeringly diverse socio-economic backgrounds that show no clear route back to residency in the suburbs. Indeed, the Nice attacker, Lahouaiej-Bouhlel, had never lived in a suburban housing estate and one of the Kouachi brothers that carried out the Charlie Hebdo attacks, Chérif, was raised in a children's home far outside of Paris. A 2014 report cited that 67% of French jihadists have come from middle-class backgrounds, and only 16% come from deprived backgrounds (Bouzar et al., 2014). Therefore, the causal link between poor areas of French cities as repositories for radicalisations and jihadism clearly does not stand up to closer scrutiny.

However, this does not mean that the more 'banal' security issues neglected by the French state are not important in facilitating terror attacks. An aspect of where the suburbs do come into play is their ability to act as vectors of general insecurity that affect the broader security landscape in France. This becomes critical when examining where the arms used in terror attacks come from, but also how and why they ended up in France and what this demonstrates about the banal security failings of the French state. Journalists have done important work in tracking where the arms came from—both the arms used in the Charlie Hebdo attack and those used in the Paris attacks came from the former Yugoslavia, brought into France via the firearms 'black market' (Douet, 2015; Franceinfo, 2016).

However, this black market does not exist to supply the tiny number of jihadists in France seeking heavy weapons. Rather, owing to the mutations in the French drugs trade, these heavy weapons have become common currency in all kinds of crime in France—something that the French state has not kept pace with. Rather it is the new, and largely unchecked 'narco-banditisme' (Sellami, 2016) that not only supplies France's cannabis, but also is a significant social phenomenon that provides employment, belonging and one of the few avenues for any kind of social mobility to working-class young men in the suburbs. This is not, however, a strictly Muslim or North African controlled trade, as can be seen by reports from Marseille that demonstrate the diversity or warring clans that include alongside North Africans, Gypsy and black groups (Sellami, 2016). Thus, these heavy arms are used not only as weapons of enforcement in regular 'score settling' (règlement de compte) killings (Valette, 2018), but also as weapons of choice in armed robberies (*Ouest France*, 2018). Thus, the banality of the use of such weapons, for example in the robbery of a jewellery store in otherwise calm and touristic Saint-Tropez (*Ouest France*, 2018), demonstrates these banal security failings. If those robbing small businesses can gain access to and use such weapons, it does not require a jihadi mastermind to gain access to the same dangerous weapons. Indeed, I have been told on numerous occasions that with the right connections and introductions it is possible to purchase a Kalashnikov in the north (quartiers nord) of Marseille for from as little as €1500—hardly a prohibitive amount for a drug dealer, jihadist or far-right activist. With an arms market as liberal and as inexpensive as this, it could be argued that it is surprising that more incidences of mass killing, terror related or not, do not occur. This secular failing to get a grip on the illegal trade in military weapons has nothing to do with colonial legacies, nor the specifics of Islam or Salafism as violent ideological movements.

Similar arguments about secular failings enabling jihadism to be devastatingly effective in France can also be seen in the failings of the central French intelligence services. Thus, in addition to banal security problems, France also has problems institutionally. The institutional context in France has rightly come under significant scrutiny in the past several years. It is important to begin by saying that security forces, including those in France, cannot stop all terror attacks (Van Puyvelde, 2015). However, this also does not mean that France's intelligence landscape has not contributed to the ability of jihadists to operate in France and carry out such complex attacks. In the wake of the recent upsurge in jihadist attacks, France has had to review its intelligence services with a view to improving their effectiveness. This has thrown up some significant failings that demonstrate that by being ineffective, the intelligence services have indirectly contributed to the ability of jihadists to carry out such deadly attacks in France by consistently letting them slip through the law enforcement net. These failings are numerous and cannot be narrowed simply to personnel failings to share intelligence, or structural, institutional issues, but rather are a combination of both. Key, however, is a bureaucratic atrophy that stifles dynamism, cooperation and effectiveness (Delbecque, 2017). Chrisafis (2016) cites a report commissioned by a parliamentary committee investigation into intelligence issues after the Paris attacks that finds a 'global failure' with the country's intelligence services. France has six intelligence services that report to different ministries (Chrisafis, 2016). This gives a 'Balkanised' institutional context where the duplication of roles and separation of services into different branches hampers co-working and breeds the kind of institutional mistrust that is hardly ideal when seeking to thwart internal security threats. Many of the attackers involved in recent French terror episodes were known to intelligence services, but failings to communicate stopped them being accurately tracked (Cornevin & Piquet, 2016).

Some of these issues can be seen at the most basic level with the monitoring system used in France for internal security threats, the 'fiche S' (S-list). Fiche S ('atteinte à la sûreté de l'état') is part of a system of categories in which individuals who are deemed wanted by the authorities are placed. Created in 1969, the entire system of lists has contained over 400,000 names in its history, including organised crime figures, escapees from prison, and political and social activists (including anarchists and ecologists), in addition to terror subjects (Laurent, 2015). As such, the list contains 21 categories which correspond with the reasons that the individual is placed on the list (Laurent, 2015). The 'S' section, which refers to those deemed a specific security danger to the state, has 16 subsections detailing why individuals have come to the attention of the authorities, with S14 corresponding to those returning from Iraq and Syria (Laurent, 2015). Being placed on this list, however, does not come with automatic obligations for the law and order authorities to watch or detail a particular individual. Thus, this is clearly not a user-friendly system, with individuals of different threat levels placed in the same category without any specific obligations placed upon law enforcement to monitor them. To rectify some of these problems, Macron's most recent attempt at improving France's security landscape has involved proposing the creation of a central anti-terrorist 'task force' (Delbecque, 2017). He proposed the creation of a new central authority dedicated solely to the investigation and prevention of terrorism that reports directly to the president and seeks to unify the fight against terror. Whether or not this just further reproduces the duplications and bureaucracy of the existing system remains to be seen. Additionally, nuanced understanding of the relationship between French Muslims and jihadism can also be gained through examining the details that emerge around the lives of the many French Muslims who have been killed in the name of their religion in recent years.

4.6   Muslim Victimhood and Nuancing 'Islamist' Terror in France

It has already been repeatedly stated that more French Muslims serve in the security services than have fought for jihadist movements (Crettiez et al., 2017). In a similar vein, in *Le Monde*, in online memorials to the dead of the Paris 2015 and Nice 2016 attacks, out of a total of 160 deaths there were a total of 15 profiles where the individuals could be read sociologically as Muslims.

This is pertinent because the profiles themselves come with important biographical details about the individuals, including their background, education and occupation. These are paradoxically details about French Muslims which are rarely divulged in the mainstream press except in the cases of the exceptionalist French jihadists such as Merah and the Kouachi brothers. Thus, in covering these examples of Muslim victimhood of jihadism there is a significant and important process of banalisation going on here. These narratives about French Muslims situate them in their daily contexts that are very far from images of Muslims seen as unable or unwilling to integrate into normal daily European lives. So often, public narratives in France about Muslims have concentrated on 'exceptionalist' debates about Halal food, prayer in the streets and many other issues that constantly situate French Muslims as exceptional to French social norms (Cesari, 2009, 2013b). In both attacks, which occurred on civilian social occasions, just as non-Muslim French people were caught up in these events, so were Muslims caught up while performing normal and banal social roles, such as socialising and staffing leisure businesses.

This process also goes beyond just covering Muslim victims through text, but also through the publication of their photographic portraits alongside their biographies. It was not possible to get permission from *Le Monde* for the reproduction of these portraits. The publication of these photos enables a 'rapport face à face' to develop by giving a human face to the victims. The ideas of Butler (2006) and Levinas (1985) exist here in their most explicit form because these are direct photos of victim's faces and thus showcase the European Muslim victim not only as individuals but also as human beings with faces. Given the context of the current discussion of French Muslims as an existential threat to state laïcité (El Hamel, 2002; Samers, 2003), the publication of these pictures alongside the biographies also goes further to banalise the French Muslim presence through building this 'rapport face à face' between reader and terror victim. An example of this is in the depiction of Muslim women both veiled and unveiled and men in similar masculine images to those usually associated with terrorists which act as powerful nuancers of both how such terror attacks can be constructed, while also showcasing the diversity of the French Muslim experience. As such, it is within the publication of these images in all of their diversity that the most progress is made in dismantling the 'good' and 'bad' Muslim dichotomy, because it sets Muslims in roles usually placed into these categories in media discourses around terrorism—as the veiled woman and the masculine, working-class North African man.

4.7 Banal Blurring: Nuancing Muslimness and the Secular in Daily Life

An interesting aspect of the biographies of the Muslim victims of terrorism is that the discussion of their daily lives and socio-economic occupations are powerful ways in which the lives of French Muslims are constructed as very 'banal'. However, 'banal' here is far from being used in a dismissive sense. Rather, exposing the everyday 'banality' of European Muslims is an important counterweight to the often exceptionalist discourse which is employed against them. The importance of the banal in identity construction is well established (Billig, 1995), but at the national level, and has been neglected both on other scales and specifically in CTS and in broader discussions of social marginalisation. This is rendered specifically important to this case by the dominant discursive context where narratives of Muslim's deviance and 'abnormality' in polemical and political discussions is well established, whether as Islamic security threats or though being depicted as working-class, violent petty criminals (G. Kepel, 2012; Wacquant, 2007). The narratives created by Muslim victimhood can contradict these established accounts because rather than situating Muslims in these violent, securitised extremes, they situate them in normal, banal, desecuritised positions in mainstream society. This occurs in the biographies in the *Le Monde* online memorials (*Le Monde*, 2015, 2016), showcasing the highly diverse range of occupations that Muslims hold in society, and therefore nuances the discussions often had around the ability of Muslims to integrate into Western societies. None of the individuals profiled in *Le Monde* are involved in overtly religious occupations but rather occupy a range of fairly banal positions in society. An Algerian victim, K. Sahbi, is profiled as a musician and teaching assistant at a middle school, whose academic excellence and affable character are commented on by ex-professors at a Paris University, the Sorbonne. This situates this individual in a very interesting position in society as not only someone that is working for the good of French children but who is also involved in an occupation as a musician that has been widely reported as banned under the so-called Islamic state in Syria. Again, this normalises and nuances the Muslim presence in France, blurring their social boundaries. This trend continues for victims such as Hodda Saadi, who managed a café, and Lamie Mondeguer, who worked as an agent for a casting company, discovering young comedians. These are banal occupations that aid in blurring the social boundaries for French Muslims by demonstrating that they are not living outside of, and in opposition to, society.

The profiles also do not present these individuals and their occupations in a vacuum where questions of religion are not raised parallel to observations about occupations. Amine Ibnolmobarak, a victim of the Paris attacks, is presented as working as an architect after migrating to France from Rabat in Morocco to study in France, with ambitions of opening a practice with his wife. One of his ex-teachers is quoted as describing him as 'a Muslim intellectual … very representative of his generation because of his openness' (*Le Monde*, 2015). Here, this is a very direct means by which the biographing of this victim discusses questions of social and intellectual position in a way that makes simplistic assumptions about group identity, and thus the possibility of constructing a particular group as a homogenous security threat, extremely difficult. Amine is a Muslim, a migrant, a professional directly contributing to society, and also a victim of a terrorism which proclaims to act in the name of his religion. These biographies demonstrate that a construction of a barrier between Islam and European values does not hold water by showing that Muslims are indeed members of mainstream society. These emerging victimhood themes nuance the way that terror events can be discussed and labelled. They challenge narratives disseminated by Islamist groups that a 'non-believing' or Christian Europe is what is being attacked when Muslim victims are so prominent in these terror episodes.

While these biographies are important means by which banal narratives about French Muslims are created, they also raise questions about re-enforcing the good Muslim/bad Muslim dichotomy. This is because, as poor socio-economic status is an important intersecting factor in the marginalisation of French Muslims with their ethnic and religious identities, the generally successful nature of the economic position of the victims covered means they sit on the positive side of the key economic cleavage that affects minorities in France. As Wacquant (2007) notes, class is a powerful and underexplored cleavage in French society where those of minority extraction who are unemployed, or who work in the grey or black economies, are marginalised on the grounds of class as well as race. The fact that those who are victims draw their blurring ability through the banality of their occupations thus highlights those who were not victims, who sit outside of mainstream economic employment. This is especially important when considering the biographies of many of the 'homegrown' French jihadists, who come from the worlds of the grey economy and have past experience of being unemployed, claiming social security benefits and/or records of petty crime such as drug dealing (Bouzar et al., 2014).

4.8 Visual Blurring: Victim's Portraits As a Means of Deconstructing Dominant Stereotypes

It is necessary to take into account the visual aspects of the social world in the construction of not only minority identities, but also in politics and international relations more generally (Hansen, 2018). The victim profiles in *Le Monde* are accompanied by photo portraits of the victims, which work in a similar but much more nuanced way. This is because they are banal portraits of the individuals in daily life and are not explicitly rendered meaning by the graphics which surround them in the same way as the Twitter images. However, they are significant because they represent the face-to-face connection that is important in the work of Levinas (1985) and Butler (2006). While in this case these pictures give a human face to the image, and thus a relatable humanity to the victims, they also make broader statements about the relation of Muslims to society in visual ways. The images that accompany the profiles show actors in postures and dress, like the Muslim veil, which have been used discursively to securitise and marginalise Muslims in France.

One of the most prominent securitising dynamics in the French, and indeed European, contexts vis-à-vis Muslims has been entrenched in a deeply gendered area—discussions around the religious dress of Muslim women. The French state's repeated attempts to regulate the public dress of Muslim women have been notable by their frequency, persistence and polemical effervescence. These legal efforts, not to mention the political debate generated in right-wing politics, have rendered the headscarf in particular a label of the problematic incompatibility of European and Islamic values. Examining the victimhood profiles with this in mind generates an interesting discussion of the ability of images to deconstruct minorities as security threats by showcasing victims in a variety of previously securitised gender roles. Thus, a form of visual desecuritisation can be observed in these images when read in tandem with the information given in the victim profiles.

It should be noted that there is a significant diversity in the way that Muslim women are depicted in these online memorials. There are those commemorated without overt religious symbols in their photos. Houda Safi, the café manager whose occupation is discussed above, can be seen in her profile not conforming to the stereotypes of the threatening Muslim woman wearing a headscarf so prominent in the securitising discourse around Muslim women in France. Once again, this banalisation of Muslims in this instance nuances public Muslim identity by demonstrating that not all Muslim women conform to this image of the veiled radical woman.

The biographies in their depictions of victimhood go beyond this banalisation and also engage with the more securitised parts of French Muslim identity in all of its diversity, including women who wear headscarves. Thus these profiles that show women in more overtly religious garb could be seen to go some way in nuancing notions of the good and bad Muslims. The indiscriminate nature of mass killings clearly does not discriminate in these cases between people on any grounds—be they religion, ethnicity, age or occupation. This means that women who visibly conform to both the 'good', secular, non-veiled Muslim woman and the 'bad' religious, veiled Muslim woman are presented together as united in their victimhood. Those who publicly wear the religious symbols of Islamic piety have been so frequently securitised as a threat to the secular republic, and the French state has been so ready to act against them (Samers, 2003). This is especially important in this case given that, as El Hamel (2002) correctly argues, the headscarf has been one of the central defining features in the debate about the integration and accommodation of Muslims under the secular republic in France for the more than a decade. This is buttressed by the humanising descriptions presented of these veiled women in the memorials as hardly threatening—Fatima Charrihi is reported here as a migrant from Morocco who believed in social mobility (insisting her children work hard at school) and who was regularly in telephone and WhatsApp contact with her family (*Le Monde*, 2016).

The profiles of the male victims also displayed photographs, and it is important to think also about how Muslim masculinities have been securitised, both in more secular, class-based terms as the French-born of migrant ethnic origin criminals (Wacquant, 2007) and the religious image of the male Islamist terrorist (Hussey, 2014). Here, however, the desecuritising potential is perhaps less obvious, given the lack of the potential for overtly religious symbols, as is the case with the women who wear the headscarf. Importantly, these should also not be overlooked due to the similarities between the images presented of men in these profiles and those of terror attackers. An example of this can be seen in the profile of Bilel Labbaoui, a victim of the Nice attack.

Here, Bilel is presented with short hair, and with a profile that details his biography as a working-class Tunisian who works in construction in Nice. This sits in contrast to those who have committed attacks in France, such as the Nice attacker Mohamed Bouhlel, who was a migrant from Tunisia who also worked a range of working-class jobs. Thus, this biography demonstrates that these working-class male individuals with similar biographical information and appearance sit on both sides of the attacker/victim dichotomy. Here again, the nuancing of Muslim identity is occurring, but rather than working to present biographical characteristics which differentiate Muslims from attackers, it works to demonstrate their closeness in class, migration status and appearance. This demonstrates that it is not just the more professional, metropolitan Muslims in France who are victims, and the attackers working-class from more marginal backgrounds, but rather indicates that the victims of the attacks come from across the entire spectrum of society.

4.9   Conclusions on Jihadism, Causality, Victimhood and French Muslims

This chapter set out to bring nuances to the position of French Muslims vis-à-vis discussion of the recent peak of jihadist violence in France. This attempted to bring together two disparate yet connected and critical facets of jihadism in France. This involved deconstructing the fallacies of causal explanations formulated and disseminated regarding the reasons an extremely small and anomalous group of French Muslims commit acts of mass murder from a staggeringly diverse set of socio-economic and religious backgrounds. As a further nuancing of the roles of French Muslims in terror attacks, this chapter also examined those who died in these acts of mass murder, apparently carried out in the name of their religion, and how the publicisation of their biographies shone a light on the far more representative banal social roles that French Muslims occupy in contemporary French society. Thus, the sociological reality remains that not only did Islamist terrorism have very little support among French Muslims, but also that many French Muslims died during acts of violence committed overtly in the name of their religion.

Vital in this analysis has been the attempts to dispel the causal myths so commonly perpetrated about jihadism in France. Using the deconstructivist tools of CTS, it has been argued that both deterministic explanations relying on France's colonial history and structural arguments about jihadism being a function of France's dysfunctional domestic politics do not hold water. The deconstruction of the empirical and ontological failings of the current Franco-centric 'grand theories' of French jihadism have been seen to commit two key empirical and conceptual errors. Firstly, they essentialise and homogenise the French Muslim population, which is actually extremely diverse socially, culturally and doctrinally. This is turn leads to essentialist and paternalistic assumptions about French Muslims that smack of colonialism. Secondly, the grand theories seek to root current French jihadism in extremely broad and far reaching social phenomena that affect huge numbers of French citizens, both Muslim and non-Muslim, without acknowledging that jihadism remains an anomaly. Grand theories do little to explain such a fringe phenomenon and these explanations do little to aid the understanding of the field of French jihadism. Indeed, not only is the current field notably poor from an explanatory perspective, but the conceptual rationale employed actually serves to further securitise the French Muslim population, already one of the most securitised in Europe (Cesari, 2013a; Eroukhmanoff, 2015). This is because arguing that broad social forces that affect much larger communities are the root cause of politically motivated mass murder inadvertently makes every socially marginalised

Muslim a potential terrorist, waiting for a cue to self-radicalise and commit acts of violence.

The second key argument of this chapter adds to the critique of these theories, because when one examines the remarkable diversity of French jihadists it becomes clear that they come from a range of backgrounds, many of which are not disadvantaged or marginalised. The emphasis of CTS literature to move away from the obsession of problem solving in traditional terrorism studies is the conceptual bedrock of this analysis, because it enables the nuancing of exactly who is the jihadist and being able to argue that the road to jihadism is extremely diverse, to the point of requiring an individual approach to understanding how and why each individual chooses to become involved in such movements. This presents significant problems for those who still seek to provide 'silver bullet' theories of frameworks for identifying and dealing with jihadism across both Europe and the broader world, because actually examining the biographies of jihadists demonstrates that no single factor will provide such a solution.

Little understood or considered by such grand theories are the far more diffuse yet structurally vital security failings of the French state when it comes to the nation and local security environments. This chapter sought to outline the more general features of the security landscape that contribute to French jihadism operating and being so deadly and effective. Institutionally, the French state was overly complex and bureaucratic in its approach to monitoring a range of terror threats, which enabled the networks involved, transnational in nature as they were, to plan and carry out attacks on French soil. Additionally, the French state has an extremely poor record in dealing with banal security concerns and has thus presided over the proliferation of heavy-grade military weapons on the streets of French cities through organised crime networks.

Turning to a discussion of victimhood of French Muslims during jihadist terror events, this chapter then sought to further banalise the role of French Muslims in these acts of violence and understand the construction of Muslim victimhood during terror events. In particular, these themes required a deeply contextual analysis to make sense in the broader framework of the security situation in France. This is because without an understanding of the discursive context, and indeed the ways that Muslims have been securitised, it is impossible to understand and assess biographical narratives for their content. These banal details of French Muslim lives exposed by victimhood open up important aspects for the nuancing of Muslim group identity in a context where both those on the far right of European politics and on the fringes of Muslim extremism set up a dichotomy whereby Islamic values do not allow Muslims to integrate into European society. This again engages with the debate about the compatibility of European and Islamic values in very important ways, in that the banal facts about the lives of these victims that emerge in the online profiles show that Muslims occupy a broad spectrum of social roles in contemporary European settings.

These banal details began with important discussions about the lack of peculiarity of Muslims in professional positions in society and thus removed their social and religious exceptionalism. These profiles demonstrate, as a collection, the 'broad church' of everyday activities that Muslims undertake in Europe. This goes a long way to nuancing group identity and thus making it difficult for a 'Muslim terrorists versus European society' dichotomy to be plausible and sustained in popular discourse. This is significant for securitisation theory as this collection of biographies goes some way to demonstrating that Roe's (2004) observation that using a group noun like 'Muslim' while trying to desecuritise is problematic may not always be the case. While group nouns are clearly problematic, a collection of biographies that detail such banal and non-exceptional Muslim practices mean that their use and desecuritisation may not be completely incompatible.

This analysis also opens a discussion about how class can contribute to the construction/deconstruction of the good/bad Muslim dichotomy. The dominance of the class cleavages in French society, particularly where they intersect with minority Muslim status, could also be a source of brightening for the good/bad Muslim dichotomy. Here, the 'good' economically active Muslim who dies in central Paris during a terror attack can be contrasted sharply with those in the suburbs without such economic opportunities who may be forced to rely on the grey or black economy to survive. This is of particular relevance when the life histories of several notable French jihadists demonstrate a life trajectory not necessarily replete with religious piety, but one that has involved significant time spent committing petty crimes.

Complementing these insights gained from the textual aspects of the published biographies, the visuals which accompanied them also demonstrate important aspects of the Muslims who were victims of these attacks. These visual portraits create an important face-to-face rapport between the victim and society. Again, context here proves key in understanding the aesthetic significance of the images at hand and specifically how they go beyond simply creating a humanised connection between victim and society to break down important dominant narratives about European Muslims.

Gendered forms, both masculine and feminine, have been of significant importance in brightening social boundaries for Muslims in France. In particular, this has been widely discussed regarding the securitised and gendered form of the Muslim woman and her choice of religious dress—in particular the headscarf. The biographical pictures nuance this gendered Islamic group identity in that several of the female victims are pictured wearing a headscarf. This engages directly with debates about the Muslim headscarf in France, as the women here wear this form of religious dress and are victims of Islamic terror. However, it is important to read the image alongside the substantive content of the profile as here the picture of a woman in a veil is accompanied by a description of an individual in society that is the polar opposite to the often discussed isolated individual existing in a parallel society. Rather, the depiction of these women as mothers and as active participants in the labour market demonstrates further the diverse ways in which French Muslims take part in mainstream society. This is not something limited to feminine forms and imagery, but is also expressed in the masculinities depicted in these profiles. Images of working-class male victims of Muslim origin also demonstrate that the highly securitised image of the working-class North African man does not have to be associated with a security threat. More broadly, however, this analysis has highlighted the necessity of further discussions of how victims, and not just Muslim victims, are depicted in terror events and what this means both for the construction of terror events, but also for the creation of broader narratives in society. In an ongoing context where the securitising of European Muslims is likely to remain strong, and where the means of communication are democratised and continually dynamic and multiplying, desecuritisation will only be rendered increasingly vital to the stability of European democracies. It is to a more thorough unpicking of the gendered dynamics around the constructions of French Muslims that this book now turns in an analysis of the different ways that gender plays a vital part in constructing contemporary French Muslims.

Bibliography

Amnesty International. (2016). *France: Upturned Lives: The Disproportionate Impact of the State of Emergency.* Retrieved October 1, 2018, from https://www.amnesty.org/en/documents/document/?indexNumber=eur21%2f3364%2f2016&language=en

Begag, A. (2011). *Arithmétique migratoire, Azouz Begag: Il y a 15 à 20 millions de musulmanes en France.* Retrieved January 5, 2018, from https://www.dailymotion.com/video/xiwsnc

Billig, M. (1995). *Banal Nationalism.* London: Sage.

Booth, K. (2007). *Theory of World Security* (1st ed.). Cambridge; New York: Cambridge University Press.

Bouzar, D., Caupenne, C., & Valsan, S. (2014). *La Metamorphose Operée Chez Le Jeune Par Les Nouveaux Discours Terroristes – CPDSI.* Retrieved from http://www.cpdsi.fr/articles-et-rapports/la-metamorphose-operee-chez-le-jeune-par-les-nouveaux-discours-terroristes/

Burgot, F. (2016). *Comprendre l'islam politique.* Retrieved October 1, 2018, from http://www.editionsladecouverte.fr/catalogue/index-Comprendre_l_islam_politique-9782707192134.html

Burnett, J., & Whyte, D. (2005). Embedded Expertise and the New Terrorism. *Journal for Crime, Conflict and the Media, 1,* 1–18.

Butler, J. (2006). *Precarious Life: The Power of Mourning and Violence* (Reprint ed.). London; New York: Verso Books.

Buzan, B., Waever, O., & de Wilde, J. (1997). *Security: A New Framework for Analysis* (UK ed.). Boulder, CO: Lynne Rienner Publishers.

Caillet, R., & Puchot, P. (2017). *Le combat vous a été prescrit.* Retrieved from http://www.editions-stock.fr/livres/essais-documents/le-combat-vous-ete-prescrit-9782234082502

Cesari, J. (2009). *The Securitisation of Islam in Europe.* Vol. 15. CEPS. Retrieved from http://aei.pitt.edu/10763/1/1826.pdf

Cesari, J. (2013a). European Conundrum: Integration of Muslims or Securitisation of Islam? *World Review.* Retrieved from https://berkleycenter. georgetown.edu/essays/european-conundrum-integration-of-muslims-or-securitisation-of-islam

Cesari, J. (2013b). Securitization of Islam in Europe: The Embodiment of Islam as an Exception. In *Why the West Fears Islam: An Exploration of Muslims in Liberal Democracies* (pp. 83–105). New York: Palgrave Macmillan US. https://doi.org/10.1057/9781137121202_5

Chrisafis, A. (2015). Charlie Hebdo Attackers: Born, Raised and Radicalised in Paris. *The Guardian.* Retrieved from https://www.theguardian.com/world/2015/jan/12/-sp-charlie-hebdo-attackers-kids-france-radicalised-paris

Chrisafis, A. (2016). *Paris Attacks Inquiry Finds Multiple Failings by French Intelligence Agencies.* Retrieved from https://www.theguardian.com/world/2016/jul/05/paris-attacks-inquiry-multiple-failings-french-intelligence-agencies

Cornevin, C., & Piquet, C. (2016). *Attentats: la longue traque d'une nebuleuse terroriste franco-belge.* Retrieved from http://www.lefigaro.fr/actualite-france/2016/03/25/01016-20160325ARTFIG   00296-attentats-la-longue-traque-d-une-nebuleuse-terroriste-franco-belge.php

Coskun, B. B. (2011). *Analysing Desecuritisation: The Case of the Israeli-Palestinian Peace Education and Water Management.* Cambridge Scholars Publishing. Retrieved from https://www.amazon.co.uk/Analysing-Desecuritisation-Israeli-Palestinian-Education-Management/dp/1443827312

Crettiez, X., Sèze, R., Ainine, B., & Lindemann, T. (2017). *Saisir les mécanismes de la radicalisation violente: pour une analyse processuelle et biographique des engagements violent, Rapport de recherche pour la mission de recherche droit et justice.* Retrieved from http://www.gip-recherche-justice.fr/wp-content/uploads/2017/08/Rapport-radicalisation_INHESJ_CESDIP_GIP-Justice_2017.pdf

Croucher, S. (2008). French-Muslims and the Hijab: An Analysis of Identity and the Islamic Veil in France. *Journal of Intercultural Communication Research, 37*, 3.

Delbecque, E. (2017). *Une 'task force' anti-terroiste à l'Elysée peut elle empêcher des attentats?* Retrieved from http://www.huffingtonpost.fr/eric-delbecque/task-force-macron-terrorisme_a_22108783/

Dell'Oro, J. L. (2015). Combien y a-t-il de djihadistes en France et quels sont leurs profils? – *Challenges*. Retrieved October 1, 2018, from https://www. challenges.fr/france/combien-y-a-t-il-de-djihadistes-en-france-et-quels-sont-leurs-profils_45504

Douet, E. (2015). *Des armes utilisées par les terroristes identifiées en Serbie.* Retrieved October 1, 2018, from https://www.rtl.fr/actu/debats-societe/attentats-a-paris-des-armes-utilisees-par-les-terroristes-identifiees-en-serbie-7780673680

El Hamel, C. (2002). Muslim Diaspora in Western Europe: The Islamic Headscarf (Hijab), the Media and Muslims' Integration in France. *Citizenship Studies, 6*(3), 293–308. https://doi.org/10.1080/1362102022000011621

Eroukhmanoff. (2015). The Remote Securitisation of Islam in the US Post-9/11: Euphemisation, Metaphors and the "Logic of Expected Consequences" in Counter-Radicalisation Discourse. *Critical Studies on Terrorism, 8*, 246–265.

Franceinfo. (2016). *Attentats terroristes en France: quelles armes ont été utilisées?* Retrieved October 1, 2018, from https://www.francetvinfo.fr/faits-divers/terrorisme/attaques-du-13-novembre-a-paris/enquete-sur-les-attentats-de-paris/attentats-terroristes-en-france-quelles-armes-ont-ete-utilisees_1374239.html

Fredette, J. (2014). *Constructing Muslims in France: Discourse, Public Identity, and the Politics of Citizenship*. Temple University Press. Retrieved from https://www.amazon.co.uk/Constructing-Muslims-France-Discourse-Citizenship-ebook/dp/B00HSFS6V0/ref=sr_1_1?ie=UTF8&qid=1538397208&sr=8-1&keywords=Muslims+in+France+%E2%80%93+Discourse%2C+Public+Identity%2C+and+the+Politics+of+Citizenship

Giry, S. (2006, September 1). France and Its Muslims. *Foreign Affairs* (September/October). Retrieved from https://www.foreignaffairs.com/articles/france/2006-09-01/france-and-its-muslims

Gunning, J., & Jackson, R. (2011). What's So 'Religious' About 'Religious Terrorism'. *Critical Studies on Terrorism, 4*, 369–388.

Hackett, C. (2017). *5 Facts About the Muslim Population in Europe*. Retrieved October 1, 2018, from http://www.pewresearch.org/fact-tank/2017/11/29/5-facts-about-the-muslim-population-in-europe/

Hansen, L. (2011). Theorizing the Image for Security Studies: Visual Securitization and the Muhammad Cartoon Crisis. *European Journal of International Relations, 17*(1), 51–74. https://doi.org/10.1177/1354066110388593

Hansen, L. (2018). Images and International Security. *The Oxford Handbook of International Security*. https://doi.org/10.1093/oxfordhb/9780198777854.013.39

Hargreaves, A. (2007). *Multi-Ethnic France: Immigration, Politics, Culture and Society* (2nd ed.). New York; London: Routledge.

Human Rights Watch. (2016). *France: Abuses Under State of Emergency | Human Rights Watch*. Retrieved October 1, 2018, from https://www.hrw.org/news/2016/02/03/france-abuses-under-state-emergency

Huntingdon, S. (1993, Summer). The Clash of Civilisations? *Foreign Affairs, 72*(3), 22–49.

Hussey, A. (2014). *The French Intifada: The Long War Between France and Its Arabs*. London: Granta.

Huysmans, J. (1998). The Question of the Limit: Desecuritization and the Aesthetics of Horror in Political Realism. *Millennium – Journal of International Studies, 27*, 569–589.

Jackson, R. (2007a). Constructing Enemies: 'Islamic Terrorism' in Political and Academic Discourse. *Government and Opposition, 42*, 394–426.

Jackson, R. (2007b). The Core Commitments of Critical Terrorism Studies. In *European Consortium for Political Research*. Retrieved from https://www.researchgate.net/publication/32031958_The_Core_Commitments_of_Critical_Terrorism_Studies

Jackson, R., Gunning, J., & Breen Smyth, M. (2007). The Case for a Critical Terrorism Studies. *Paper of the American Political Science Association*.

Jacob, E. (2016). *La population musulmane largement surestimée en France*. Retrieved from http://www.lefigaro.fr/actualite-france/2016/12/14/01016-20161214ARTFIG00214-la-population-musulmane-largement-surestimee-en-france.php

Jarvis, L. (2011). 9/11 Digitally Remastered? Internet Archives, Vernacular Memories and WhereWereYou.org. *Journal of American Studies, 45*(4), 793–814. https://doi.org/10.1017/S002187581100096X

Kepel, G. (2012). *Banlieue de la République*. Paris: Institut Montaigne.

Kepel, G. (2017). *Terreur dans l'Hexagone: Genèse du djihad français*. Folio.

Kepel, G., & Jardin, A. (2017). *Terror in France: The Rise of Jihad in the West*. Princeton, NJ: Princeton University Press. Retrieved from https://www.amazon.fr/Terror-France-Rise-Jihad-West-ebook/dp/B01M3XAUKO/ref=sr_1_fkmr0_1?ie=UTF8&qid=1538394128&sr=8-1-fkmr0&keywords=kepel++jardin+2015

Khosrokhavar, F. (2014). *Radicalisation (fiche technique)*. Les éditions de la maison des sciences de l'home. Retrieved from http://www.editions-msh.fr/livre/?GCOI=27351100399910&fa=details

Laurent, S. (2015). Terrorisme: qu'est-ce que la 'fiche S'? *Le Monde*. Retrieved from http://www.lemonde.fr/les-decodeurs/article/2015/08/31/terrorisme-peut-on-sanctionner-les-personnes-faisant-l-objet-d-une-fiche-s_4741574_4355770.html

Le Monde. (2015). *Le mémorial du 'Monde' aux victimes des attentats du 13-Novembre*. Retrieved from http://www.lemonde.fr/attaques-a-paris/visuel/2015/11/25/enmemoire_4817200_4809495.html

Le Monde. (2016). *Le mémorial du 'Monde' aux victimes de attentats de Nice*. Retrieved from http://www.lemonde.fr/grands-formats/visuel/2016/10/06/le-memorial-du-monde-aux-victimes-des-attentats-de-nice_5009546_4497053.html

Levinas, E. (1985). *Ethics and Infinity: Conversations with Philippe Nemo*. Pittsburgh: Duquesne University Press.

Mavelli, L. (2013). Between Normalisation and Exception: The Securitisation of Islam and the Construction of the Secular Subject. *Millennium, 41*(2), 159–181. https://doi.org/10.1177/0305829812463655

McCulloch, J., & Pickering, S. (2009). Pre-Crime and Counter-Terrorism: Imagining Future Crime in the 'War on Terror'. *The British Journal of Criminology, 49*, 628–645.

Ouest France. (2018). Braquage à la Kalachnikov: 500 000 E de bijoux volés. Retrieved from https://www.ouest-france.fr/societe/faits-divers/saint-tropez-braquage-l-arme-lourde-500-000-eu-de-bijoux-voles-5481474

Roe, P. (2004). Securitization and Minority Rights: Conditions of Desecuritization. *Security Dialogue, 35*, 279–292.

Roy, O. (2015, January 10). *There Are More French Muslims Working for French Security Than for Al Qaeda*. Retrieved September 1, 2018, from https://www.huffingtonpost.com/olivier-roy/paris-attack-muslim-cliches_b_6445582.html

Roy, O. (2017). *Jihad and Death: The Global Appeal of Islamic State*. London: Hurst and Co. Retrieved from https://www.amazon.co.uk/Jihad-Death-Global-Appeal-Islamic/dp/1849046980

Rumelili, B. (2013). Identity and Desecuritisation: The Pitfalls of Conflating Ontological and Physical Security. *Journal of International Relations and Development, 18*, 52–74.

Sagemen, M. (2014). The Stagnation in Terrorism Research. *Terrorism and Political Violence, 26*, 565–580.

Samers, M. E. (2003). Diaspora Unbound: Muslim Identity and the Erratic Regulation of Islam in France. *International Journal of Population Geography*, 9(4), 351–364. https://doi.org/10.1002/ijpg.292

Schmid, A. P. (2013). Radicalisation, De-Radicalisation, Counter-Radicalisation: A Conceptual Discussion and Literature. *Review, ICCT Research Paper*. Retrieved from https://www.icct.nl/download/file/ICCT-Schmid-Radicalisation-De-Radicalisation-Counter-Radicalisation-March-2013.pdf

Sellami, S. (2016). Le vrai visage du narco-banditisme a *Marseille, La Parisien* online at http://www.leparisien.fr/faits-divers/le-vrai-visage-du-narco-banditisme-a-marseille-02-05-2016-5760745.php

Senni, A. (2016). *Les banlieues, des fabriques de djihadistes? La faute aux politiques. Il est temps d'agir.* Retrieved October 1, 2018, from http://leplus.nouvelobs.com/contribution/1500213-les-banlieues-des-fabriques-de-djihadistes-la-faute-aux-politiques-il-est-temps-d-agir.html

Valette, N. (2018). *Un homme tué par des tirs de Kalachnikov à Marseille le soir du réveillon.* Retrieved October 1, 2018, from https://www.francebleu.fr/infos/faits-divers-justice/un-homme-tue-par-des-tires-de-kalachnikov-a-marseille-le-soir-du-nouvel-1514771178

Van Puyvelde, D. (2015). *We Can't Expect Intelligence Services to Prevent Every Terrorist Attack.* Retrieved from https://theconversation.com/we-cant-expect-intelligence-services-to-prevent-every-terrorist-attack-36676

Wacquant, L. (2007). *Urban Outcasts: A Comparative Sociology of Advanced Marginality.* Retrieved from https://www.amazon.co.uk/Urban-Outcasts-Comparative-Sociology-Marginality/dp/0745631258/ref=sr_1_3?ie=UTF8&qid=1517652872&sr=8-3&keywords=wacquant

Williams, M. C. (2003). Words, Images, Enemies: Securitization and International Politics. *International Studies Quarterly, 47*(4), 511–531. https://doi.org/10.1046/j.0020-8833.2003.00277.x

Zappi, S. (2015, October 22). Le djihadiste, nouvel épouvantail des banlieues françaises. *Le Monde.* Retrieved from https://www.lemonde.fr/banlieues/article/2015/10/22/le-djihadiste-nouvel-epouvantail-des-banlieues-francaises_4794877_1653530.html

5

Gender, Orientalism and Muslims in France: Culture, Masculinity, Violence and Sexuality

5.1 Introducing the Intersection of Gender, Orientalism and Islam in France

Anissa Kate and Yasmine Latife—two names that, at least partially, suggest origin in the Muslim world. Perhaps these two women are the subject of some kind of controversy over the regulation of women's dress? Perhaps they are two women who were forced to remove 'offensive' swimwear on a Mediterranean beach during the summer months? To my knowledge, neither of these things have occurred. Rather, in quite stark contrast, these two women are actually two of the top-selling French pornographic actresses of the past two decades—Anissa being of French Algerian origin and Yasmine born in Morocco before moving to France. It might seem quite paradoxical, and perhaps even provocative, to bring two porn actresses into the equation when discussing French Muslims and femininity, given that Islam as a religion hardly condones the consumption, let alone the production, of such films. However, in 2017 the most popular porn search term in France according to Google Analytics was for women of North African origin (France 24, 2017).

© The Author(s) 2019
J. Downing, *French Muslims in Perspective*,
https://doi.org/10.1007/978-3-030-16103-3_5

This observation opens up a broader conversation about the ways in which new 'orientalised' forms of the exotic and erotic 'internal other' are created and disseminated in the contemporary era. If we are to take seriously the assertion of the critical school of cultural studies that studying culture gives important insights into the way that forms of power are shaped and deployed (Procter, 2004), then no cultural forms should be off limits to sociological or political analysis. This is rendered especially important given the increasingly mainstream positionality of erotic content. The proliferation of the internet means that pornography is accessible to ever larger and more mainstream audiences, and is far from being the domain of old men purchasing dubious magazines or videos from specialist sex shops. Free streaming pornography sites mean that, regardless of one's normative stance on pornography, it is more and more part of the mainstream entertainment landscape—an observation that applies to the French context (Paveau, 2014). This renders it ever more important for sociological analysis in the ways that its choices of scenarios, characters and plots construct, reinforce and redefine the sociological formations and norms. It has long been established that porn has its history, cinematic form and set of discourses (L. Williams, 1989). This is especially important here because the construction of the feminine 'other' in the orientalist tradition has historically been intertwined with notions of eroticism. However, this line of enquiry has yet to be taken up with regards to how orientalism continues in contemporary forms of eroticism. While this makes for somewhat uncomfortable research, and perhaps uncomfortable reading, it remains necessary to understand the sociological forms that contemporary forms of eroticised orientalism continue to be reproduced two centuries after the production of the well known orientalist paintings of Muslim women in imaginary harems and hammams of the East. In the contemporary era, the harem has been replaced with the suburban tower block, and the passive oriental woman has been remade as a working-class, suburban French woman of Muslim origin.

These cultural creations of an orientalised internal other do not stop at women, however, and neither should an analysis of gender only be concerned with femininities. In popular culture in France, there are also ways in which masculinities are also orientalised and intersect in interesting ways with notions of class, religion and ethnic background. While women are eroticised, the exotification of men is through their depiction as the internal 'savage', 'barbaric' criminal. Scholarship has expanded on the ways that categories of marginalisation have been created for French Muslim men, even prior to the recent focus on Islamist terrorism, through the intersection of class and gender to create the threatening, aggressive stereotype of the suburban male (Dikeç, 2007; Hargreaves & McKinney, 1997; Wacquant, 2007). This chapter seeks to shine a light on how these forms of masculinities are taken, Islamised and reproduced in mainstream French culture. For source material, this chapter uses more orthodox material for sociological analysis in terms of the popular French television drama 'Les Engranages'. This piece of cultural output constructs French Muslims through an intersection of class, masculinity, criminality and religion to create the character of the 'Muslim gangster'. This example is far from unique and has become a common trope in French cultural output. However, the example analysed here is illustrative of the components that come together to form this broader trend.

5.2   Conceptualising Gender, Orientalism and Muslims in France

It is evident from some of the discussions begun above concerning the contemporary constructions of gender regarding French Muslims that a wide set of concepts are required to understand the complex forms which come together to produce orientalist, exotic and eroticised forms yet within a contemporary French setting. This offers insights because rather than dealing strictly with the 'other', located somewhere in an imaginary Orient, contemporary forms of gender orientalisms are rather concerned with an internal other, located in an imagined internal space. This 'space' of the internal other, typified by the marginalised suburban housing estate, is key because its relative isolation from mainstream society is not completely imagined, nor is it created by geographical distance between the metropole and the colonised territory somewhere in Asia or Africa. Rather, it exists in structures that Wacquant (2007) identifies as the 'dual cities' in France, where the suburban housing estates exist in isolation from the rest of the city. During research on a number of issues in France, it was consistently expressed to me by those of Muslim origin that they were constantly quizzed about what life was 'really' like on these estates, whether they actually had an experience of living in them or not. Thus, these spaces are internal spaces of the orientalised 'other' are intimately linked to forms of ethnic, class and increasingly religious social forms of existence and belonging, as seen in Kepel's (2012) assertions that the French suburbs, in their abandonment by the central state, are becoming increasingly 'Islamised'.

It has been over 40 years since Edward Said wrote *Orientalism*, which defines approaches to Third-World and post-colonial studies to this day. Important within this and connected closely to the approaches set up in this book, Said (1978) was overtly a social constructivist who drew on discourse as the central 'data' for his ground-breaking work. Here the examination of the orientalist paintings of the eighteenth and nineteenth centuries that did so much to inform the Western world of the paradoxically situated savagery, decadence, piety and profanity of the Middle East delivered these messages through visual and cultural stories. This opens the door to the far broader interpretation of orientalism as a set of cultural practices and cultural misrepresentations of non-Western societies (Chua, 2008). This follows closely work done on the need to bring the 'visual' into the discussion of politics and international affairs (Hansen, 2011) that sees the visual world as important, and perhaps even more important than words, in creating 'discourse' in the social world. Indeed, in the multimodal, saturated and ubiquitous media environment that we find ourselves in at the start of the twenty-first century, a chapter such as this that seeks to look at the gendered constructions of an identity group such as French Muslims needs to take account of a multitude of source materials, both in terms of genre and medium, to make any sense of how sexuality, gender, violence, race and religion intersect in ways remarkably similar, yet strikingly different, to those depictions of harems and Arab cavalry that shaped the imperial gaze on the Orient. Indeed, this chapter's argument is that the gendered, external other, has been replaced by the gendered internal other—with the harem and the hammam as the exotified environment replaced by the concrete tower blocks of the suburban estate. Thus, in this sense orientalism moves from being about the misrepresentation of the non-Western world (Chua, 2008), to being about the cultural practices and misrepresentations of those *within* Western societies who have some connection, no matter how tenuous, to the non-Western world.

While discussions of such popular cultural forms are important in discussions of 'banal' forms of identity construction (Billig, 1995), this discussion is differentiated from the broader discussion of cultural nationalism in the following chapter, as the discussions here do not fit the classification argued for by Zimmer (2003) that the nation is formed in this way at the confluence of culture and politics. Here, this culture is not overtly connected to politics and is as such part of the broader discursive landscape of the ways in which French Muslims are constructed. This draws heavily on the cultural turn in sociology in the 1970s, which remains hugely influential in not just allowing sociologists to understand the broader role that popular culture takes in defining social reality, but fundamentally shifted the discipline of sociology (McLennan, 2014). This shift drew heavily on critical theory about the nature of the social world and how power is located all around us, shaping, often subconsciously, what we do, how we act and what we aspire to (McCoy, 1988). Of particular importance here is Foucault, whose work enables sociologists to see power as 'productive as well as coercive, situational as well as pervasive' (McCoy, 1988). For Foucault, the media was extremely important in offering an avenue for cultural forms of power to be broadcast and projected into society (McCoy, 1988). Within this, Hall speaks about culture as not something to be simply appreciated and studied, but a 'critical site of social action and intervention, where power relations are both established and potentially unsettled' (Procter, 2004). Thus, while it is necessary to examine the creation of national narratives at the confluence of culture and politics (Zimmer, 2003), in examining national identities, and broader identity constructions, all forms of culture have much larger roles. In this vein, Nash (2001) argues for the need for a cultural turn in political sociology. The relations between state and society should not be taken as the key concern of political sociology but rather ideas by Foucault on the power and domination expressed through cultural output should be a key concern (Nash, 2001).

It should be reiterated that the sociological approach being taken here is to analyse the idea of the 'French Muslim' in this context as something that is not simply constituted by adherence to a particular religion, but rather is something which is intimately linked to, and co-constituted by, a range of race and class identities. A key conceptual point of this chapter will be its quest not simply to examine gender, race or sexuality as separate entities, experienced discretely, but rather to employ the intersectional approach to the study of gender and identity pioneered by the radical black feminists of the post-civil rights USA, who took issue with feminism as articulated in a vein that ignored the heterogeneity of the female experience—in particular excluding experiences of black working-class women (inter alia Crenshaw, 1989; Hooks, 1987) As such, it was imperative to find a way to think about a feminism which does not assume all women's experiences of patriarchy are the same. Within this, it was necessary to find a way to integrate other identity categories that lead women to experience different kinds of exclusions. In the same way that the 'humanist' French revolution had neglected women in its founding document, which was gendered only to articulate the rights of men, leaving women politically, civilly and social subservient, first-wave feminism neglected to be concerned with the female experience outside of the white, middle-class woman. This does not mean to say that non-white women did not play a significant role in articulating female struggles, but had to do so within a context of European imperialism and slavery which sets them in very different social, political and material landscape to movements such as the suffragettes, who were concerned with gaining the vote for women.

Indeed, on the other side of the coin, when looking internally within black liberation and anti-colonial struggles, discussions of gender and women's issues remained subservient to the material and political goals of liberation from white supremacy. As such, narratives about 'blackness' deployed both by the racist right and the civil rights activists themselves assumed that 'black' meant 'black man' and not 'black woman' or 'black homosexual'. The prominent civil rights ideologue W. E. B. de bois saw the benefits of an intersectional approach to examining race, class and nation in explaining the problematic position of blacks in the USA, but did not include gender and relegated this to what feminists consider the 'private' sphere. Thus, hidden away in the private sphere, gender questions are depoliticised and hidden from the more 'public' normative discussions of what constitutes the good life and a just polity. It is indeed the destruction of such a divide and the quest to politicise the private that defines almost two centuries of feminist thought and action (Pateman, 1989) and as such its neglect remains a significant blot on the copybook of many radical emancipatory movements. This is not limited to the anglophone world, evidenced by the somewhat ambiguous relationship to women's emancipation seen in the Algerian liberation struggle. As Vince (2015) correctly argues, we need to be nuanced here as it is not simply that once the war ended, women were 'sent back to the kitchen' in the new anti-colonial state. However, many of their pre-war concerns were neglected, alongside many other national non-gender related issues, once the new state began to concentrate more on authoritarian rule rather than improving the social, political and economic lot of the new nation. Many of the women who were integral to the anti-colonial struggle, as rural guerrilla fighters or urban bomb makers, were not rewarded with the utopian promises of the anti-colonial struggle (Vince, 2015). Thus, even in the discourses and practices of some of the twentieth century's most active and revolutionary independence movements, that sought to cast away the literal and metaphorical shackles of both trans-Atlantic slavery and European maritime settler colonialism, women remained marginalised and oppressed by the multiple and overlapping forms of domination both inside and outside these movements.

It is within this context that intersectionality intervenes to de-homogenise the experiences of women who had been unproblematically treated as one mass by earlier iterations of feminism that were mainly concerned with the political emancipation of white women. Thus, intersectionality seeks to identify the interlocking systems of power which come together to oppress different kinds of women in different ways. Even taking colour out of the equation, disabled white women, and indeed white women who convert to Islam, have very different experiences of patriarchal oppression than those of able bodied, non-identifiably religious, white women.

Within a context of majority–minority relations in France, where the minority is the recipient of significant discursive and material exclusion from the national narrative, intersectional feminism engages directly with the question of how a 'colour-blind' feminism can be used as a tool of white dominance. For example, the bans in France concerning the 'burkini', headscarf and full-face veil have explicit feminist justifications in their construction as a means by which women can be 'liberated' from the apparently oppressive aspects of the Islamic faith in being forced to wear certain garments as a function of religious duty. However, this 'feminist' concern with women's dress does not see the need for internal reflection on the oppressive norms that non-Muslim women may face in France, such as the obsession with being thin, the need to wear dangerous high heel shoes on cobble-stoned streets or the significant sexual harassment.

Here, feminism is used as the justification for the need for the French legislature to decide how to regulate the dress of a certain section of the female population defined as 'outsiders' on the basis of religion, race and cultural background. It is within this context that Al-Saji (2008) argues for a racialisation of Muslim women, in that the convergence of ideas about their need for 'liberation' from the veil in contemporary France stem from similar ideas in the colonial era in Algeria and that this gives rise to a form of cultural racism. This highlights the ways that the category Muslim, in this case when considering gender roles, has taken on a 'racial' element and cannot be examined sociologically as simply a religious category.

Interestingly, the defining images of the burkini ban scandal missed several nuances of beach life in Mediterranean France that would have better contextualised the absurdity of such a ban and how it actually moves beyond the 'objective' discussion of female garments and into the realm of direct discrimination based on 'read' racial, cultural and religious characteristics. Owing to the seemingly perpetual 'freshness' of the waters of the Mediterranean, whose surface temperatures never get to anything comparable to that of the human body's resting temperature of 37 degrees centigrade, swimmers, divers and those involved in water sports face the risk of losing significant body heat even in July and August, and are thus required to wear neoprene wetsuits while in the water, which often cover the head and even the hands and feet in the case of those scuba diving. The French police and indeed the local municipalities that banned the burkini never saw this as a concern, and neither did those who advocated it on ridiculous 'hygiene' grounds. Thus, the visibly white women users of the Côte d'Azur beaches wearing wetsuits were never apprehended by the police to de-robe to prove their membership of the republican community. The secularism law of 1901, which forbids religion to enter French political life for very good reasons, does not see the beach as a battleground of political secularism, thus the Supreme Court swiftly and sensibly overturned the ban on the grounds that it was unconstitutional. As such, both Muslim women who want to wear clothes to cover their bodies, and non-Muslim women who want to wear wetsuits to avoid hyperthermia can now do so without fear of police harassment.

When Paul Gilroy (2002) posed the rhetorical observation that there 'ain't no black in the union jack', for some there still remains room in the tricolour only for blanc and not the beur nor the black. This relates closely to the notion advocated by Sayad (1999) of the migrant suffering a 'double absence', in that they are no longer in their country of origin, nor completely assimilated within the host society. This again needs to be modified for the context into which this book intervenes, because the Muslim diaspora in France often exists in a place where the country of origin is France yet at the same time they are not fully considered French, thus perhaps here there is something more than a double absence, because those who are forced to feel an absence in France are not only migrants, with many being born in France and having lived in no other country. In this situation, Muslim women seek adjustments and accommodation from laïcité for them as no longer external 'immigrants' or 'foreigners' but rather as fully-fledged French citizens of Muslim faith (Lutrand & Yazdekhasti, 2011). Thus, it must be both conceptually and empirically avoided to talk about an 'Islamic' or 'Muslim' feminism in France as, like Muslims themselves and their opinions on a large range of social and political issues, there exists no one answer from Muslims to today's social and political questions. Muslim women and Muslim feminism are no different and it is worth reiterating that the only constant and 'truth' about French Muslims is their complexity, diversity and variations in social practices and opinions.

It is within this context that it is necessary to be extremely nuanced and careful when it comes to discussing the forms of feminism that have emerged around these issues, as a crude typology of a 'Muslim feminism' is misleading because of its homogenising tendencies. New forms of Muslim feminist organisations founded in France and across Europe are notable for their significant diversity of ideas and lack of homogeneity (Fournier, 2008). The much broader church of feminism, whether defined as 'Muslim' or not, is marked as a field within which there is significant conflict over a wide range of issues which affect women (Dot-Pouillard, 2007). As such, these conflicts have included various forms of Islamic feminism that seek freedom to wear the veil, see the veil as a 'reactionary' instrument (Dot-Pouillard, 2007), see its banning as further evidence of the racism and colonial thinking in France; see it as an important liberating statement for women (Dot-Pouillard, 2007), and often see it as a discussion that excludes women, with the men in charge of politics making decisions about what should be done to both ensure the liberty of the public sphere and establish what is appropriate public dress for women (Dorlin, 2010).

This conflict and diversity are at least in part due to the public discussion around the status, life experience and political mobilisation of Muslim women in France, which has been far more profound and wide reaching than the recent bans on women's clothes such as the national burka ban and the local-level burkini ban. Rather, the empirical and the normative dimensions to how the lives of French Muslims women unfold, and indeed how they *should* be structured, have been the subject of fierce political, social and ideological battles in France for decades. This has drawn in activists, commentators and individuals from a wide range of political persuasions and economic positions to contribute to a wide range of political debates in the public realm.

A point of entry that gives important context to the broader discussions of the intersections of class, culture and religion in gender-based struggles in France is around the 2003 creation of the NGO 'Ni Putes Ni Soumises' (NPNS) which roughly translates as 'neither whores nor submissives'. This association was created to, among other things, agitate for women's rights in the isolated suburban housing estates. It was argued that the hyper-masculine environment of the poor and relatively lawless housing estates were key factors in enabling the physical, sexual and emotional abuse of women (Amra & Zappi, 2004). This led to protests across France against the mistreatment of women (Ni Putes Ni Soumises, 2005), and to the publication of a 'Guide to Respect', which looks at the experiences of both men and women in these toxic forms of social relations. The extent of some of the horrific instances of violence in these areas of French cities were given form and substance through the work of Samira Bellil (2003), who published a memoir of her horrific experiences of being subjected to repeated gang-rapes by men in her neighbourhood, such women being referred to as 'tournants' or 'pass around'. This memoir lifted the lid not only on the horrors of physical and sexual abuse, but also on what Bellil (2003) referred to as a conspiracy of silence, where the victims were encouraged not to go to the police for fear of reprisal from the perpetrators. The bravery of Bellil's work earned her the honour of being named a 'new Marianne', and also having a primary school posthumously named after her in the Parisian suburb of Seine-Saint-Denis. NPNS was founded by Fadela Amara, who had been involved in working for the rights of women from poor areas of France since the 1980s, and who had also been instrumental in organising the march in 2002 that gave rise to the NPNS slogan. The march was provoked by another important and tragic event where a French Muslim woman, Sohane Benziane, living in a poor suburb, was set on fire by her ex-boyfriend because she had found a new partner.

To more fully outline the politics and social position of NPNS, the organisation and its founders created several publications. In 'La Racaille de la République' (The Scum of the Republic) (Abdi & Amara, 2006), NPNS outlines where they see the current state of minorities in France. Their specific platform draws a lot on the structural problems of contemporary France—including a rise in violence in the suburbs, an increased inequality of chances for those of minority origin—while also denouncing what they see as an increase in 'religious' discourses. This establishes them as not wishing to fully disrupt the current order in France, but rather seeking a reform of existing state, social and economic structures to better level the playing field for minorities.

However, NPNS does not have a monopoly on ideas around how the feminist struggle should be structured in the French case, and the appearance of the Parti des Indigènes de la République (the Party of the Indigenous of the Republic, PIR) represented the emergence of a different strand of thought. Drawing heavily on ideas of anti-imperialism, and colonial and post-colonial theory, the party has been the subject of significant controversy in France and has been alleged to be homophobic, anti-semitic and racist towards white French people. The ideas of the party and its spokesperson, Houria Bouteldja, have received significant attention in recent years in France. The PIR has a significantly different point of departure from previous movements such as the NPNS, in that they more fundamentally question the structures of French society. Their point of departure is strongly rooted in anti-colonial ideologies (Bouteldja, Khiari, Ewanjé-Epée, & Magliani-Belkacem, 2012), and they pitch themselves as a continuation of anti-colonial struggles. Here, the idea follows that France was a colonial state, and remains very much a colonial state, with society structured on hierarchies of class, status and white privilege (Bouteldja et al., 2012). Here, it is necessary to nuance this idea of 'white privilege', in that it is not simply reducible to origin or skin colour, but rather takes account of far more profound questions of citizenship, status, class and other social categories (Bouteldja, 2016). In an interview, Bouteldja identifies herself as 'white' due to her privileged position in society—having a passport, union rights and a job (Mechaï, 2018). She also articulates ideas about the structure of French society that mirror strongly the hierarchies of colonialism, in that she sees the privileged white men at the top and the Roma at the bottom, due to their recent marginalisation in France (Mechaï, 2018). In contrast to the stance of NPNS, the PIR connect the struggle of minority women to the struggles of minorities in France more generally through militant anti-colonial ideology. Interestingly, their designation of what to call the internal 'other' is important, because this choice of terminology goes some way to understanding this contrasting view of society and what needs to be done about it. NPNS use the term 'racaille', while PIR use the term 'indigène'. 'Racaille' is a term intimately linked to the French context and made famous by Nicolas Sarkozy when he used it to describe rioters in the wake of the 2005 riots (Jobard, 2006). The term 'indigène', however, has very different connotations in that it is intimately linked to the colonial era and the suppression of the rights of those colonised by European powers. Here, both movements seek to settle France's minorities social problems through bringing an end to the discrimination faced by minorities, with NPNS advocating a reform of the current system, and PIR preferring an approach of, in their own words, 'revolutionary love' (Bouteldja, 2016).

Thus far in this discussion as presented here, men have appeared only as those who are either trying to set the agenda within the French government for how women should dress, or as the aggressors that commit unspeakably horrific violent acts against women. This would be an extremely misleading picture, with the rhetoric around specifically Muslim men as sexual predators against European women becoming a staple of European xenophobic discourse in the past decade. However, intersectional forms of gender experiences are also repressive to men. A straightforward example in France is that those who are still disproportionately likely to be the victims of police harassment are those who are defined by a different set of intersectional gender characteristics (Dikeç, 2007; Hargreaves, 2007; Wacquant, 2007). These are the men of ethnic minority origin in France whose gender is the basis of a very different form of discursive construction not as the exotic, passive woman without agency, but rather as the dominant, violent and morally corrupt exotic man. Thus, in the way that the orientalist conceptions of Muslim women as erotic and exotic are reproduced in contemporary French culture, the same goes for the historical stereotypes of the savage, barbaric and aggressive oriental man. Here, masculinities will also be an important basis upon which intersectional forms of oppression are constructed in France, sharing many characteristics with the experiences of those of minority ethnic origin in places such as the UK, Holland and the USA, to name only a few. Here, the conceptual nuance is that an intersectional approach is not reducible to analysing the various overlapping facets of one's social experience, but rather seeking to analyse how they interact. The prima facie arguments of feminism ignore the fact that masculinity can be an important form of oppression and not just a signal of membership of the 'patriarchal elite' of the privileged half of humanity born into male bodies.

When examining both masculinity and femininity from an intersectional perspective in this context, post-colonial theory is particularly relevant because of the hangover of concepts of the non-white other which emerged during the French imperial project. However, these ideas should not be viewed as static, pristine heirlooms of the nineteenth and twentieth centuries, but rather as extremely dynamic and changing narratives that make sense of the inferiority of the non-white subject in new ways grafted onto the cultural, historical and social changes of the times. For example, the construction of the violent and criminal young man of 'Arab' origin owes much now to a notion of a suburban underclass with a penchant for expensive sportswear and loud motor scooters.

These brief examples serve to illustrate Crenshaw's point that intersectionality works in different arenas of social life—the structural, political and representational. While this chapter will concentrate on 'representational intersectionalism' (Crenshaw, 1989), in terms of the social construction of representations of French Muslims, it should be kept in mind that this discussion is not an abstract discussion of symbolic politics, irrelevant to the 'real' world, because systems of symbolic oppression are always intertwined with structural and political forms of oppression. The Muslim woman on the beach in a burkini and the young North African man wearing a tracksuit in the suburbs of Paris are harassed for different reasons by the coercive apparatus of the state because they are symbolically oppressed in addition to being the subjects of structural and political forms of marginalisation.

These observations led to the selection of the source material used here. There is already a good body of scholarship on feminist movements in France, and the debates within French feminism and its contending conceptions of what women's liberation means vis-à-vis Muslim women and the veil. There also exists a significant literature on the structural oppression of Muslim men in terms of experiencing disproportionate attention from the police forces. To examine both of these issues from a discursive perspective, that is, to examine how these contemporary intersectional gender constructions are being reproduced, this chapter draws on the discussed.

5.3   Exotifying and Eroticising the Muslim Woman in France: Beurette and French Pornography

This connection was made by reporting over recent years that one of the top search terms in France for online pornography was the term 'Beurette', a slang term for a young woman of French-Arab extraction (France 24, 2017). This rare glimpse in the mainstream into the highly racialised world of pornography shone the light on a prominent subcategory of production in France which connects class, gender and orientalist notions about the North African woman in important intersectional ways. Analysing this slightly unorthodox material thus gives key insights into the constructions of gender and contemporary forms of orientalism.

The point of departure for this chapter when thinking empirically about gender, orientalism and imperialism in contemporary France is in the term 'beurette'. The deconstruction of this term will also shed significant light on the need to adopt an intersectional approach to be able to make sense of the complex and overlapping layers of meaning that construct these terms in their vernacular use in the French context. Discussions of this term (perhaps the best work on the early emergence and usage of the term is Souilamas, 1999) are by no means new, as the term itself has been in use for some considerable time. However, the term is used across a number of contexts, some rooted in the banalisation of the North African presence in France, and sometimes used by women of North African origin themselves. In this vein, Kemp (2009) argues that the term is used in a context about liberation but in a retrogressive context that constructs Arab women as requiring emancipation rather than giving them agency—a thread all too common in the discourses. But this account is remarkable because it looks at this problematic slightly apart from a context of religion per se—here it is more the secular and sociocultural aspects of the women's experience that are considered. This is significant because this designation of the North African woman in the first instance is not related specifically to the membership of any particular religious group per se.

However, as well as having banal aspects to its application and definition in the French context, it also has other highly eroticised connotations. In French rap videos the beurette is analogous to the 'video girls' of US rap, where they are used in degrading and sexualised ways as accessories to the male rappers in the videos. Here, there develops a representation of the 'black Maghreban female' which creates and reproduces degrading and sexualised stereotypes (Ramdani, 2011). This also stretches to questions of the construction and stereotyping of North African women in French literature, which draws on many of these exotified and erotic themes (Ireland, 2001). Indeed, during field research in France, a range of these sexualised stereotypes emerged, including an idea of the French North African woman as 'Fatima Lopez' owing to a construction of the second and third generation, working-class North African woman as vulgar, working-class and highly sexualised due to their dress and attitude, which referenced the hip-hop culture of the USA. However, in a world where erotic content can be beamed directly onto one's laptop and tablet for free, the eroticisation and exotification of the French North African woman goes much further and gets much more explicit in the numerous outputs of French pornography which directly reference themes not only of the North African woman in the abstract, but ones which directly link her to religion, class and ethnicity in important ways.

Including pornography as a source material for the discursive production of gendered roles in France does not come without significant controversy as porn studies itself, despite porn becoming mainstream in France as elsewhere (Paveau, 2014), remains a niche field. While having roots in US sociology of the twentieth century, it remains still in the margins. Pornography as a matter of academic interest has been treated in the main from a pathological perspective. As such, there is no dearth of studies that discuss issues such as exposure of underage adults to the material (Wolak, Mitchell, & Finkelhor, 2007) or investigate the behavioural consequences of prolonged use by adults (Zillmann, 1989). There remains a significant dearth of academic and sociological literature that asks the important questions about pornography. L. Williams (2014) identifies the over-representation of gay porn in studies, and shows the real lack of serious single-author scholarly works.

This lack of enquiry is paradoxical because on the one hand sociology, and sociologists more generally, have rarely shied away from covering phenomenon on the fringes of society or aspects of social life that are considered 'taboo'. And on the other hand, sociologists have not neglected to broaden the scope of discourse studies away from simply reading texts to opening up a cornucopia of interesting and robust methodologies to understand and analyse the visual and multimodal means by which discourse is structured and disseminated in the contemporary era. Pornography somehow sits in both of these camps. As such, porn rather has a specific history, cinematic form, and has been long established as a key part of discourses on sexuality (L. Williams, 1989). However, it still remains understudied for the ways in which it can open up broader insights into discourses on a range of social and political issues. This is especially true in the French context, where porn studies arrives late, imported from the anglophone world into the French context (Landais, 2014). An example of this lag between the anglophone and francophone context can be seen in the landmark publishing of an anthology of translations of key works from English into French in 2015 (Vörös, 2015), alongside other original works by Paveau (2014). Studies have thus not kept pace with the changing reality in France, where pornography has become a banalised theme in media discourses, both in print and on TV (Paveau, 2014). Arguments have recently been made in French media outlets that porn is an important means by which power relations in society can be understood (Florian Vörös, quoted in Arnau, 2018). This resonates with observations made in other contexts that pornography 'may reify systematic oppression while also empowering marginalised subjects to disrupt these systems in unique ways' (Smith & Luykx, 2017), and it is again surprising that sociologists have not made more interventions into this realm. The few articles that do exist point towards the importance of race within this field and the ability of pornographic productions to significantly reproduce dominant forms of racism in systematic and erotic ways. This could be in the valuing of black women less than white women (Reece, 2015), and also the marginalisation of black male performers and those that choose to work with them in processes of 'racial dodging' (Landes & Nielsen, 2018).

This is evidence that in line with the existing concept of pornography as something on the fringes, academic enquiry is yet to catch up with it as increasingly a feature of the mainstream. For example, both the recent Stormy Daniels controversy around her affair with President Trump, and the transformation of French pornographic actress Clara Morgane to a mainstream singer and TV presenter, demonstrate that the division between the 'mainstream' culture of society and the deviance of pornography is breaking down. Pornography is also no longer a marginal feature of the social landscape but is increasingly mainstream. Once the preserve of the margins, the mainstreamisation of pornography, or indeed the 'pornographisation' of the mainstream, through the proliferation of porn on the internet, have rendered it a much more familiar social phenomena than even a decade or two ago. Indeed, some have argued that porn represents the new 'shared experience'.

Additionally, it has significantly evolved and produced and reproduces numerous discourses about a wide range of social issues. It should be stated from the outset that in analysing pornography in this chapter, this book does not seek to take either a normative or a moral stance on the sex industry, its treatment of women, or the increasing availability of pornography to audiences both young and old. There is significant work done on this already, and it is beyond the scope of this book to attempt to add to these debates in a work concentrated on the constructions and reconstructions of a social group in a European country. Rather, this book takes a much more pragmatic approach to pornography as a source material which requires some unpacking before moving on. Regardless of our personal views, pornography is a large, and increasingly mainstream, feature of the social landscape that studies have identified is growing in acceptance especially among the young (Carroll et al., 2008). In a similar vein to violent video games or genres of music that could be argued to glorify and glamorise violent lifestyles, they remain important parts of the social world and require us to take account of their theoretical and empirical implications in shaping notions in society of gender roles, social norms and forms of economic organisation. Pornography in this chapter will therefore be treated in this vein, as a piece of discourse that this chapter will argue can shed important light on the construction of intersectional gender identities and broader discourses around women and sexuality. It sheds light on two intersectional constructions of femininity that are necessary to understand when we think about how female Muslims are constructed in France. The world of French pornography interestingly buttresses ideas already laid out earlier in this book around the complex nature of constructions of contemporary Muslimness in France through the intersection of religion, gender and class in constructions of Muslim women. There is not simply one, unidirectional trajectory to how the Muslim women featured in these films are constructed, but rather there are variations that need careful consideration in understanding how this emerging social force shapes, mirrors and even confounds other constructions of the Muslims woman.

One variety of ways in which Muslim femininity is exoticised and orientalised in contemporary French pornographic videos is through an
'ethnicisation' of the female actresses. This takes a range of aesthetic forms
that are necessary to understand in further comprehending the means
with which femininity, ethnicity and Muslimness are exotified in erotic
production. It should be acknowledged here that not every instance of a
woman of Muslim origin taking part in such films is labelled as such and
nor do they always draw on overtly ethnicising themes. Those who have
found significant success, such as Anissa Kate and Yasmine Latif, make
the majority of their films without there being any overt discussion of
their origins, and the themes deployed do not directly discuss them as
North African or Muslim women. Thus, it would not be empirically correct to argue that the only, or indeed the dominant, means by which
Muslim women are represented are overtly as such. This does not, however, negate the fact that one of the key selling points of these actresses is
their minority ethnic origins. This observation simply goes to show once
again that constructions of Muslimness in contemporary France do not
just occur under specific banners that label them as such, but rather mesh
with far more banal forms of construction.

These are important framing points because there is no one fixed way
in which new forms of orientalist constructions of Muslim women occur
in French pornography. In line with sociological observations that
'Muslim' as a social category is constituted by a far wider range of facets
than simply the religious, there are the intersections of class and race.
This is where the setting of such films demonstrates the broader point
made that the harems and hammams of the orientalist era have been
replaced with the concrete of the contemporary tower block.

In several of these films, Muslim women have their femininity constructed through the lens of them as women of Arab origin that are
marked out by their class position. In particular, this takes the form of
women performing roles of under-class, suburban women in films that
particularly market themselves as such, with titles such as 'Sluts from the
estate'. Here, these women act out the roles of women from France's
high-rise suburban housing estates and act out scenes that situate them as
involved in a world of criminality, loose sexual morality and where
women trade on, and in turn are used for, their ability to provide sexual

favours to hyper-masculine men. Class and race come together to exotify the woman of Muslim origin that is obscured from view; in this case, not by the social or moral norms of Islamic family values which are conspicuous by their absence. Rather, here she is obscured from view through being on the wrong side of the dominant class, social and security cleavages of French urban life between the 'safe' middle-class, white society both suburban and urban, and the dangerous suburbs. The Muslim women is exotified in secular terms through the thrill of giving a view into a world hitherto opaque to the casual observer.

This occurs in a number of ways and reproduces key themes about poverty and exploitation of minority ethnic women in France. Muslim women are exoticised in French pornography through their depiction in class and economic deprivation terms as residents of the poor housing estates in French suburbs, the 'banlieues'. The film 'Sluts of the suburbs', released in 2012 by the small French company HeXagone, begins with graphics of a stylised housing estate and is followed by a scene of the three female protagonists running into a high-rise building. The story follows the three girls—Manon, Samia and Adella—who set themselves up as escort girls online, overtly because they cannot find sufficient money to leave their housing estate. JTC Video also released a film which eroticises and orientalises French Muslim women from a class perspective without specifically identifying them as Muslims in 'Zahia and her Friends'. Here, the plot follows Zahia arriving back in Paris from an unknown destination. She attempts to organise an evening out with two of her friends, one called Aaliya, but Aaliya is stopped from joining them by her domestically violent boyfriend. Interestingly here, no reference is made to being Muslim per se beyond the girls' names and their obviously working-class, second or third generation North African backgrounds. There are also no symbolic references to traditional forms of the exotification of North African or Islamic femininity—no veils, no belly dancing. Rather, in these films it is enough to reference class and geographical segregation in the suburbs to construct a notion of French Muslim femininity that is appealing to the exotic and erotic fantasies of the wider audience.

Other films, however, do deploy symbols more traditionally associated with the exotification of North African women, such as belly dancing, and do more to directly discuss and address the ethnic origins of these women in countries in the Middle East and North Africa. In these, there is the modernisation and reproduction in French pornography of the exotic 'oriental' woman. Here, women are 'marked' as having a 'unique' selling point, offering an opportunity to gaze upon the oriental woman, who is usually hidden under a veil and kept away from the gaze of the occidental man. They appear in belly-dancing costumes in films that feature important performative aspects of orientalism that would seem at home in orientalist paintings of fictitious eighteenth-century harems. An example of this occurs in a film by the production company Jacquie et Michel. The growth of the group Jacquie et Michel demonstrates that pornography in France, as in many societies across the world, is not only extremely successful, but is ever more in the mainstream of culture and society. Begun in 1999 by a school teacher Michel as a photo-sharing website, the company now has ten shops across French cities and even sells branded merchandise in hypermarket chains such as Auchan. Additionally, the first copy of its paper magazine sold around 27,000 copies on its launch in 2016. The company has also sponsored football teams. It produces films across a wide range of themes, many of which play to a theme of amateurism and scenes shot at least partially in public locations. One of these demonstrates how gendered themes of ethnicity are used in orientalist ways to exotify the actresses. The film begins with an actress named 'Paloma' arriving in Marseille to be met by the production team. As she is interviewed in the home of the crew, the subject of her ethnicity emerges. She describes herself having a mix of Moroccan and Turkish ancestry, with the production crew getting her to recite the company tagline in North African dialect Arabic, where she says that she speaks very good Arabic. Later on, Paloma performs a belly dance to North African music. Thus, here there is a far more overt and direct engagement with more traditional orientalist themes such as the exotified woman performing a belly dance. This is directly following in the vein of the orientalist paintings of the nineteenth century that sought to eroticise and exotify the Muslim women by allowing outsiders to gaze upon them as they perform activities that would have not traditionally been observable. This construction of gendered roles of French Muslims is not simply something that occurs in terms of the creation of exotified forms of femininities, but also for masculinities, but in importantly different ways that continue to echo, and also modify, constructions that date from the ori-entalist era of the nineteenth century.

5.4 Masculinity, Class and Crime: The 'Muslim Gangster' in French Popular Culture

If the term 'beurette' was our analytical point of departure for the con-struction of Muslim women in popular culture, then it makes sense that a discussion on constructions of masculinities begins with the male equivalent 'beur', and a discussion of the ways in which particular kinds of masculinities in the French cultural narrative are particularly applied to the construction of French Muslims. Before we fully unpack this term and begin to think about how its use and connotations differ from how the feminine equivalent is deployed, it is necessary to highlight the mul-tifaceted ways in which masculinities are important in the contemporary French discourse on Muslims. It should be noted that masculinities, like their feminine equivalents, are constructed in a variety of ways in con-temporary France vis-à-vis French Muslims, even when they have received comparatively less attention within the sociological field of enquiry. There is clearly, therefore, a need to bring masculinities more fully into focus when examining issues of gender in France (Guénif-Souilamas & Macé, 2006). Masculinities have been the subject of a flurry of scholarship which accurately portrays the reality that there is not one masculinity but a series of masculinities, which are hard to define because of their con-stantly dynamic and diverse nature (Connell, 2005). Thus, any analysis of masculinities, real or constructed through culture, must be rooted in the context in which they are being reproduced. Scholars have done valu-able work on how this plays out in contexts as wide as education systems (Ghaill, 1994), and in penal systems skewed towards targeting and imprisoning men from marginalised social groups and backgrounds (Messerschmidt, Tomsen, & Tomsen, 2018).

Recent years have also seen much scholarship emerge on the specific examination of masculinities in Muslim diaspora contexts. This has uncovered some very interesting observations about how Muslim masculinities are constructed, with a paradoxical discourse emerging where Muslim men are constructed as both effeminate and academic, but at the same time toxically masculine and extreme patriarchal (Hopkins, 2006). Indeed, much of the scholarship on Muslim masculinities that goes on to influence the policy agenda has been criticised for being poorly theorised (Kalra, 2009). These observations are relevant, given the highly securitised contexts in which the discussion of Muslim masculinities occurs in a Western context, where their constitutions are interrogated as explanations for phenomena such as sexual violence (Dagistanli & Grewal, 2016) and terrorism (Aslam, 2012). Explaining acts of mass violence with recourse to the idea that it is the product of masculine disempowerment is extremely problematic due to the tiny amount of potentially 'disempowered' men who actually commit acts of violence. Much more interesting and well thought out are the discussions around the 'moral panics' created by reports of sexual violence committed by Muslim men, which build on previous orientalist tropes about Muslim men being perverse and sexually deviant (Dagistanli & Grewal, 2016). French feminism can construct young men of ethnic minority origin who rape and veil women as a 'problem', from whom women of ethnic minority origin need to be saved (Guénif-Souilamas & Macé, 2006). Thus, we can already see how this references two of the key milestones in contemporary social discourse that brings the position of Muslim women in French society into clear focus—the regulation of women's religious dress, and also the feminist movements that have emerged such as NPNS in response to conditions of insecurity in the suburbs that have left women vulnerable to sexual violence.

Moving back to terminology, the term 'beur' does not have the same layers of pejorative meaning heaped onto it as the term 'beurette'. Rather different language is deployed against young men of immigrant origin that unites them across racial lines in a way that beurette does not, due to its specific situation within the context of post-colonial, post-migration immigrant women. Perhaps an alternative pejorative term that enables the dissection of the depiction of young men of migrant, and often Muslim, origin is 'racaille', whose unpacking demonstrates some of the key ways in which Muslim masculinities, alongside those of other working-class minority youth in France, are constructed. Although this term has been in vernacular use in France for some time, it found fame in the urban riots of 2005 in the now infamous comments of Nicolas Sarkozy about the need to clean the 'racaille' from the suburbs with a pressure washer (Jobard, 2006). In this context, the term was used to dehumanise those who took part in the riots and treat them as a mass of irrational individuals requiring coercive actions to stop them inflicting carnage on broader French society. As Azouz Begag said, the 'racaille' are synonymous with those who 'frighten everyone … and ignore traffic lights just as they challenge all other codes of social conduct' (Pulham, 2005).

However, this is not the only way to understand how the term 'racaille' intersects with masculinity to construct what it means to be a young Muslim man in France. Rather, the term has a complex meaning and presents multiple layers of marginalisation vis-à-vis the French Muslim community in an almost completely secular sense. Here, it has become a term internalised by youths of immigrant origin themselves to describe not just the criminal lifestyle prevalent in the popular discourse around the term, but a linguistic, sartorial and lifestyle orientation (Doran, 2004). In fact, many of the youths interviewed in this work identified with the construction of racaille in nuanced and multifaceted ways—rejecting the criminal elements of it, choosing to not use language or wear clothes epitomic of the lifestyle in formal public settings (Doran, 2004). This discussion of the ways in which other social categories combine with a notion of being Muslim come together in France to construct identity is an extremely dynamic and diverse field of social life that remains understudied. There is undoubtedly important work also to be done on the ways in which class, race and religion intersect with masculinities in the wake of the wave of Islamist terror attacks in France since 2012, where the majority of attackers were indeed men. Indeed, broader discussions about the danger of radicalisation have pushed questions of how and why male French Muslims have chosen to plot terror attacks and travel to the Middle East to fight for ISIS. This is not simply an issue which affects men, however, as discourses around construction of jihadi brides and the women who have played important roles in terror attacks, and who have travelled overseas to join ISIS, are also important.

This section of the chapter seeks to contribute to the field of understanding how Muslim masculinities are constructed in French culture through an analysis of the emergent character of the 'Muslim gangster'. This seeks to build on recent discourse vis-à-vis the political problems of the suburbs of French cities being dominated by the spectre of an 'Islamisation' discussed both by politicians both on the left and right (as identified by Geisser, 2007) and also by scholars and policy makers (an example of this can be seen in the work of Kepel, 2012). This layers on top of the masculine stereotypes of the 'racaille', the baggage of the possibility of an Islamist threat and begins to become visible in public culture through the intersection of Islam and criminality. While this section of the chapter seeks to move beyond an analysis of French pornography, as male characters are not given centre stage, it is worth noting that the roles that Muslim men play in these films, even if they are marginal, re-enforce the analysis that these films serve as a contemporary means by which one can gaze into the world of the internal other. These men are hyper-masculine and toxically masculine individuals who control and abuse the women in the films. This occurs in the two films analysed above. In the first, 'Zahia and her Friends', the woman's boyfriend arrives and stops her from seeing her friends before slapping her and forcing her to perform a sex act. This trope is repeated in 'Sluts of the suburbs' where it is the men who control the women and intimidate them as they walk around their housing estate. Therefore, these roles re-enforce the notion that Muslim men in these areas of France are something that the women there need to be protected from (Guénif-Souilamas & Macé, 2006). The films act as a mirror for dominant, marginalising narratives about Muslim men. Interestingly, again here they are not explicitly described as 'Muslim' in the first instance, as far less of their biographical information is given than for the female characters—indeed heterosexual male consumers of these films are not seeking to gaze into the hidden world of these men. However, this re-enforces the argument that the idea of being a Muslim in France is constituted by a far more diverse range of social characteristics and categories than simply the obviously religious.

Where masculinity also gets attention, and also gets fleshed out more fully as characters are far more developed, are in more mainstream forms of French cultural output. In this regard, this chapter seeks to build on this scholarship by examining how these concepts of Muslim masculinities feed into, and are re-enforced by, constructions in popular culture that bring together criminality, class, race and religion. Here, there emerges a fictitious and orientalist Islam of criminality. Building on the old orientalist trope of the savage non-Western man, stories are constructed whereby Muslim gangsters, who are paradoxically pious and culturally very conservative, also mix freely elements of the sacred and the profane in the execution of their violent criminal conspiracies as a matter of course. This buttresses the more secular image of the 'racaille' juvenile delinquent, while also giving it a significant religious dimension that was previously not so present. It is interesting here that alongside literature that emerges which discusses concerns about the 'Islamification' of the French suburbs (G. Kepel, 2012), a parallel discourse emerges in popular culture which depicts an 'Islamification' of the criminality which exists in such places.

This kind of portrayal of the Muslim gangster occurs in the French TV crime thriller 'Engranages' (shown in English under the name 'Spiral'). This series is a mainstream hit in France, being broadcast on Canal+, and has had the rights for broadcast sold all over the world, including to BBC4 in the UK. As such, this is not a fringe piece of cultural production and illustrates that these depictions are not limited to the fringes of French culture but rather penetrate into the mainstream. Season two of this series centres on the activities of a drug-smuggling crime gang of Moroccan origin, the Larbis, and their criminal operations around Paris. This follows a rather similar criminal plot line to other crime related films, including a discussion of the role of the police, portraying how criminals operate and depicting those that act outside of the system of social order (Mason, 2002; Rafter, 2006). Additionally, it is important to note that the depictions of diaspora groups in the roles of criminals is nothing new in the genre of crime cinema more broadly, with the African-American or Italian gangster in US films an old trope (Chan, 1998; Mason, 2002). However, there is a lack of a discussion about how Muslim criminals are constructed in the French context and how this draws on notions of ethnic and religious group identity as an integral part of not just the plot of the series more generally, but more specifically how these concerns shape and frame their criminal activities.

This is where the French output connects important aspects of a notion of French Muslimness with specific kinds of criminality in some very interesting ways. There is a construction of a specific kind of 'French Muslim gangster'—not simply a gangster of North African origin but rather one where Islamic themes are present consistently alongside their criminal activities. This is of significance in understanding constructions of French Muslims, because this particular construction is not just about someone of minority ethnic origin committing crimes. Rather, there are direct connections made between the two gangster brothers and Islamic institutions, seeing them for example making donations to a particular Imam for a mosque. This directly brings Islamic themes into a discussion of criminality. Also significant are the ways that these notions of the Muslim gangster intersect with questions of gender, because these figures are overwhelmingly men, with Muslim women playing marginal roles within the narrative, whether these are highly sexualised roles such as prostitutes, materialistic gangsters' wives or pious, religious dress wearing family members. Within this, there are specific representations that point at specific ways that the Muslim gangster is constructed.

In one particular plot line, the two gangster brothers, Mustafa and Farouk, hold a birthday party for a young girl, to which they invite two corrupt lawyers that have been working for them. This is depicted as a traditional North African Islamic family setting—musicians are playing North African music on drums, belly dancers are dancing and people are drinking mint tea poured from Moroccan teapots. Additionally, the dialogue takes place against a backdrop of groups of women in traditional North African dress, their hair covered with headscarves. The dialogue also turns to the details of the involvement of the criminals and their money with specifically Islamic activities. At one point, the corrupt lawyer explains to his new recruit that an Imam is in attendance (Imam Saïd) because the crime family is financing the building of a new mosque. This constructs the gangsters as more than just criminals of North African origin but rather criminals of that origin who still have a specifically Islamic involvement with the social world through the construction of Islamic religious buildings with the laundered money from their drugs empire. The scene also depicts this as something far from benign, and propped up with violence, as while the party is going on upstairs the scene moves to the basement where drug money is being processed for money laundering and someone is being brutally tortured. Thus, within this small example, of which the series contains many others, there are several markers of French Muslimness which appear and are directly connected with criminality. As such, these forms of popular drama are important means by which narratives about French Muslims are created and disseminated. This involvement of a particular Islamic narrative builds on previous discussions and stereotypes of the minority ethnic criminal 'racaille' (Jobard, 2006) that did not have a particular religious connotation. Here, the question of religion is grafted onto this construction of criminality to move the discourse from one that is dominated by ethnic/racial characteristics to one which also contains a specifically religious element in the construction of a Muslim gangster. Thus, as scholars argue that certain aspects of society are becoming 'Islamised' (G. Kepel, 2012), it is also the case that marginalising narratives about France's minority ethnic population are also becoming 'Islamised'. Additionally, as scholars have argued about the securitisation of Islam being a key aspect of contemporary European discourse (Jocelyne Cesari, 2013), this example also demonstrates that this occurs not just in the realm of terrorism but in that of societal insecurity more broadly in terms of the discussion of Muslims being an existential threat to the social order—not simply due to terrorism or religion, but because of their involvement in criminal activities. Taking this back to questions of orientalism and masculinity, this example also presents an interesting means by which previous ideas of the 'savage' oriental man is modified and reconstructed in the contemporary era. If the savages of the previous era were Arab cavalry men in rural, semi-arid landscapes (Said, 1978), in a similar vein to the constructions of femininities for the internal 'other', the new savage is the gangster, and the new environment of the internal other is the concrete housing estate. Thus, these two, highly gendered, orientalist constructions both show a similar trend, in that the deserts and harems of the nineteenth century have been replaced by the suburban housing estate as the key context in which the outsider can 'gaze' into the savagery of the 'other'.

5.5   Conclusions on Gender, Class and Orientalism

This chapter has sought to demonstrate that interrogating the question of gender in relation to French Muslims is indeed a complex and multifaceted process. In and of themselves, the political rumblings around gender in France, whether these concern the regulation of women's dress or the associations created such as NPNS to agitate for women's rights, could easily fill an entire monograph. However, this chapter has attempted to open up a discussion of how gender also plays an important role in the broader discursive construction of French Muslims. Thus, the key analytical point that this chapter has sought to drive home has been that to understand the ways that gendered roles play out requires casting the net much wider. Here, popular culture provides an important means by which further understanding can be gleaned about how orientalist forms of gender construction occur, and how the idea of culture being seen as a key lens through which one can gaze at the other can be applied in a very contemporary sense.

This is in no way to diminish the importance of gendered forms of political mobilisation by Muslims in contemporary France, which have been diverse and numerous. This chapter began by drawing attention to the diverse ways in which gendered forms of political mobilisation have occurred in French Muslim populations. Here, it is important not to deploy the term 'Islamic feminism', as if it is one homogenous block, or claim that Muslims only political mobilise on gendered groups around overtly 'Islamic' feminist movements. The picture on the ground is indeed much more diverse. The emergence of NPNS represents a movement where Muslim women mobilised against the insecurity and sexual violence of the French suburbs without overtly doing so around any kind of religious markers or agenda. This challenges further essentialist notions that to examine Muslims as a social group can only be done by examining mobilisations or political or cultural discourses only that overtly name check Islamic themes. This is far from the case. Indeed, the emergence of more recent forms of feminist discourse from the Parti des Indigènes de la République further buttresses this assertion. This is because while the party addresses more overtly Islam related issues, such as the banning of religious symbols and the wearing of the full-face veil, they can hardly be topologised as a strictly Islamic movement. Their use of radical, post- and anti-colonial theory and ideologies once again shows the complexities of the mobilisation undertaken by French Muslims in that again this mobilisation occurs in ways which are very diverse and draws on a wide range of political and ideological influences. However, analysing how gender relates to, and is an integral part of, the construction of discourse around contemporary French Muslims requires a more wide-ranging analysis than simply looking at forms of political mobilisation.

Rather, we must examine more broadly how popular culture creates and disseminates narratives that construct gendered Muslims roles in certain ways. The key argument that this chapter has attempted to make is that following in the orientalist tradition, certain forms of popular culture act as a means by which one can gaze on the 'other'. In this case, it is an internal other, which rather than existing in exotic poses in hammams, harems and deserts, does so against a backdrop of the concrete forms of the French suburban estate. This context, which is as much constituted by geographical, class and ethno-racial markers, exists as a world apart that mainstream French society is fascinated with, but has no direct experience of, nor is ever likely to have. Wacquant (2007) discusses this in terms of Paris being a 'dual city' of city proper and poor suburbs which exist apart, and create a line across which few transgress. This operates in an imaginary sense, where the curiosity about this parallel, and in the words of the orientalist, 'savage' world creates a market for cultural forms which offer the outside the ability to gaze into this weird and mysterious world through the safety of a screen.

This is highlighted by the popularity of pornography in France, which allows the viewer to gaze on the erotic nature of the 'beurette' or the French born women of North African origin. However, examining these films does not just enable, as scholars have argued for many years (inter alia Williams, 1989), an understanding of the nature of contemporary sexual relations. Rather, analysing these films in the vein of the critical cultural turn in society enables a much broader analysis of the power and cultural relations in society. Here, digging deeper than just the erotic nature of these films enables an understanding of the ways in which

Muslim women are constructed in a much wider sense, even when they are not name checked as 'Muslim' but rather are presented in ethnic and class based terms as the young, sexually exploitable and available women of the housing estates. These women are controlled by abusive partners and go into sex work to escape the socio-economic deprivation of their immediate environments. In other contexts more is overtly made of their exotic origins, where the women discuss their origins and perform belly dances to exhibit their oriental eroticism. However, both the overtly 'oriental' and the more class-based depictions of these women follow in the orientalist tradition of offering the outside an ability to gaze into an erotic and exotic world where they can see the 'reality' of the otherwise unknown exotic woman.

When turning to questions of the constructions of masculinity vis-à-vis Muslim men in France, the men in these erotic films demonstrate some important entry points into understanding how they are constructed. While men play marginal roles compared to the women in these films, owing to them being produced for a heterosexual market, they do however perform roles which show them being controlling and misogynistic. They verbally harass, exploit and control the Muslim women in the films, demonstrating how such films reproduce the problematic stereotypes of Muslim men in France as something women need to be protected from (Guénif-Souilamas & Macé, 2006). However, these are not the only ways that Muslim men are constructed in popular culture. In more mainstream forms of culture than pornography they play important roles that build on previously articulated forms of class and criminality. Analysing season two of the hit TV series 'Engranages' offers an insight into how notions of criminality, long constructed vis-à-vis ethnic minorities in France, have become 'Islamised'. While the idea of the working-class, minority ethnic criminal 'racaille' has long been a common trope in France, even used by Nicolas Sarkozy during his tenure as interior minister, it was one which was largely secular. While these young men were criminal and of minority ethnic extraction, they were not specifically 'Muslim' per se. As scholars have discussed both the Islamisation of Muslim communities in France (G. Kepel, 2012) and the increased focus on 'Muslims' in the discourse as security threats (Jocelyne Cesari, 2013), it appears that cultural output is also following suit in constructing minority ethnic origin criminals as 'Muslim gangsters'. The criminals in the material analysed are not just of North African origin, but also give money to an Imam to build a new mosque, and are seen torturing a rival in the basement while a family gathering goes on upstairs. As such, following on from other cultural contexts where criminals have been constructed as having specific backgrounds, such as the African-American and Italian-American gangster in the USA (Chan, 1998; Mason, 2002), in the French cultural landscape there is an emergence of a particularly Muslim form of gangster. Linking this back to themes from the orientalist paintings of the nineteenth century, the 'savage' Arab cavalry man in the desert has been replaced by the 'savage' criminal of the concrete suburbs. However, in a broader sense, this chapter also opens up the discussion of French Muslims to a far wider discussion of their construction in broader cultural fields. The next chapter of this book seeks to build on this analysis by examining how French Muslims, again whether labelled as such explicitly or not, are caught up in the paradoxes of the construction or reconstruction of French cultural national identity in the contemporary era.

Bibliography

Abdi, M., & Amara, F. (2006). *La Racaille de la République… Ni Putes ni Soumises*. Paris: Le Seuil.

Al-Saji, A. (2008). Voiles racialisés: la femme musulmane dans les imaginaires occidentaux. *Les ateliers de l'éthique/The Ethics Forum, 3*(2), 39–55. https://doi.org/10.7202/1044595ar

Amra, F., & Zappi, S. (2004). *Ni Putes Ni Soumises*. Paris: La Découverte.

Arnau, M. (2018). Les Porn Studies, qu'est-ce que c'est? *Playboy France,* (8), 38–39.

Aslam, M. (2012). *Gender-Based Explosions: The Nexus Between Muslim Masculinities, Jihadist Islamism and Terrorism*. UNU Press. Retrieved from https://collections.unu.edu/view/UNU:2519

Bellil, S. (2003). *Dans l'enfer des tournantes*. Paris: Folio.

Billig, M. (1995). *Banal Nationalism*. London: Sage.

Bouteldja, H. (2016). *Les Blancs, les Juifs et nous: Vers une politique de l'amour révolutionnaire*. Paris: La Fabrique Editions.

Bouteldja, H., Khiari, S., Ewanjé-Epée, F. B., & Magliani-Belkacem, S. (2012). *Nous sommes les indigènes de la République*. Paris: Editions Amsterdam.

Carroll, J. S., Padilla-Walker, L. M., Nelson, L. J., Olson, C. D., Barry, C. M., & Madsen, S. D. (2008). Generation XXX: Pornography Acceptance and Use Among Emerging Adults. *Journal of Adolescent Research, 23*(1), 6–30. https://doi.org/10.1177/0743558407306348

Cesari, J. (2013). European Conundrum: Integration of Muslims or Securitisation of Islam? *World Review.* Retrieved from https://berkleycenter. georgetown.edu/essays/european-conundrum-integration-of-muslims-or-securitisation-of-islam

Chan, K. (1998). The Construction of Black Male Identity in Black Action Films of the Nineties. *Cinema Journal, 37*(2), 35–48. https://doi. org/10.2307/1225641

Chua, D. (2008). Orientalism as Cultural Practices and the Production of Sociological Knowledge. *Sociology Compass, 2*(4), 1179–1191.

Connell, R. W. (2005). *Masculinities.* Cambridge: Polity.

Crenshaw, K. (1989). Demarginalizing the Intersection of Race and Sex: A Black Feminist Critique of Antidiscrimination Doctrine, Feminist Theory and Antiracist Politics. *University of Chicago Legal Forum, 1989*, 139.

Dagistanli, S., & Grewal, K. (2016). Perverse Muslim Masculinities in Contemporary Orientalist Discourse: The Vagaries of Muslim Immigration in the West. In *Global Islamophobia: Muslims and Moral Panic in the West.* Routledge, London, UK.

Dikeç, M. (2007). *Badlands of the Republic: Space, Politics and Urban Policy.* Oxford: Blackwell Publishing.

Doran, M. (2004). Negotiating Between Bourge and Racaille: Verlan as Youth Identity Practice in Suburban Paris. In *Negotiation of Identities in Multilingual Contexts.* Clevedon: Multilingual Matters.

Dorlin, E. (2010). 33. Le grand strip-tease: féminisme, nationalisme et burqa en France. In *Ruptures postcoloniales* (pp. 429–442). La Découverte. Retrieved from https://www.cairn.info/resume.php?ID_ARTICLE=DEC_BANCE_2010_01_0429

Dot-Pouillard, N. (2007). Les recompositions politiques du mouvement féministe français au regard du hijab. Le voile comme signe et révélateur des impensés d'un espace public déchiré entre identité républicaine et héritage colonial. *SociologieS.* Retrieved from http://journals.openedition.org/sociologies/246

Fournier, L. (2008). Le 'féminisme musulman' en Europe de l'Ouest: le cas du réseau féminin de Présence musulmane. *Amnis. Revue de civilisation contemporaine Europes/Amériques, 8.* https://doi.org/10.4000/amnis.593

France 24. (2017). *Transgressive But Popular: Egypt's Taste for 'Arab Porn'.* Retrieved November 12, 2018, from http://observers.france24.com/en/20170818-transgressive-popular-egypt-taste-arab-porn

Geisser, V. (2007). Des Voltaire, des Zola musulmans...? Réflexion sur les 'nouveaux dissidents' de l'islam. *Revue internationale et stratégique, 65,* 143–156. https://doi.org/10.3917/ris.065.0143

Ghaill, M. A. (1994). *The Making of Men: Masculinities, Sexualities and Schooling.* Milton Keynes: McGraw-Hill Education (UK).

Gilroy, P. (2002). *There Ain't no Black in the Union Jack: The Cultural Politics of Race and Nation.* London: Routledge.

Guénif-Souilamas, N., & Macé, E. (2006). *Les féministes et le garçon arabe.* La Tour-d'Aigues (Vaucluse): Editions de l'Aube.

Hansen, L. (2011). Theorizing the Image for Security Studies: Visual Securitization and the Muhammad Cartoon Crisis. *European Journal of International Relations, 17*(1), 51–74. https://doi.org/10.1177/1354066110388593

Hargreaves, A. (2007). *Multi-Ethnic France: Immigration, Politics, Culture and Society* (2nd ed.). New York; London: Routledge.

Hargreaves, A., & McKinney, M. (Eds.). (1997). *Post-Colonial Cultures in France* (1st ed.). London; New York: Routledge.

Hooks, B. (1987). *Ain't I a Woman: Black Women and Feminism.* Retrieved March 23, 2018, from https://www.amazon.co.uk/Aint-Woman-Black-Women-Feminism/dp/0861043790/ref=sr_1_cc_1?s=aps&ie=UTF8&qid=1521806924&sr=1-1-catcorr&keywords=Ain%27t+I+a+Woman%3A+black+women+and+feminism

Hopkins, P. E. (2006). Youthful Muslim Masculinities: Gender and Generational Relations. *Transactions of the Institute of British Geographers, 31*(3), 337–352. https://doi.org/10.1111/j.1475-5661.2006.00206.x

Ireland, S. (2001). Negotiating Gender in the Work of Women Writers of Maghrebi Immigrant Descent. *Nottingham French Studies, 40*(1), 52–62. https://doi.org/10.3366/nfs.2001.007

Jobard, F. (2006). Chapitre 2: Sociologie politique de la 'racaille'. In *Émeutes urbaines et protestations* (pp. 59–80). Presses de Sciences Po (P.F.N.S.P.). Retrieved from https://www.cairn.info/emeutes-urbaines-et-protestations-une-singularite%2D%2D9782724609921-p-59.htm

Kalra, V. S. (2009). Between Emasculation and Hypermasculinity: Theorizing British South Asian Masculinities. *South Asian Popular Culture, 7*(2), 113–125. https://doi.org/10.1080/14746680902920874

Kemp, A. (2009). Marianne d'aujourd'hui?: The Figure of the beurette in Contemporary French Feminist Discourses. *Modern & Contemporary France, 17*(1), 19–33. https://doi.org/10.1080/09639480802639751

Kepel, G. (2012). *Banlieue de la République.* Paris: Institut Montaigne.

Landais, É. (2014). Porn studies et études de la pornographie en sciences humaines et sociales. *Questions de Communication,* (26), 17–37.

Landes, X., & Nielsen, M. E. J. (2018). Racial Dodging in the Porn Industry: A Case with No Silver Bullet. *Porn Studies*, 1–16. https://doi.org/10.1080/232 68743.2018.1435302

Lutrand, M.-C., & Yazdekhasti, B. (2011). Laïcité et présence musulmane en France: des dynamiques d'influence réciproque. *Cahiers de la Méditerranée, 83*, 327–335.

Mason, F. (2002). *American Gangster Cinema: From 'Little Caesar' to 'Pulp Fiction'*. Berlin: Springer.

McCoy, T. S. (1988). Hegemony, Power, Media: Foucault and Cultural Studies. *Communications, 14*(3), 71–90. https://doi.org/10.1515/comm. 1988.14.3.71

McLennan, G. (2014). Sociology, Cultural Studies and the Cultural Turn. In J. Holmwood & J. Scott (Eds.), *The Palgrave Handbook of Sociology in Britain* (pp. 510–535). London: Palgrave Macmillan UK. https://doi. org/10.1007/978-1-137-31886-2_23

Mechaï, H. (2018). *French-Algerian Activist Houria Bouteldja: 'The Left Is Struggling in France'*. Retrieved October 6, 2018, from https://www.middlee- astmonitor.com/20180319-french-algerian-activist-houria-bouteldja-the- left-is-struggling-in-france/

Messerschmidt, J. W., Tomsen, S., & Tomsen, S. (2018, April 9). *Masculinities and Crime*. https://doi.org/10.4324/9781315622040-8

Nash, K. (2001). The 'Cultural Turn' in Social Theory: Towards a Theory of Cultural Politics. *Sociology, 35*(1), 77–92. https://doi.org/10.1177/ 0038038501035001006

Ni Putes Ni Soumises. (2005). *Le guide du respect*. Paris: Cherche Midi.

Pateman, C. (Ed.). (1989). Feminist Critiques of the Public/Private Dichotomy. In *The Disorder of Women: Democracy, Feminism and Political Theory*. Stanford, CA: Stanford University Press.

Paveau, M.-A. (2014). Un objet de discours pour les études pornographiques. *Questions de Communication, 2*(26), 7–15.

Procter, J. (2004). *Stuart Hall*. London: Routledge.

Pulham, S. (2005, November 8). *Inflammatory Language*. Retrieved February 15, 2018, from http://www.theguardian.com/news/blog/2005/ nov/08/inflammatoryla

Rafter, N. H. (2006). *Shots in the Mirror: Crime Films and Society*. Oxford: Oxford University Press.

Ramdani, K. (2011). Bitch and Beurette: When Femininity Rhymes with Freedom. *Volume !, 8*(2), 13–39.

Reece, R. L. (2015). The Plight of the Black Belle Knox: Race and Webcam Modelling. *Porn Studies, 2*(2–3), 269–271. https://doi.org/10.1080/232687 43.2015.1054672

Said, E. (1978). *Orientalism.* New York: Pantheon Books.

Sayad, A. (1999). *La double absence: des illusions de l'émigré aux souffrances de l'immigré.* Paris: Liber.

Smith, J. G., & Luykx, A. (2017). Race Play in BDSM Porn: The Eroticization of Oppression. *Porn Studies, 4*(4), 433–446. https://doi.org/10.1080/23268 743.2016.1252158

Souilamas, G. (1999). *Des beurettes aux descendantes d'immigrants nord-africains.* Paris: Grasset.

Vince, N. (2015). *Our Fighting Sisters: Nation, Memory and Gender in Algeria, 1954–2012.* Retrieved March 23, 2018, from https://www.amazon.co.uk/ Our-Fighting-Sisters-Algeria-1954-2012-ebook/dp/B012DLLXWM/ref=sr _1_1?ie=UTF8&qid=1521805565&sr=8-1&keywords=Our+Fighting+Sist ers%3A+Nation%2C+Memory+and+Gender+in+Algeria%2C+1954-2012

Vörös, F. (2015). *Cultures pornographiques: Anthologie des Porn Studies.* Paris: Editions Amsterdam.

Wacquant, L. (2007). *Urban Outcasts: A Comparative Sociology of Advanced Marginality.* Retrieved from https://www.amazon.co.uk/Urban-Outcasts-Comparative-Sociology-Marginality/dp/0745631258/ref=sr_1_3?ie=UTF8 &qid=1517652872&sr=8-3&keywords=wacquant

Williams, L. (1989). *HARDCORE: Power, Pleasure and the 'Frenzy of the Visible'.* Los Angeles: University of California Press.

Williams, L. (2014). Pornography, Porno, Porn: Thoughts on a Weedy Field. *Porn Studies, 1*(1–2), 24–40. https://doi.org/10.1080/23268743.2013.863662

Wolak, J., Mitchell, K., & Finkelhor, D. (2007). Unwanted and Wanted Exposure to Online Pornography in a National Sample of Youth Internet Users. *Pediatrics, 119*(2), 247–257. https://doi.org/10.1542/peds.2006-1891

Zillmann, D. (1989). Effects of Prolonged Consumption of Pornography. In *Pornography: Research Advances and Policy Considerations.* Hillsdale, NJ: Lawrence Erlbaum Associates.

Zimmer, O. (2003). Boundary Mechanisms and Symbolic Resources: Towards a Process-Oriented Approach to National Identity. *Nations and Nationalism, 9*(2), 173–193. https://doi.org/10.1111/1469-8219.00081

6

The Cultural Paradoxes of Frenchness: Cultural Nationalism, Social Boundaries and French Muslims in Broader Discursive Perspective

6.1 Introducing National Identity, France and Muslims

The year 2018 marked a particularly celebratory year for France. After being plagued by jihadist violence since 2015 and a brutal 2017 presidential election which offered a choice between far-right, xenophobic Marine Le Pen and untested and unpopular centrist Emmanuel Macron, France finally had a reason to celebrate. Les Bleus lifted the World Cup for the second time, closing a neat, 20-year hiatus from winning in top flight football since Zidane and co. lifted the cup in 1998. However, during this moment of national triumph, social media had other, more contrary ideas, about how the French victory should be celebrated.

Tweets exchanged highlighted very well the paradox of French society, as discussed in Chap. 2 on the state, and its lack of acceptance of hybridised identities. A particular tweet exchange began when sports social media giant @Sporf tweeted the names of French players highlighting their ancestral background (in a very crude and essentialising way—Mbappé has both Algerian and Cameroonian parentage and was born in France—so perhaps three flags would be more suitable). However,

© The Author(s) 2019
J. Downing, *French Muslims in Perspective*,
https://doi.org/10.1007/978-3-030-16103-3_6

Benjamin Mendy replied clearly to this, stating that regardless of their ethnic origins the players were French. Additionally, some on social media sought to highlight the African make-up of the team, or that it was a contribution made by the Third World to France through graphical memes. Thus, there are many ways of discussing the make-up of the French national team.

The polemic did not stop here, with the tweet above depicting France taking the World Cup from a boat of black refugees, the kind of image that has become iconic of the recent migrant crisis in the Mediterranean Sea. Here, the accompanying hashtag #frafrica seeks to make a hybridisation again considering the background of the players. This may seem like a facetious example with which to begin a chapter on cultural nationalism and how the remaking of French nationhood has direct implications for French Muslims. To a certain extent it is—but it does bring our attention to a very important aspect of the remaking of the nation that this book is yet to analyse fully. While Chap. 2 takes into account the state, and how its structures deal with notions of ethnic and religious difference, and Chap. 5 deals explicitly with issues of the construction of gendered roles within popular forms of culture, there is a domain somewhere in-between these two that has direct implications for how the boundaries of the national community are made. Anderson (2006) highlighted the importance of shared narratives delivered in newspapers as a key means by which membership of the 'imagined community' is defined, and Billig (1995) sought to bring into this question of national belonging the question of the daily rituals of nationhood. It is within this context that the work of Zimmer becomes important to this chapter, because of his observation that the construction of national identity is 'public … taking place at the interface of culture and politics' (Zimmer, 2003, p. 174). Thus, discussions of national football are a key example of this—in that it has been in France a key domain by which 'culture' has a very close relationship with culture. This goes much deeper than simply Twitter memes suggesting that Africa (and indeed other European countries) should be credited with giving France the players that lifted trophies in 1998 and 2018, which a discussion about how politics has criticised the racial make-up of the French team for being too 'foreign' will show. This is a discussion which has direct implications for the position of French

Muslims within the national narrative because they are not simply implicated in the very visibly labelled 'Muslim' discussions which take place about nationhood in France—such as those over halal food in schools, prayer in the streets or the banning of the veil. Thinking that these are the only issues which influence Muslim feelings of belonging to the French state would take an extremely limited, homogenised and essentialising view of what defines national belonging not only for French Muslims but human beings more generally. Rather, there are a number of identity categories and broader concerns which come together for any individual in their nation belonging at any particular time. This is why it is necessary to get a full picture of how ongoing debates about the nation in France have important consequences for the French Muslim community.

It is well known and understood across the political sciences that France exists as a case of a 'secular' state in the specific sense that insists on 'assimilation' rather than multiculturalism to integrate citizens of migrant origin. This book has already explored in an institutional and state sense how this has played out for French Muslims at many different levels of the state and international governance. However, taking a constructivist, discursive position on politics, social relations and the construction of the nation enables us to see quite clearly that the state is but one of many ways and means with which social boundaries are constructed. There are a multitude of other ways in which national identity is constructed, which creates important paradoxes for French Muslims, alongside other post-colonial migrant communities. Thus, in a book on French Muslims from a discursive perspective it is important to attempt to consider some of the ways in which these paradoxes of nationhood have occurred over the past decades when constructing key aspects of French national identity and the relationships which Muslims have to it. An entire book, let alone a chapter, would be insufficient to provide an exhaustive list of the ways in which this has taken place, given the plethora of 'banal' (Billig, 1995) ways through which national identity is formed. Indeed, much has already been written about the specifically religious ways in which public discourse has brightened social boundaries for Muslims in France—such as the Burka ban, the burkini ban and controversies about praying in the streets.

However, these processes continue, and take different yet equally important forms in subtler and less overtly religious domains. A key observation about discussing Muslims as a social group that this study has already emphasised is that the category is far from a solely religious one and as such to capture the full discursive experience an analysis needs to cast its net wider into areas which are less obviously signposted as 'Muslim' issues, such as protest, the discursive construction of rap music and even discussions about the loyalty and composition of the French national football team. In a case of such an expansive field, the scholar has no choice but to make well rationalised and deductive case study selections that illustrate the broader, significant, points within the field. This chapter thus seeks to take contrasting examples of the broader, banal and cultural ways in which the French nation has been defined, and how Muslims, in one sociological form or another, have been cast as the 'other', even while paradoxically conforming to broader French cultural norms and practices otherwise valorised when enacted by white French counterparts. It is necessary to nuance the category of Muslim as deployed here as many of the examples may not seem, and neither empirically are, examples which involve Muslims only, but rather cast a far broader net which connects French Muslims to the broader 'brightening' of social boundaries vis-à-vis post-colonial migrants of a mixture of class, racial and religious backgrounds. Indeed, 'de facto' multicultural France, like all multicultural societies, does not exist in discrete units where homogenous 'Muslims' exist in solitude next to, and never interacting with, homogenous 'blacks', 'whites' or indeed any other social category. Far-right political statements to this effect empirically do not hold water. A broad range of social interactions, including but not limited to friendships, marriages, economic interactions, membership of the same rap subculture, university, office or even marijuana-dealing operations mean that the barriers between Muslims and non-Muslims are extremely porous. This chapter will attempt to tease out the ways in which the marginalisation of Muslims in the broader cultural sense sits alongside broader marginalisation of non-white, or indeed even working-class, groups.

This analysis has selected three examples of the ethnicisation of French national identity construction in the broader field of the intersection of politics and culture (Zimmer, 2003). These three, seemingly disparate, examples have been chosen to demonstrate the less obvious, banal ways in which national identity is constructed in an ethicised way in the public realm, which works to exclude French Muslims alongside their post-colonial migrant non-Muslim compatriots. This is important to understand because, and correctly so, a lot of attention is given to the ways in which the official actions of the state, as discussed here in Chap. 2 of this book, work in exclusionary ways. While this is a significant aspect of the creation and re-creation of French national identity in an exclusionary, organic manner, it fails to fully engage with the multitude of ways that broader discursive processes in the field of culture work in a similar way. Thus, as in the case of nationalism, while the state remains relevant it can never capture the full story, and scholars need to tread the well-established path of moving beyond the political chambers and law courts into broader society to understand the multifaceted ways that national identity is constructed in paradoxical and exclusionary ways.

The first paradox of national identity construction in France that demonstrates how the intersection of politics and culture ethicise French identity and serves to exclude those of migrant origin can be seen in the reaction to, and coverage of, the 2005 suburban riots. On the surface it seems clear that such an anti-systemic action would be, and possibly even normatively should be, condemned and constructed as outside of the national narrative. However, the paradox here can only be seen in comparative perspective, where other events of anti-systemic direct political action, from the revolution of 1789 to the riots of May 1968 and most recently the action by the yellow vest 'gilets jaunes' have been incorporated into a history that defines such direct action as a key part of Frenchness. Additionally, it is not just the fact that the 2005 riots have not found their place alongside these other events in the national narrative that demonstrates the de facto ethnicisation of Frenchness in the public cultural sphere, but also the racialised way in which they were covered. This demonstrates the primacy of the 'othering' of the rioters in 2005 on ethnic, racial and religious grounds, even when studies have found that white French rioters also took part (Body-Gendrot, 2013).

However, the intersection of politics and culture does not stop here in the ways in which it works to make paradoxical exclusions in French society. France has never shied away from embracing and celebrating artists who produce controversial material or lead controversial lives. Whether this is epitomised in the 'belle époque' lives of painters such as Henri de Toulouse-Lautrec, or the more contemporary lives of controversial artists of immigrant origin such as Serge Gainsbourg. However, the paradox emerges in the reception and coverage of French rap music, which has been one of the commercially most popular art forms in contemporary France. However, it has been the subject of several legal cases concerning the freedom of expression of rap artists in ways that other art forms have not. Herein lies the essence of the second paradox of cultural nationalism in that a form of popular culture associated with recent migrant waves is not deemed at times publicly as acceptable to the national narrative. While clearly not all French rappers are of French Muslim origin, a number of the most prominent are. Additionally, rap has been an important form of public culture which has been one of the few open to expressions of Islamic idioms and themes, and where it has been possible to make commentaries on multicultural French life. Thus, here politics has got involved in a field of culture outside of the boundaries of the state to attempt to define French rap, its subjects, idioms and artists as legally unacceptable to the norms of French artistic expression.

Finally, this chapter examines the French national football team and the paradoxical rejection that it has received due to its racial make-up in the 20 years between its two World Cup triumphs in 1998 and 2018. Again, not a solely French Muslim domain, a number of the great and good of both French World Cup winning teams were, or have converted to become, French Muslims. Additionally, when victorious, the French national team has been constructed as an almost exceptional vehicle of socio-economic and personal advancement to those of post-migrant origin, especially those of poor socio-economic status. However, closer inspection both around the World Cup wins, but also during the 'lean' years where the team was not successful, demonstrates the paradoxical means by which the national team is subject to critique and construction that marginalises those of non-white backgrounds. While the cases of this paradoxical construction of national identity are unfortunately plural, one that stands out is the controversial proposition to have quotas for ethnic minority players to limit their number in the team. The irony of the proposition of negative quotas in such an important national body, while refusing to create positive quotas to fight socio-economic discrimination, is clear. However, going deeper it is emblematic of broader existential discussions around the national team and its 'Frenchness' being compromised by being 'too black'. Here, we can see another way in which culture and politics intersect to create a national identity which is de facto racialising and exclusionary under the de jure umbrella of radical colour-blind equality.

6.2   Conceptualising National Identity, Muslims and France

Nationalism and the construction of national identity has been the subject of considerable, and indeed highly varying, scholarship since the early- to mid-twentieth century. Key in this is the endeavour to understand how a specifically European system of land and maritime empires fell, and gave way to a new form of organisation—the 'nation state'—which through post-colonial settlement was exported across the globe. Clearly, one does not have to look far to see that the 'nation'—however defined culturally, linguistically, religious or otherwise—and the boundaries of the state do not match in any cases across the globe. Every state has 'minorities', religious or ethnic, whose integration is often a preoccupation of central, regional and local governments. France, regardless of claims to cultural unity, is an excellent example of historical fallacy of the nation state—indeed its current obsession with assimilationist policies is not actually the product of Muslim immigration, but rather stems from the need to integrate its highly cultural, religious and linguistically diverse regions into a common notion of 'Frenchness' that has neither been easy nor non-contested (E. Weber, 1976). Indeed, one of the famous mantras repeated about the exceptionalism of my adopted home city, Marseille, is that the cannons in the Fort Saint Jean, built in 1660 and now part of the MuCem (Museum of European and Mediterranean Civilisations), were pointed at the town rather than out to sea, because it was thought that an internal uprising was a greater threat to France's territorial integrity than any invasion from the Mediterranean Sea.

Taking the discussion away from France for a moment, for a plethora of key writers, urbanisation and the technological and social developments of urban forms of governance, media and capitalism are central in the emergence and salience of nations and nationalisms. For Gellner (1983), urbanisation was a vital element of the social disjuncture that facilitated the embracing of national identities, as individuals moved from the isolation of the 'in-turned village' to the more cosmopolitan city. Recent work by Leerssen (2015) has attempted to explain the role of 'urbania' as a theatre of cultural nationalism between the imperial 'megalomania' and the provincial Ruritania of Gellner's (1983) earlier work. Here, it is the culture performances and manifestations taking place in the urban sphere that go on to inform and shape the nation. The centrality of cultural forms is also not lost in perhaps the most famous work on nationalism, Anderson's (2006) *Imagined communities*. For Anderson, the idea of the development of a 'print capitalism' to spread the stories of the nation is vital in the way that shared narratives gave meanings to a community so large we could never meet all of its members. Two observations can be made about these two theories—they do not talk about the state per se but rather how narratives give meaning to abstract ideas of community. This is not to say that the state is not important, nor that it is not discussed extensively in the nationalism literature, such as the insightful work of Breuilly (1994).

Here, it should be acknowledged that the state, due to its central role as a container of power, has the infrastructural and social power to dictate the terms of the game and the role individuals play within it (Breuilly, 1994). Nowhere is this more obvious than in France, where this book has demonstrated the power of the 'rules of the game' laid down by laïcité and assimilation have defined the French political field. However, we can see from the plethora of authors above that place importance on the role of public culture in defining the nation, that the state is neither where the story begins, nor where it ends. This chapter seeks to go beyond the state, and to look at the more 'banal' (Billig, 1995) forms of cultural narratives that inform the French 'imagined community' (Anderson, 2006) for French Muslims. Both empirically and theoretically this opens up a possible 'Pandora's box' of examples that could be explored. However, the three examined here have been selected in an attempt to show some of the paradoxes present between the 'civic' and 'ethnic' construction of the French nation even present in the field of public culture, beyond the state yet reproducing important discursive, political and material hierarchies and disadvantages for a multiplicity of post-colonial migrants, a large number of which are French Muslims. To effectively be able to do this, it is appropriate to unpack a little further these notions of the civic and the ethnic, how they work beyond the boundaries of the state and inform more diffuse and public constructions of French national identity.

To understand these changed processes in the production and reproduction of French national identity it is vital to examine the emergence of concepts of civic and ethnic nationalism and how these offer important insights that can be used here. Conceptually, with the diversity and elusiveness of capturing and explaining exactly what nationalism and nation formation are, as touched on above, early scholars have resorted to ideal type distinctions (Kohn, 2005; Zimmer, 2003). These, however, were quite state focused and examined principles such as nationality laws, the institutional arrangements of church and state, and the state's official procedures for the treatment of minorities. An example of such work is the comparative analysis of French and German citizenship conducted by Brubaker, where he argues that 'in the French tradition, the nation has been conceived in relation to the institutions and territorial frame of the state where Revolutionary and republican definitions of nationhood and citizenship-unitarist, Universalist and secular' (Brubaker, 1998). It is this kind of view that has caused the definition of the French nation as 'civic', stemming from the original work of Kohn (2005), who defined France against what he termed the 'ethnic' state policies of Germany, which were much more focused on descent and blood than those of France. While the civic–ethnic distinction in the study of nations has been widely critiqued, it 'does grasp important aspects of modern history, but does so in certain ways' (Calhoun, 2007, p. 117). In this analysis, the traditional view of the institutional arrangements and state values of post-1789 France (with the exceptions of the Vichy government of 1940–1944, and indeed the racial hierarchies imposed during the French imperial project), based as they are on universalist rights, are an example of a post enlightenment attempt at forging a national identity not on religious commonality or even common descent, but on a common adherence to values, with its secular republican values forming the basis for its national identity (Kohn, 2005). However, these theories totally miss exactly the kind of more diffuse, cultural and public national identity construction that this chapter seeks to tease out. This de jure understanding of national identity is thus clearly lacking.

Therefore, a far broader conceptual definition of where national identity construction and reconstruction occurs is required. This draws heavily on the cultural turn in sociology in the 1970s, which remains hugely influential in not just allowing sociologists to understand the broader role that popular culture takes in defining social reality, but fundamentally shifted the discipline of sociology (McLennan, 2014). This shift drew heavily on critical theory about the nature of the social world and how power is located all around us, shaping, often subconsciously, what we do, how we act and what we aspire to (McCoy, 1988). Of particular significance here is Foucault, whose work enables sociologists to see power as 'productive as well as coercive, situational as well as pervasive' (McCoy, 1988). For Foucault, the media was extremely important in offering an avenue for cultural forms of power to be broadcast and projected onto society (McCoy, 1988). Within this, Hall speaks about culture as not something to be simply appreciated and studied, but as a 'critical site of social action and intervention, where power relations are both established and potentially unsettled' (Procter, 2004). Thus, while it is important to examine the creation of national narratives at the confluence of culture and politics (Zimmer, 2003), examining national identities, and identity constructions more broadly, all forms of culture have much larger roles. In this vein, Nash (2001) argues for the need for a cultural turn in political sociology. Thus, the relations between state and society should not be taken as the key concern of political sociology, but rather Foucault's ideas on the power and domination expressed through cultural output should be a key concern (Nash, 2001).

These ideas have long been taken up by scholars of nationalism who have been concerned with thinking about how notions of 'culture' become important in questions of nationhood (Hutchingson, 1982). This is, however, no straightforward task, as the transformations required for the nation to become coherent necessitate the privileging of certain cultures over others (E. Weber, 1976) or indeed the wholesale destruction of the 'folk' cultures of the in-turned villages (Gellner, 1988). Thus, what exists in the creation of nationhood is neither the wholesale destruction of previous cultures nor the 'invention' of coherent new 'national' culture, but rather a process of bricolage where some aspects of previous cultures are privileged, reinterpreted and remade, combined with novel cultural narratives of the nation (Smith, 2005) in a constantly dynamic and relational process of social construction. It is aspects of these cultural narratives which decide what is 'in' or 'out' of the national narrative (Yoshino, 1992). 'Culture' per se, in the form of cultural nationalism is prima facie neither civic nor ethnic (Nielsen, 1996). How culture defines who is 'in' or 'out' of the nation is never a given, and no particular narrative defines inclusion in a fixed or given way.

These ideas are significantly developed in later works on nationalism that give us further insights into the ways in which cultural national identity is constructed with implications for the French case. In the work of Zimmer (2003), a far broader definition of national identity is found. For him, the definition and redefinition of nationhood is 'public ... taking place at the interface of culture and politics' (Zimmer, 2003, p. 174). All three examples analysed in this chapter are important examples of how these processes unfold in different ways in that they connect to important, yet diverse aspects of French culture, yet are deeply political and have had direct involvement from the state in some way. Thus, in France the definition of national identity is far more diffuse than the institutional arrangements of the state, and occurs in the media (television, newspapers), through the arts, and through the discourse in society concerning the interpretation of public events and the boundaries of national culture.

These examples can be seen as 'symbolic resources' that can be deployed in different ways to conceptualise 'national identities in terms of dynamic processes' (Zimmer, 2003, p. 177). It is necessary to distinguish between 'the mechanisms which social actors use as they reconstruct the boundaries of national identity' and 'the symbolic resources on which they draw when they reconstruct these boundaries' (Zimmer, 2003, p. 178). For this analysis, the most important aspect of this framework is that the symbolic resources on which nationalists draw can be seen as value neutral, that is, 'nationalists create new ideological syntheses from available cultural idioms and resources' (Zimmer, 2003, p. 179). A highly relevant example that highlights this difference is the widespread use of the term 'civic nationalism'. 'Civic' encompasses for Zimmer not just a definition of national identity, but the confusion of both a particular symbolic resource of institutions and values with a specific mechanism of identity construction, which he denotes as voluntarism (Zimmer, 2003, p. 179).

This illustrates that the use of the symbolic resources of institutions and values does not automatically equate with an attempt to construct a particular form of national identity. While these particular symbolic resources have a history of being used in the construction of particular types of national identities, and may even lend themselves to creating a particular type of national identity and solidarity, owing to their particular properties, like all resources they can be deployed in a number of particular ways. In short then, this concept allows us to move away from the mistake of thinking that the presence of a particular resource, in this case institutions and values, dictates what type of national identity can be constructed. It is in fact the other way around, where a particular construction or reconstruction of national identity can reinterpret resources and give them new meanings, 'creating new ideological synthesis from the available cultural idioms and resources' (Zimmer, 2003, p. 179). For Zimmer, this could be for the creation of either an 'organic' or 'voluntarist' boundary mechanism. Here, 'organic' denotes a nation conceived of as determined by ethnic descent and tradition, while 'voluntarist' denotes a nation conceived of putting human will above naturalistic criteria (Zimmer, 2003, p. 175). This separation of resources with their meaning, and the type of national identity that they are used to create is conceptually very useful, as it frees the scholar from the potential straightjacket of only being able to argue that recourse to common values is something that would create an ethnically neutral national identity, or vice-versa. It is this that forms a vital underpinning to the main argument of this book.

Within this framework it opens up the possibility that national identity construction can operate in very contrasting ways. In France, you can have a de jure national identity based on voluntarist forms of belonging, alongside which can operate de facto forms of national identity construction that are organic and exclusionary. Thus, what emerges is a form of 'cognitive dissonance' when examining national identity construction for minority communities in France because, while they are repeatedly told that French national identity construction operates in a voluntarist manner, where 'human will operates above naturalistic criteria' (Zimmer, 2003, p. 175), they are repeatedly exposed to the opposite, where shared heritage and ethnicity prove more salient.

This is where questions of social boundaries become important, because what is happening here within the construction of the national narrative is the increasing salience of certain kinds of exclusionary boundaries for minorities within the reconstruction of a national identity which is de jure hostile to such processes. There exists a well-developed literature on sociological boundary making (Alba, 2005; Bhabha, 2006). However, Alba's concept of bright and blurred boundaries again becomes useful here in both theoretical and empirical terms. It explains how and why boundaries between minorities and national identity may be brightened or blurred with significant implications for the constructions of collective identities. For Alba, a 'bright' boundary is where there is 'no ambiguity in the location of individuals with respect to it' (Alba, 2005). As such, through processes of social construction, this is a boundary that is sharp, concrete and difficult for an individual to transgress. However, boundaries can also be 'blurred'—where the relationship across the boundary is ambiguous (Alba, 2005). Here, 'individuals are seen as simultaneously members of the groups on both sides of the boundary' (Alba, 2005). Alba sees this is an important process for French Muslims in that their existence has been constructed as a problem through the 'organic' deployment of the boundary mechanism of laïcité as a means to further differentiate Muslims from mainstream society, paradoxically while they are actually key and mostly banal features of the social and cultural landscape in France. It is to using empirical examples to demonstrate this that this chapter now turns.

6.3   From the Revolution of 1789 to the Riots of 2005 and the Gilets Jaunes: The Ethnicisation of the Merit of Civil Unrest in the French National Narrative

The first example that will be discussed here of how French Muslims are excluded in the cultural national narrative of contemporary France involves examining the various ways that different events of civil unrest have been constructed as central to the French national narrative or not. This may seem somewhat disconnected from specifically Muslim issues, of which there clearly are many which constantly emerge both polemically (such as prayers in the street) and politically (such as the regulation of women's clothes) that are more visibly 'Muslim'. However, not only have these events been well examined from the perspectives of Muslims and the discursive means by which they are othered in the French narrative, but simply looking at these overtly 'Muslim' issues is problematic. Not only is this an extremely simple premise—that the best data to define Muslim inclusion in a society is only examining overtly Muslim issues— but it also does not consider the diverse social identity categories that make up contemporary Muslim identity in France—whether these are racial, class or some mix of both. This is especially important for the contemporary reality of French Muslims as an extremely well settled population, who actually have no problem identifying themselves as French and as such have much more invested in being part of the French national identity than simply issues around religious dress. Rather, to examine the different ways that they are marginalised, an analysis requires an examination of how they are caught up in the bigger debates and dynamics of French contemporary nationhood in ways which may not on the surface be so overtly 'Muslim' but which are none the less significant. From a journalistic standpoint, Reuters made a point in 2005 of not calling the rioters 'Muslim rioters', despite pressure from segments of its readership to do so (Heneghan, 2007). They make a distinction between using the term 'Muslim' when Muslims are engaged in overtly Muslim issues or protests, but not when they are engaged in issues not overtly 'Muslim' (Heneghan, 2007). Journalistically this makes a good point, because of the ethics of reporting and the choices that need to be made when simplifying complex issues for both limited publication space and also for 'lay' readers who may not want, or need, extensively nuanced information but rather a well-informed brief about a situation. They also make the important point that Muslims are not simply 'Muslims' but are also 'male or female, football fans or music lovers' (Heneghan, 2007). These are very valid empirical points and it is not the point of this chapter to wrongly label the 2005 riots as 'Muslim' or 'Islamic' because they were not. However, what is important here is examining the paradoxes of

French nationhood where post-colonial immigrant communities, Muslims included, are marginalised using broader cultural symbols.

This is essential because one way which exclusion works for French Muslims from parts of an otherwise celebrated facet of the national narrative comes in the form of the stigmatisation of forms of protest and direct action when these are carried out by members of post-colonial migrant communities. This is perhaps the most overtly political example that this chapter deals with, because it involves something that is directly concerned with politics—civil unrest, which any state would be obliged to intervene to prevent. The French suburban riots of 2005 represented one of the largest examples of civil unrest in post-Second World War Europe and resulted in the country declaring a state of emergency. However, it is also significant because while not bringing together culture and politics in an obvious way, the spectre of civil unrest against forms of oppression and power are actually deeply intertwined in the French national narrative from a discursive perspective, and indeed the discussions of the riots of 1968 and the violent revolution of 1789 are part of the French cultural narrative. The ethnicisation of the legitimacy of public protest can be seen in the depiction of the current yellow vest (gilets jaunes) crisis in France. Headlines abound situating the latest spike of French civil unrest within the broader construction of the recurring protests so important in the French national narrative. Within this, comparisons are frequently made with the May 1968 protests, even if this is to say that there are few commonalities (BFMTV, 2018). Other coverage goes as far as to situate the unrest within a broader historical trajectory with the revolution of 1789 and the protests of 1968 (RTL, 2018). Conspicuous by its absence here are any discussions that also situate the 2005 suburban riots within this broader national history of protest. Indeed, during TV appearances to discuss the yellow vest movement, I had to constantly prompt anchors that civil unrest in France also occurred in 2005 and that if we are to seriously discuss the role of discontent in the formation of protest movements in France, we cannot simply exclude a series of events which produced a national state of emergency—the first declared in twenty-first-century France.

Political civil unrest holds quite a privileged position in the French national narrative. This begins with the revolution of 1789, seen as 'crowning the age of enlightenment' (Calhoun, 2007, p. 118), giving as it did the 'rights of man' and the idea of republican rule upon which modern French politics is based. This is because of its sweeping aside of the oppressive, absolutist ancien regime to be replaced by government based on enlightenment values of formal equality before the law and the rights of man, alongside the separation of church from state. During the Second World War, the free French forces, based in Algiers and led by General de Gaulle, carried on fighting against the axis forces after the armistice was signed by the Vichy government in 1940. Their manifestation in occupied France was the French Resistance, a network of resistance fighters drawn from across socio-economic and religious divides, with the common goal of disrupting German rule in France, and aiding allied liberation. These activities played an important part in French national pride after the war ended, as they stood in stark contrast to the collaborationist nature of the Vichy regime and other individuals within France. However, it is not just in historically exceptional times that popular protest has been valorised as a key means for the lifting of oppression and the betterment of French society. More recently, the student-led riots of 1968 not only brought France to a standstill but were a key defining national moment that was a continuation of the trend of events of direct action and protest to be important parts of the French national story. These events culminated in protests and a general strike that involved 11 million workers and lasted for two weeks, and was seen as one of the only examples in post-Second World War Europe where a major democratic state was on the verge of a revolution (Amos, 2005). However, this was not just an event that was about labour laws and material concerns. It took a far broader set of grievances to the streets including, but not limited to, imperialism, capitalism, and the constrictions of traditional French society (Singer, 2002; Tarrow, 1993). Thus, these events and protests were about a broader national soul searching and redefinition of what it meant to be French at a particular critical juncture in history. These are very similar sentiments, and indeed forms of action in terms of direct protest in the streets, that have been recurring features in France since the 1990s, however with very different discursive frames applied to them than May 1968.

These periods of unrest have been recurring since the 1980s, where the 'hot summer' of 1981 brought a new form of violent protest to the streets of French cities. Here, the Minguettes housing estates of Lyon saw a new form of confrontation between French youths of migrant origin engaged in burning cars and confronting French law enforcement (Jobard, 2009). This summer gave a new form to political mobilisation of second generation French Muslims of North African origin who sought to find a solution to the problems of poverty, unemployment and discrimination faced by those in a similar position of marginalisation in French society.

This violence repeatedly reoccurred later in the 1980s, the 1990s, with the peak intensity occurring in 2005. The 2005 disturbances were sparked by the deaths at an electricity substation of two youths, who were apparently hiding there after being pursued by the police. Interestingly, these two victims demonstrate the heterogeneity of the French Muslim population—one youth was of Tunisian origin and the other was from Mauritania (Canet, Pech, & Stewart, 2015). It was after these two deaths that suburban rioting reached its crescendo in 2005, when this incident was the catalyst for rioting on a national scale (Hargreaves, 2007). Their intensity, spread and duration was unprecedented in peace-time Western Europe, with an estimated €200 million worth of damage and over 2900 arrests, taking place over 20 nights in 274 French towns and cities, causing the president to declare a national state of emergency (Sahlins, 2006). Understandably, these events have focused analysis of French cities on the multiple dysfunctions of the immigrant-rich suburbs where these riots took place. This has rightly pinpointed the causes of the riots as local police brutality, poor upkeep of large estates, and the lack of opportunities for socio-economic advancement for those from minority ethnic backgrounds (Dikeç, 2007; Hargreaves, 2007; Moran, 2011; Sahlins, 2006). Thus, a failure of governments on both the left and right to deal with issues presented by inter-generational poverty, entrenched joblessness in post-industrial areas and overt discrimination against those of migrant origin were key motivations for the rioters (Dikeç, 2007; Hargreaves, 2007). However, lifting the lid and coming back to the ethnic diversity of the rioters briefly illuminated by the two victims, Muslims of North and West African origin rioted alongside non-Muslims, including those of French Caribbean descent and also white, working-class

French people (Canet et al., 2015). Barring ethnic discrimination, which however given its class-based element shares significant similarities with previous forms of entrenched privilege, these are problems not greatly differentiated from those motivating previous generations of French demonstrators, whether in the French Revolution or the riots of May 1968. However, this portrayal and reception are very different.

While the previous history of civil unrest in France has been celebrated as an integral part of the national narrative of fighting tyranny, the riots in French suburbs have been labelled as 'anti-republican pogroms' and their organisers as 'scum' (Amos, 2005; Lacroix, 2005). This demonstrates the paradoxical construction of different forms of unrest in very different ways, depending on the constitutions of those who are committing the acts of unrest, as the riots of 2005 in common with earlier disturbances demonstrate plenty of commonalities with past events of civil unrest. Thus here, it is clear that from a discursive perspective, the riots of 2005 have been constructed differently. The multicultural cast of rioters in 2005, rather than being constructed as part of the broader genealogy of those who in the French national narrative are labelled as heroes of the public good, are rather constructed as 'scum' seeking to undermine the very political and social fabric of France itself. Thus, here the social boundaries of the rioters were 'brightened' in that their boundary with the rest of society is depicted in such a way as they are outside of society.

The events of 2005 involved youths rioting against the oppression, lack of opportunities and alienation of their environments. They also rioted against an oppressive ancien regime, under which they had suffered direct violence from the instruments of the state, whose priority has been to enrich itself while neglecting the poor. These are all common themes with the revolution of 1789 and the May 1968 disturbances. The only differing factor is ethnicity; those rioting in 2005, while having 'white French' members in their ranks, are estimated to have been made up mainly of Franco-Arab and Franco-African youths, born and raised in France and unhappy at the discrimination they faced and their lack of socio-economic opportunities. However, it is an important nuance to this picture that working-class people of white French origin also took part in these riots and thus it is a far broader phenomenon than simply riots by minority ethnic youths (Body-Gendrot, 2013).

Therefore, in terms of national identity construction, while France celebrates its republican tradition of civil unrest with the noble purpose of fighting for the values of freedom and against oppression, this example demonstrates that this is not a given. Rather, Zimmer (2003) correctly argues that 'symbolic resources' have no fixed value contents per se, and while in certain contexts they can be used to construct voluntarist forms of national belonging, they can also be used to exclude. In this particular case, therefore, rather than being constructed as part of the broader national tradition of direct political action by French citizens unhappy with their lot, the rioters were instead constructed as apart from society, with some commentators even going as far as to Islamise the riots and the rioters themselves (Roy, 2005). This demonstrates the overlapping issue that French Muslims face in the way that their national inclusion is constructed, in that it is not simply on religious terms using overtly religious polemics. Rather it occurs in much more diverse and subtle ways, where exclusion is produced in discursive formations that overlap and mix notions of race, religion and class. Thus, the inclusion, or indeed exclusion, of French Muslims occurs in discursive ways which require the analysis of much broader strokes than simply the ways which directly name check a symbol, example or social practice which are clearly 'Muslim'. This is a key observation as this continues when examining the ways in which French hip-hop has been constructed as a subculture 'apart' from French society in ways that other forms of controversial subcultures have not.

6.4 Acceptance and Non-Acceptance of Subcultures: French Rap As Outside of Cultural Norms

In 2018, a rapper called Médine announced he would play two shows in October in the Bataclan theatre, site of the death of 90 victims during the 13 November 2015 terror attacks in Paris. This created a massive polemic because a rapper who has critiqued laïcité and who has spoken about jihad in his music was going to play at a concert hall so central to France's worst terror attack. Indeed, the French Muslim, Franco-Tunisian lawyer Samia Maktouf attempted to have the concerts banned, primarily on public order grounds, but also due to the memory of the victims, even though this is not covered by any laws in the same way that public order is (Dagorn, 2018). Maktouf has been active against Islamist groups, writing a book whose title translates as 'I will defend life as much as you preach death' (Maktouf, 2017), and has been labelled an apostate and received death threats for her work (Bongiovanni, 2018). Médine announcing dates at the Bataclan also led to anonymous individuals unofficially printing portraits of the attack victims and sticking them to walls in central Paris near the concert hall alongside slogans of 'No to the Islamist rapper Médine at the Bataclan' (Tervé, 2018). Already, this particular issue involves French Muslims in a number of roles on different sides of one of the most significant events in recent French social and political history—the Islamic terrorists, the Muslim victims of attack, a Muslim rapper and a Muslim lawyer. What unites all of these disparate actors is a cultural phenomenon that from the outset has engaged a wide range of French Muslims and has been a key means by which Islamic themes have been articulated in a range of different ways (Durand, 2002; Hammou, 2014; J. M. Prévos, 1996; Sweedenburg, 2001; Van den Avenne, Gascquet-Cyrus, & Kosmicki, 1999). That cultural form is French rap.

This example also demonstrates how culture in this case becomes connected with politics and judicial processes, thus making the link which Zimmer (2003) argues is so important between cultural forms and politics. While extremely popular in France and selling to a wide range of audiences, Muslim, non-Muslim and from across the race and class spectrum, this is not the first time that French rap has come up against legal challenges. The Médine example may seem like an extreme, and somewhat specific and unique case, but there is a further reaching issue with French rap as a rebellious subculture that has not been embraced into the national cultural narrative in the same way that other forms of rebellious subcultures have been in France. In the same way that it is necessary to nuance how a notion of French Muslims relates to the questions of rioting in 2005, it is also necessary, if not somewhat obvious, to nuance the relationship between French Muslims and rap music. Clearly French rap is not solely a Muslim phenomenon, nor are all French Muslims rap fans. However, it is one of the cultural forms in the contemporary French landscape that has been the most free to articulate themes of French Muslim identity in the realm of public culture, and has given French Muslims authorship over this process in ways that few other avenues of public culture have (Sweedenburg, 2001).

However, French rap is not the first modern musical form that has involved significant, and controversial, output from those of migrant origin. France has a long tradition of taking in artistic talent from other parts of the world and adopting them as French cultural icons. There is no problem, for example, with seeing Charlotte Gainsbourg and her mother Jane Birkin as key parts of contemporary French culture, even though Charlotte was born in London, and her mother holds a British passport and is notorious for her misuse of the French language. More significant in this sense, is the acceptance and celebration of Charlotte's father, Serge Gainsbourg. Serge was a first generation immigrant, of Russian Jewish parents that left Russia in 1917 due to the revolution. Both Serge and his family were forced to wear yellow stars under the Nazi occupation. After the occupation ended, he went on to have a successful musical career, and became a national cultural icon, with the then French president commenting, 'He was our Baudelaire, our Apollinaire ... He elevated the song to the level of art' (Simmons, 2001). This acceptance was not behaviour dependent, and endured despite numerous acts of controversy, such as lewd lyrics, vulgar language on prime-time TV, his song about incest with his daughter, and the burning a 500-franc note live on TV (Simmons, 2001). Although he defies placement in a single genre, Gainsbourg is an example of an important recurring theme in French culture. This theme is the adoption, incorporation and then ownership of foreign cultural forms. In this case, his example shows how rock, an art form originating and most popular in the USA and UK at the time, was taken up in France, adapted to the cultural landscape of France, then becoming an accepted and celebrated part of the cultural landscape. As outlined earlier, this cultural landscape is vital in the construction and reconstruction of national identity, and in the case here, how social boundaries become blurred to accept foreign forms of culture and their producers with roots outside of the hexagon. However, this history obscures the modern reality; underneath this veneer of acceptance exist strongly brightened cultural boundaries, where culture such as rap, created by members of certain immigrant groups are seen as outside the boundaries of acceptance.

French rap, due to its mix of commercial success, and the high participation from minority ethnic groups makes it difficult to have a sustentative discussion of contemporary French national identity without discussing this art form in a substantive manner. This is because the reception of such a phenomenon, in light of the reception of other controversial artists and art forms of immigrant origin, such as Gainsbourg discussed above, demonstrates how the cultural boundaries of French national identity are being constructed and reconstructed.

Rap, or 'rhymed storytelling accompanied by highly rhythmic, electronically based music' (Rose, 1994), originated in the social crisis of 1970s' New York. In France, scenes emerged as early as the 1980s in the two capitals of French rap, Paris and Marseille (Perrier, 2010, p. 15). However, rap really became established in the mainstream with the success, beginning in 1991, of the 'three pillars of French rap' (Perrier, 2010, p. 15): IAM (Marseille), MC Solar (Paris) and Supreme NTM (Paris). In the eyes of art critics and hip-hop's international fan base, France had now become rap's second home, owing to these successes in record sales in France, the quality of the French artistic production, rap's public popularity and the sheer number of acts in France (Perrier, 2010, p. 15). The art form has seen significant commercial success in France, with IAM selling 3.5 million albums (Future.fr, 2011), including 1.5 million of their album 'L'École du micro d'argent', making it the most successful album in French rap history, and 2.5 million sales for Supreme NTM. Added to this, the artists themselves have been overwhelmingly 'des jeunes issus de l'immigration' (Bachman and Basier, 1985). Rap, as mentioned above, originated in the USA, and once in France, like many other alien cultural forms before it, it quickly became stylistically 'acclimatised, transformed and adapted to the reality of France … a reality different from the reality of the United States' (Perrier, 2010, p. 15). This difference stems from two key factors. Firstly, it has a very different history of external colonialism instead of domestic slavery, meaning that rap artists in France came from France's ex-colonies, their parents or grandparents coming to France either for economic reasons, or because of the political necessities of complicity under colonialism (from example the Algerian Harkis). Secondly, the urban arena of French rap was not the economically depressed inner-city of the USA, but the desolate and isolated suburbs of French cities.

This specifically neglects the fact that French rap is a cultural phenomenon that reflects the social realities of its context, where 'the poetic power of French rap is nourished from the daily' (Perrier, 2010, p. 17). As such, the environment in which this art form is produced affects the finished product (Sberna, 2008, p. 14), in as much as the sentiments in the surrounding environment affect what it addresses. Scholars of French rap have rightly asserted its importance as 'a means of interpreting a social reality' (Sberna, 2008, p. 7), rap acts as an 'articulation' of the theme of a city, or of distinct districts of that city (Sberna, 2008, p. 12), and a means of discovering the state of a society (Sberna, 2008, p. 13). Scholars have attempted to understand how rap does this through similar methodological means to this study, through a detailed discourse analysis of its lyrics (Pecqueux, 2007). Here, a similar methodological approach has been taken on a much larger data set to discuss the relationship between rapper and audience in French rap, but again neglecting the issue of boundary making (Pecqueux, 2007). There are also works which deal directly with questions of scene making and the specifics of the subculture in Marseille (Valnet, Cachin, AKA, & Maéro, 2013). Even here, however, scant attention is given to the specific boundaries, symbols and conflicts of the local play out in specific contexts of French rap and how these differ.

This is even more remarkable given the current state of scholarship on rap in other contexts such as the USA, where primacy is given to investigating these more specific questions of boundary and place making in rap music. Beyond the observation that rap more generally is important in identity formation (Krims, 2000), specifically in negotiating a range of diaspora identities (Flores, 2000), it should be noted that paying attention to the lyrics and discourse created are key to understanding a cultural form where the spoken word is highly prized (E. Richardson, 2006). Rap lyrics thus make important inroads into discussing a myriad of themes—including but not limited to gender, race, ethnicity and economic status (Perrier, 2010; E. Richardson, 2006; Sberna, 2008). Other scholars have attempted to attach this to the local, where rap specifically expresses local concerns about belonging and citizenship (Bennet, 1999). This theme of rap's relationship to urban space is specifically highlighted as important: 'rap music takes the city and its multiple spaces as the foundation of its cultural production' (Forman, 2004). It addresses and interacts with these spaces to create 'alternative maps' to urban space (Forman, 2004, p. 202). Some have even argued that rap artists be treated as 'urban ethnographers' (Beer, 2014), and thus their lyrical output as ethnographic texts of specific urban, spatial and temporal settings. As such, rap lyrics are ripe to be used to examine how social structures, collective norms and patterns of social change are constructed and negotiated in the urban sphere.

The reception of French rap has not been the same as previous patterns of incorporation, as seen in other cases such as rock and Serge Gainsbourg. Some observers have argued for French rap to have its place in France's modern 'beaux arts', as a prime example of the poetry of our times (Perrier, 2010, p. 13), this against a backdrop of criticism and non-acceptance, which, in the words of French rapper Oreslan, have meant that rap is 'not accepted as "culture" by a large part of the [French] population' (Sayare, 2009). During the disturbances of 2005, for example, a proposed action by 200 French MPs would have seen seven French rap acts prosecuted for inciting violence (Muggs, 2005). There have also been numerous attempts by right-wing groups, such as the National Front, to prosecute rap acts for their music's lyrical content (Muggs, 2005). As recently as 2009, Orelsan had his album banned from several French public libraries, due to controversy over its lyrical content, based on a song about lovers' spite (Sayare, 2009). It has also been historically difficult to organise large tours with French rap groups because in France 'concert promoters … rely heavily upon state funding, they have been reluctant to book acts so often at odds with the government' (Sayare, 2009). This difference in treatment, between controversial French musical figures such as Gainsbourg and rap groups such as NTM has led to accusations of racism, summed up by the lawyer Guillaume Traynard: 'At a certain point, what they accept from a Franco-French artist they don't accept from an artist of North African origin' (Sayare, 2009). This has clear implications for the construction, and reconstruction, of modern French national identity.

This is especially relevant when one examines the relationship between French rap and its articulation of Islamic themes. Rap has developed as an important means in France by which those in the diaspora attempt to appropriate, create and mediate idioms, vernaculars and forms of identification in the highly complex context in which they find themselves (Drissel, 2009). As such, examining French rap from this perspective, it is clearly an important means by which questions of homeland, migration, discrimination, religion and colour are re-examined for the French context (Durand, 2002; Hammou, 2014; J. M. Prévos, 1996; Sweedenburg, 2001; Van den Avenne et al., 1999). This includes the Islamic themes and the connection of France with the black and Islamic worlds. An example of this, and the broader discussions of multiculturalism and local pride that connect rap to French Muslims in ways less obvious, can be found in the work of the Marseille rap group IAM. This connects to observations that Marseille rap is using a 'black Mediterranean' connection between Marseille and Egypt as a coded means to construct connections between Marseille, and thus France, and the Islamic world (Sweedenburg, 2001). Not only did the leading member of IAM, Akhenaton, convert to Islam, but the group more generally expressed through their lyrics the historical connections between Marseille and Islamic North and West Africa as a means to demonstrate that not only is multiculturalism in the city a historic fact, but also something that should be championed in the modern era in the face of increasing support for the far-right, anti-immigrant, politics of the National Front (Sweedenburg, 2001).

This is a theme that emerges on a track where the same group, IAM, appeared with the famous Algerian singer Khaled entitled 'Oran—Marseille' on his album 'Sahara' in 1996. Here, the rappers discuss Marseille as a place where 'the odors of couscous, tajine, prunes, mafé, yassa, fresh fish, pasta ... multiple ethnicities cohabiting naturally, the cultures, the walls, dance like in a watercolor'. This articulation is indicative of the idiom of Marseille rap of the connectedness to the Mediterranean world of the city—a recurrent theme in the work of the group IAM that makes imaginative renderings of Marseille as a place connected to the Mediterranean and all of its cultural constituents—Africa, Islam, and ancient Egypt amongst others (A. Prévos, 2001; Sweedenburg, 2001). To a certain extent, this also constitutes an interesting reinterpretation of Marseille's colonial designation as 'The Door to the South' ('Marseille Porte du Sud', Londres, 1926) that was the entry point to not only France's overseas empire in Asia and Africa, but also the starting point of many famous journeys made by Europeans to other continents. Here, it is these colonial connections, with all their negative connotations, that lead to the current city being populated by those immigrants and their descendants from North and West Africa so important to Marseille hip-hop—including the members of the group IAM, such as Malek Sultan and Imhotep who were both born in Algiers—the former to Muslim Arab parents and the latter to European settler parents.

This includes the emergence of discussions of the multicultural nature of France in addition to expressing pride in the rapper's home city. This can be seen in a track on the 1991 album by IAM entitled 'I come from Marseille' (Je viens de Marseille). On this track, the group refers to Marseille as the 'mythical, mystical nightmare of xenophobes … city of 10,000 cities … But do not get me wrong, the country where I come from has nothing to do with the wonders—I am from Marseille'. This goes further and connects to the image of the city as a place of Mediterranean mixity which has historically constituted the city from its founding myth as the result of a marriage between Protis the Greek and Gyptis the Ligurian princess (Temime, 1999). This also continues today in the urban policy of the city in using an image of being part of the Mediterranean and by default multicultural to side-step the French republican insistence on being French first and foremost (Downing, 2015).

This comparative difference of acceptance between two controversial art forms in France, produced by actors with roots outside of the hexagon, demonstrates something very interesting about constructions of national identity in contemporary France. The acceptance of artists such as Gainsbourg, regardless of his immigrant origin and controversial style, gives examples of how the cultural field in France can blur social boundaries in ways which make it open to producers from a variety of backgrounds. However, the complicated relationship to public cultural acceptance that has marked French rap, in spite of its huge commercial success, demonstrates that the cultural field, and its relationship with politics, can also brighten social boundaries and construct certain forms of culture as outside of acceptable social norms. Thus, the construction of rap in this way at times demonstrates how French Muslims, like their non-Muslim counterparts in the rap scene, are subject to a significantly more problematic relationship with cultural acceptance in the national cultural narrative.

6.5 The Ugly Sides of the Beautiful Game: The Politicisation of Race and Religion in the French National Football Team

Zinadine Zidane, N'golo Kante, Paul Pogba and even Theirry Henry. Four of the biggest names to ever be associated with French football, central in delivering France's two World Cups, exactly 20 years apart. And all of them either raised as, or at one time or another becoming, French Muslims. The French national team has not only been extremely successful at times, but has been one of the key means by which the wider world has had an insight into the multicultural nature of French society and both the historical and contemporary diversity of French society. Indeed, it is not just Muslims that have nuanced contemporary national identity in the national team, but a host of African, Caribbean and white French players with roots in other European countries—such as Robert Pirès, born to a Portuguese father and Spanish mother in Reims. However, this apparent harmony in such a key vehicle for 'banal' nationalism (Vidacs, 2011) has experienced its dark moments, because like all key cultural sites for the contestation and redefinition of the nation, it has both attempted to brighten and blur social boundaries in quite paradoxical ways. For a facet of public culture that has included so many French Muslims in such prominent positions, it is necessary for a chapter on the construction of French Muslims in diffuse cultural forms of nationalism to take account of how the national team has done this.

This is not an observation that is limited to France or to the specifics of the French national team, as all national teams are important in defining the nation. This is regardless of whether culturally diverse, as in post-migration states such as France, and whether or not they contain players from social and religious minorities such as French Muslims. This is because of the centrality of large sports events in contemporary life, which are much more than sport—the spectacle and the media coverage surrounding them is highly relevant (Tomlinson & Young, 2006). They also provide opportunities for the articulation, contestation and indeed redefinition of the complexities of national and local identities (Tomlinson & Young, 2006). Football can also be an important national sport because of its ability to create 'flat', 'horizontal' loyalties to the nation that cut across class, regional, race and religious social cleavages, albeit often with masculine overtones (J. Williams, 2017). National football is a key site for ongoing processes of banal nationalism, where the nation is defined and reproduced through daily practices such as supporting the national team (Vidacs, 2011). However, this does not mean that national teams are not themselves contested sites of nationalism—most notably through the many incidents of racism in football. When the black British player Cyrille Regis was called up to the England team in the 1980s, he was famously sent a bullet in the mail, after years of enduring racist chants during domestic games (Sports Journalist Association, 2010). Thus racism, in addition to hooliganism, are two ugly facets to a sport often referred to as the beautiful game.

The significance of football in redefining national identity is not lost on former players of the French national team. The straight-talking former captain of the French national team, Zinadine Zidane, recently said of the 1998 World Cup win that 'it was not about religion, the colour of your skin, we didn't care about that, we were just together and enjoyed the moment' (Vice Media, 2018). This echoes the sentiment of the times, that a multicultural team of united 'black, blanc, beur' (Hargreaves, 2007) players had united under the cause of the French national team to lift the World Cup for the first time in French history. This gives insight into the public performance of Frenchness in football, where in this case triumph on the football field demonstrated that integration had been successful in France and anyone could reach the top of French society. Zidane himself had grown up on Marseille's infamous estate 'La Castellane' (Kazi-Tani, 2018), seen as one of the toughest estates in one of France's toughest cities. However, this moment of multi-racial, multi-religious, multi-class triumph in French football did not signal an end to either the impoverishment of minority communities in suburban housing estates racial controversies in French football that have caught French Muslims in the wider net of discrimination. While the multicultural team led by Mbappé triumphed again in Russia in 2018, these two victorious moments neatly book-end 20 years where race, class and by extension the role of French Muslims have taken far darker discussions. These two key trends demonstrate the discursive way that, even in a nation with an overtly colour-blind, assimilationist national policy, the composition and the management of the national team have operated on very different, discriminatory principles. Firstly, there were significant polemics on the exit in 2012 that concentrated on the 'loyalty' of non-white players to the national side.

This series of polemics on the racial backgrounds of French players occurred both during the 1998 World Cup run and also during the less successful 2010 campaign. In 2010, the French team crashed out of the tournament in South Africa at the group stage, winning no games. Behind the scenes, the coach had terrible relations with the players, resulting in star Nicolas Anelka being banned for 18 games for screaming obscenities at the manager, Raymond Domenech, and team captain Patrice Evra having an on-field bust up with the fitness coach, Robert Duverne (Hytner, 2010). However, rather than question the work of these two white men and their incompetence in managing the national side, blame fell quickly on the players, whose commitment to the French team was questioned. This was not the usual rumblings about spoilt and overpaid players, but rather took on a distinctly sinister and racial tone where the ethnic and class backgrounds of the players were questioned directly in public.

These questions and issues did not just represent a dysfunctional moment in French football, because questions about the French team's ethnic credentials have a much longer political trajectory. Questions about the ethnic make-up of the team were mentioned as early as 1998, just after the victory against Brazil, when the far-right leader Jean-Marie Le Pen argued that black and Arab players had been selected from ethnic groups to placate France's multicultural population, despite them playing vital roles in the win (Dely, 1998). However, after 2010 this took on a much more public, mainstream appearance when the philosopher Alain

Finkielkraut called the team a 'gang of thieves with mafia morals' (Marc, 2010). While this only referred to the footballers by their presumed class backgrounds as children of France's crime-ridden, suburban housing estates, it was obvious that this had a more racial tone as these suburban designations are also synonymous with black and Arab youths in France. Marine Le Pen waded into the fray, arguing that the problem with the national team was down to them having 'another nationality in their hearts' (Marianne, 2016). Thus, it was deemed that the class and racial background of the French players of ethnic origin meant that they could not be loyal to the French team nor embody the discipline and good sportsmanship required of a national team.

However, the discussion of these issues does not stop here, neither chronologically nor in the realms of the polemic. Rather, this continued in an extremely worrying way when in 2011 the technical head of the French team was embroiled in accusations of stating a need for 'racial quotas' for the French national team, to limit the number of black and Arab players (Arfi, Mathieu, & Hajdenberg, 2011). This was also worryingly linked to discussions of how the racial background of the players determined their style of play, with black players being seen as big and strong, and white players small, more intelligent and more skilful (BBC, 2011). This worryingly echoes the racial hierarchies constructed under the colonial empire (Camiscioli, 2009), not to mention being discursively extremely ironic to be proposed in a country where racial statistics are banned.

The world of contemporary French football is indeed a murky one, which makes some elements of accusations about racism in the selection of the national team hard to substantiate due to the ongoing complexity of sexual scandals relating to players in the team. This is the case with the star striker Karim Benzema, who has been repeatedly left out of the national side despite excelling at Real Madrid (Foot Mercato, 2017). Accusations of racism have been made here by both Benzema himself but also ex-French international player Samir Nasri (Europe1, 2017). However, the story is far murkier than simply a star player being left off the national team because of his origins, as he served a suspension for his alleged involvement in the blackmail of a fellow French player over a sex tape, in addition to being caught up in controversy over the use of underage prostitutes in a Paris nightclub (BBC, 2014). While none of these charges have resulted in a prosecution, they have significantly damaged the reputation of the player with the French side. However, he is not the only player of North African origin to be left off, or under-used, by the French national team. Nasri, Benzama and Hatem Ben Arfa are three North African players whose exclusion from star roles in the national team have caused controversy in recent years, with both former French international Eric Cantona and French-Moroccan comedian and actor Jamal Debbouze accusing the French team of leaving out players on racial grounds (Lichfield, 2016). Regardless of the uncertainties around these exclusions, whether they have been made on racial, personal, legal or football grounds, or some combination of any number of these, may be never possible to ascertain. However, what can be seen from examining the French national team as a vehicle for the rebuilding of the nation at the intersection of culture and politics, is that it is a key point at which national identity has been remade in exclusionary ethnic terms. This has even been the case when the multi-ethnic national team triumphed, but has intensified in years of poor success.

6.6 Conclusions on the Paradoxes of Cultural Nationalism, French Muslims and National Identity

This chapter has demonstrated the importance of examining cultural nationalism when seeking to understand the profound ways in which the construction of national identity in France can operate in exclusionary ways for French Muslims alongside other post-colonial minority groups. Importantly for the broader study of Muslims, this has been done without actually examining an overtly 'Muslim' issue—such as the banning of religious symbols or the many polemics which construct Muslims as 'others' in France, such as about halal meals in schools or prayers in the streets. This is key in the broader discussions of Muslims sociologically because it is essentialist and condescending if scholars put Muslims in a conceptual and empirical prison whereby they only care about issues that are clearly labelled Muslim. In a context such as France, where Muslims are not only extremely racially, ethnically and socially diverse, they are also a very settled and French population. Thus, they are implicated in a variety of different cultural and national debates which go far beyond the obviously Muslim issues. This analysis thus selected three important examples of French national identity construction in the broader field of the intersection of politics and culture (Zimmer, 2003). These three, seemingly disparate examples have been chosen to demonstrate the less obvious, banal, ways in which national identity is constructed in an ethnicised way in the public realm, which works to exclude French Muslims alongside their post-colonial migrant non-Muslim compatriots. This is important to understand because, and correctly so, a lot of attention is given to the ways in which the official actions of the state, as discussed in Chap. 2, work in exclusionary ways. While this is key aspect of the creation and re-creation of French national identity in an exclusionary, organic manner, it fails to fully engage with the multitude of ways that broader discursive processes in the field of culture work in a similar way. Thus, as in the case of nationalism, while the state remains important, analysing only state structures can never capture the full story, and scholars need to tread the well-established path of moving beyond the political chambers and law courts into broader society to understand the multifaceted ways that national identity is constructed in paradoxical and exclusionary ways. Thus, this account of the multifaceted ways in which cultural nationalism in the public realm can work in an exclusionary way should be read as complementary to Chap. 2 on the state, to demonstrate that processes or marginalisation operate in more profound symbolic ways that are not solely reliant on the political cultural of laïcité. During my research in France, it has often been explained to me that the preservation of laïcité is critical to ensuring the stability of French society that the unintended, undesirable outcomes of not having structures to tackle structural racial and religious discrimination is almost acceptable collateral damage. However, regardless of our normative position on laïcité and the French assimilationist system, reading its outcomes in tandem with the broader structures of cultural nationalism demonstrate that marginalisation and racism work in France in far more diverse discursive ways in the public realm—not just in the case of French Muslims but for those who are defined as 'others' in society for a number of reasons.

It is erroneous to consider the riots of 2005 to be 'Muslim' in any way other than some of the diverse mix of rioters were Muslims. However, the paradox here can only be seen in comparative perspective, where other events of anti-systemic direct political action, from the revolution of 1789 to the riots of May 1968 have been incorporated in a history that defines such direct action as a key part of Frenchness. Additionally, it is not just the fact that the 2005 riots have not found their place alongside these other events in the national narrative that demonstrates the de facto ethnicisation of Frenchness in the public cultural sphere, but rather the racialised way in which they were covered. This demonstrates the primacy of the 'othering' of the rioters in 2005 on ethnic, racial and religious grounds, even when studies have found that white French rioters also took part.

However, the intersection of politics and culture does not stop here in the ways in which it works to make paradoxical exclusions in French society. France has never shied away from embracing and celebrating artists who produce controversial material or lead controversial lives, as seen with Serge Gainsbourg. However, the paradox emerges here in the reception and coverage of French rap music which has been one of the commercially most popular art forms in contemporary France. However, it has been the subject of several legal cases about the freedom of expression of rap artists in ways that other art forms are not. While clearly not all French rappers are of French Muslim origin, a number of the most prominent are. Additionally, rap has been an important form of public culture which has been one of the few open to expressions of Islamic idioms and themes and where it has been possible to make commentaries on multicultural French life. Thus, here politics has got involved in a field of culture outside of the boundaries of the state to attempt to define French rap, its subjects, idioms and artists as legally unacceptable to the norms of French artistic expression.

Finally, this chapter examined the French national football team in the 20 years between its two World Cup triumphs, 1998 and 2018. Again, not a solely French Muslim domain, a number of the great and good of both French World Cup winning teams were, of have become through conversion, French Muslims. Additionally, when victorious, the French national team has been constructed as an almost exceptional vehicle of socio-economic and personal advancement to those of post-migrant origin, especially those of poor socio-economic status, origin. However, closer inspection both around the World Cup wins, but also during the 'lean' years where the team was not successful, demonstrate the paradoxical means where even the national team is subject to critique and construction that marginalises those of non-white backgrounds. While the cases of this paradoxical construction of national identity are unfortunately plural, one that stands out is the controversy where it was proposed to have quotas for ethnic minority players to limit their number in the team. The irony of the proposition of negative quotas in such an important national body, while refusing to create positive quotas to fight socio-economic discrimination, is clear. However, going deeper it is emblematic of broader existential discussions around the national team and its 'Frenchness' being compromised by being 'too black'. Thus, here we can see another way in which culture and politics intersect to create a national identity which is de facto racialising and exclusionary under the de jure umbrella of radical colour-blind equality.

Bibliography

Alba, R. (2005). Bright vs. Blurred Boundaries: Second-Generation Assimilation and Exclusion in France, Germany, and the United States. *Ethnic and Racial Studies, 28*(1), 20–49.

Amos, D. (2005). *Sarkozy at the Centre of French Riot Debate* [Online]. Retrieved from http://www.npr.org/templates/story/story.php

Anderson, B. (Ed.). (2006). *Imagined Communities: Reflections on the Origin and Spread of Nationalism*. London: Verso.

Arfi, F., Mathieu, M., & Hajdenberg, M. (2011). *Les quotas discriminatoires dans le foot français*. Retrieved October 9, 2018, from https://www.mediapart.fr/journal/france/dossier/les-quotas-discriminatoires-dans-le-foot-francais

Bachman, C., & Basier, L. (1985). Junior s'entraine tres fort, ou le smurf comme mobilisation symbolique. *Langage et société, 34*, 57–68.

BBC. (2011). French Football Suspends Official. *BBC News*. Retrieved from https://www.bbc.com/news/world-europe-13236864

BBC. (2014, January 20). French Players in Prostitution Trial. *BBC News*. Retrieved from https://www.bbc.com/news/world-europe-25802279

Beer, D. (2014). Hip-Hop as Urban and Regional Research: Encountering an Insider's Ethnography of City Life. *International Journal of Urban and Regional Research, 38*(2), 677–685. https://doi.org/10.1111/j.1468-2427.2012.01151.x

Bennet, A. (1999). *Hip Hop Am Main: The Localization of Rap Music and Hip Hop Culture*. Media.

BFMTV. (2018). *Mai 68, gilets jaunes: une comparaison qui a ses limites*. Retrieved February 9, 2019, from https://www.bfmtv.com/societe/mai-68-gilets-jaunes-une-comparaison-qui-a-ses-limites-1583488.html

Bhabha, H. K. (2006). Cultural Diversity and Cultural Differences. In B. Ashcroft, H. Griffiths, & F. Tiffin (Eds.), *The Post-Colonial Studies Reader*. London: Routledge.

Billig, M. (1995). *Banal Nationalism*. London: Sage.

Body-Gendrot, S. (2013). Urban Violence in France and England: Comparing Paris (2005) and London (2011). *Policing and Society, 23*(1), 6–25. https://doi.org/10.1080/10439463.2012.727608

Bongiovanni, F. M. (2018). *Europe and the End of the Age of Innocence*. Cham: Springer.

Breuilly, J. (1994). *Nationalism and the State*. University of Chicago Press. Retrieved from https://www.press.uchicago.edu/ucp/books/book/chicago/N/bo3619074.html

Brubaker, R. (1998). *Citizenship and Nationhood in France and Germany*. Cambridge, MA: Harvard University Press.

Calhoun, C. (2007). *Nations Matter: Culture, History, and the Cosmopolitan Dream*. London: Routledge.

Camiscioli, E. (2009). *Reproducing the French Race: Immigration, Intimacy and Embodiment in the Early Twentieth Century*. Durham, NC: Duke University Press.

Canet, R., Pech, L., & Stewart, M. (2015). France's Burning Issue: Understanding the Urban Riots of November 2005. In M. T. Davis (Ed.), *Crowd Actions in Britain and France from the Middle Ages to the Modern World* (pp. 270–292). London: Palgrave Macmillan UK. https://doi.org/10.1057/9781137316516_17

Dagorn, G. (2018, June 12). Le rappeur Médine au Bataclan: la polémique en quatre questions. *Le Monde*. Retrieved from https://www.lemonde.fr/politique/article/2018/06/12/le-rappeur-medine-au-bataclan-la-polemique-en-quatre-questions_5313815_823448.html

Dely, R. (1998). Le Pen: 'la Coupe du monde, est un détail de l'histoire'. *Nouvelle diatribe provocatrice du leader du FN. – Libération.* Retrieved October 9, 2018, from https://www.liberation.fr/france/1998/07/13/le-pen-la-coupe-du-monde-est-un-detail-de-l-histoire-nouvelle-diatribe-provocatrice-du-leader-du-fn_243689

Dikeç, M. (2007). *Badlands of the Republic: Space, Politics and Urban Policy.* Oxford: Blackwell Publishing.

Downing, J. (2015). Understanding the (Re) Definition of Nationhood in French Cities: A Case of Multiple States and Multiple Republics. *Studies in Ethnicity and Nationalism, 15*(2), 336–351.

Drissel, D. (2009). Hip-Hop Hybridity for a Glocalized World: African and Muslim Diasporic Discourses in French Rap Music. *The Global Studies Journal, 2*(3). Retrieved from https://www.academia.edu/1591080/Hip-Hop_Hybridity_for_a_Glocalized_World_African_and_Muslim_Diasporic_Discourses_in_French_Rap_Music

Durand, A.-P. (2002). *Black, Blanc, Beur: Rap Music and Hip-Hop Culture in the Francophone World.* Lanham, MD: Scarecrow Press.

Europe1. (2017). *Pour Nasri, Benzema, Ben Arfa et lui sont victimes d'un racisme ambiant.* Retrieved November 24, 2018, from http://www.europe1.fr/sport/pour-nasri-benzema-ben-arfa-et-lui-sont-victimes-dun-racisme-ambiant-3458684

Flores. (2000). *From Bomba to Hip-Hop: Puerto Rican Culture and Latino Identity.* New York: Colombia University Press.

Foot Mercato. (2017). *Equipe de France: Karim Benzema règle ses comptes avec Didier Deschamps.* Retrieved October 9, 2018, from http://www.footmercato.net/equipe-de-france/equipe-de-france-karim-benzema-regle-ses-comptes-avec-didier-deschamps_214107

Forman, M. (2004). Represent: Race, Space and Place in Rap Music. In M. Forman & M. A. Neal (Eds.), *That's the Joint! The Hip-Hop Studies Reader.* New York: Routledge.

Future.fr. (2011). *IAM sort un triple album pour célébrer ses 20 ans.* Retrieved from http://joga.future.fr/actualites/article-886-iam-sort-un-triple-album-pour-celebrer-ses-20-ans.html

Gellner, E. (Ed.). (1983). *Nations and Nationalism.* London: Blackwell.

Gellner, E. (Ed.). (1988). *Plough, Sword and Book: The Structure of Human History.* London: Collins Harvill.

Hammou, K. (2014). *Une histoire du rap en France.* Paris: Editions Découverte.

Hargreaves, A. (2007). *Multi-Ethnic France: Immigration, Politics, Culture and Society* (2nd ed.). New York; London: Routledge.

Heneghan, T. (2007, November 29). *Why We Don't Call Them 'Muslim Riots' in Paris Suburbs*. Retrieved October 20, 2018, from http://blogs.reuters.com/faithworld/2007/11/29/why-we-dont-call-them-muslim-riots-in-paris-suburbs/

Hutchingson, J. (1982). *The Dynamics of Cultural Nationalism: The Gaelic Revival and the Creation of the Irish Nation State*. Crows Nest, Australia: Allen and Unwin.

Hytner, D. (2010). World Cup 2010: France Revolt Leaves Raymond Domenech High and Dry. *The Guardian*. Retrieved from https://www.theguardian.com/football/2010/jun/20/france-raymond-domenech-nicolas-anelka

Jobard, F. (2009). An Overview of French Riots: 1981–2004. In D. Waddington, F. Jobard, & M. King (Eds.), *Rioting in the UK and France. A Comparative Analysis* (pp. 27–38). Willan Publishing. Retrieved from https://hal.archives-ouvertes.fr/hal-00550788

Kazi-Tani, S. (2018). *Sports | Football: de la cité de la Castellane aux étoiles du Real, Zinédine Zidane ce héros made in Marseille | La Provence*. Retrieved October 9, 2018, from https://www.laprovence.com/article/sports/4988951/de-la-castellane-au-real-zinedine-zidane-un-heros-made-in-marseille.html

Kohn, H. (2005). *The Idea of Nationalism*. New Brunswick, NJ: Transaction Publisher.

Krims, A. (2000). *Rap Music and the Poetics of Identity*. Cambridge: Cambridge University Press.

Lacroix, A. (2005). Alain Finkielkraut: 'The Illegitimacy of Hatred'. *Le Figaro*. Retrieved from http://www.lefigaro.fr/debats/2005/11/17/01005-20051117ARTFIG90264-alain_finkielkraut_the_illegitimacy_of_hatred.php

Leerssen, J. (2015). The Nation and the City: Urban Festivals and Cultural Mobilisation. *Nations and Nationalism, 21*(1), 2–20. https://doi.org/10.1111/nana.12090

Lichfield, J. (2016, May 31). France Accused of Excluding Players of North African Origin from Euro 2016 Squad. *The Independent*. Retrieved from http://www.independent.co.uk/sport/football/international/euro-2016-france-accused-of-excluding-players-of-african-origin-from-squad-for-tournament-a7058371.html

Londres, A. (1926). *Marseille porte du Sud*. Paris: Arléa.

Maktouf, S. (2017). *Je défendrai la vie autant que vous prêchez la mort*. Neuilly-sur-Seine: Michel Lafon.

Marc, J. (2010). *Finkielkraut: 'L'équipe de France est une bande de voyous avec une morale de mafia'*. Retrieved October 9, 2018, from http://www.agoravox.tv/tribune-libre/article/finkielkraut-l-equipe-de-france-26725

Marianne. (2016). *Comment le débat sur l'équipe de France de football s'est racialisé depuis 1998*. Retrieved October 9, 2018, from https://www.marianne.net/societe/comment-le-debat-sur-lequipe-de-france-de-football-sest-racialise-depuis-1998

McCoy, T. S. (1988). Hegemony, Power, Media: Foucault and Cultural Studies. *Communications, 14*(3), 71–90. https://doi.org/10.1515/comm.1988.14.3.71

McLennan, G. (2014). Sociology, Cultural Studies and the Cultural Turn. In J. Holmwood & J. Scott (Eds.), *The Palgrave Handbook of Sociology in Britain* (pp. 510–535). London: Palgrave Macmillan UK. https://doi.org/10.1007/978-1-137-31886-2_23

Moran, M. (2011). Sarkozy Versus the Banlieues: Deconstructing Urban Legend. *Journal of Franco-Iberian Studies*, Special Issue: 'Beyond Hate: Representations of the Parisian Banlieue'.

Muggs, J. (2005). *Should French Hip Hop Take the Rap for Rioting* [Online]. Retrieved from http://www.telegraph.co.uk/culture/music/rockandjazzmusic/3648576/Should-hip-hop-take-the-rap-for-rioting.html

Nash, K. (2001). The 'Cultural Turn' in Social Theory: Towards a Theory of Cultural Politics. *Sociology, 35*(1), 77–92. https://doi.org/10.1177/0038038501035001006

Nielsen, K. (1996). Cultural Nationalism, Neither Ethnic Nor Civic. *Philosophical Forum, 28*(1–2), 42–52.

Pecqueux, A. (2007). *Voix du rap: Essai de sociologie de l'action musicale*. Paris: Editions L'Harmattan.

Perrier, J. (2010). *Rap Francais: Dix Ans Après*. Paris: Poche.

Prévos, A. (2001). Post-Colonial Popular Music in France: Rap Music and Hip-Hop Culture in the 1980s and 1990s. In *Global Noise: Rap and HipHop outside of the USA*. Middletown, CT: Wesleyan University Press.

Prévos, J. M. (1996). The Evolution of French Rap Music and Hip Hop Culture in the 1980s and 1990s. *The French Review, 69*(5), 713–725.

Procter, J. (2004). *Stuart Hall*. London: Routledge.

Richardson, E. (2006). *Hiphop Literacies*. Retrieved from https://www.amazon.co.uk/Hiphop-Literacies-Elaine-Richardson/dp/0415329272

Rose, T. (1994). *Black Noise: Rap Music and Black Culture in Contemporary America*. Hanover, NH: Wesleyan University Press.

Roy, O. (2005). Intifada des banlieues ou émeutes des jeunes déclassés? *Esprit*, (12).

RTL. (2018). *VIDÉO – Les gilets jaunes mènent-ils un combat historique?* Retrieved February 9, 2019, from https://www.rtl.fr/actu/debats-societe/video-1789-mai-1968-les-gilets-jaunes-menent-ils-un-combat-historique-7795794100

Sahlins, P. (2006). *Civil Unrest in the French Suburbs.* New York: Brooklyn.

Sayare, S. (2009, August 26). French Rap as a Flash Point. *The New York Times.* Retrieved from https://www.nytimes.com/2009/08/27/arts/27iht-rap.html

Sberna, B. (Ed.). (2008). *Une sociologie du rap à Marseille.* Broché.

Simmons, S. (2001). *An Extract from Serge Gainsbourg: A Fistfull of Gitanes* [Online]. Retrieved from http://www.guardian.co.uk/books/2001/feb/02/culture.features

Singer, D. (2002). *Prelude to Revolution: France in May 1968.* Cambridge, MA: South End Press.

Smith, A. D. (2005). The Genealogy of Nations: An Ethno-Symbolist Approach. In A. Ichijo & G. Uzelac (Eds.), *When Is the Nation?* London: Routledge.

Sports Journalist Association. (2010). *Regis on Big Ron, Racism and Death Threats Sent with a Bullet.* Sports Journalists' Association. Retrieved September 13, 2018, from https://www.sportsjournalists.co.uk/other-bodies/football-writers/regis-on-big-ron-racism-and-death-threats-wrapped-in-a-bullet/

Sweedenburg, T. (2001). Islamic Hip-Hop vs. Islamophobia: Aki Nawaz, Natacha Atlas, Akhenaton. In *Global Noise: Hip Hop Outside of the USA.* Middletown, CT: Wesleyan University Press.

Tarrow, S. (1993). Social Protest and Policy Reform: May 1968 and the Loi d'Orientation in France. *Comparative Political Studies, 25*(4), 579–607. https://doi.org/10.1177/0010414093025004006

Temime, E. (Ed.). (1999). *Migrance: Histoire des migrations à Marseille.* Paris: Editions Jeanne Laffite.

Tervé, C. (2018). *Des familles de victimes du Bataclan dénoncent la récupération de leurs portraits contre la venue de Médine.* Retrieved September 12, 2018, from https://www.huffingtonpost.fr/2018/07/04/medine-au-bataclan-des-familles-de-victimes-denoncent-la-recuperation-de-leurs-portraits-pour-la-deprogrammation-du-concert_a_23474648/

Tomlinson, A., & Young, C. (2006). *National Identity and Global Sports Events: Culture, Politics, and Spectacle in the Olympics and the Football World Cup.* Albany: SUNY Press.

Valnet, J., Cachin, O., AKA, & Maéro, J.-P. (2013). *M.A.R.S. Histoires et légendes du hip-hop marseillais* (1st ed.). Paris: Wildproject Editions.

Van den Avenne, C., Gascquet-Cyrus, M., & Kosmicki, G. (1999). *Paroles et Musiques à Marseille: Les voix d'une Ville*. Paris: Editions L'Hartmann.

Vice Media. (2018). *Zinedine Zidane Shares His World Cup Memories – VICE Video: Documentaries, Films, News Videos*. Retrieved from https://video.vice.com/en_uk/video/vice-zinedine-zidane-shares-his-world-cup-memories/5b3b81eebe407726cc522301

Vidacs, B. (2011). Banal Nationalism, Football, and Discourse Community in Africa. *Studies in Ethnicity and Nationalism, 11*(1), 25–41. https://doi.org/10.1111/j.1754-9469.2011.01105.x

Weber, E. (1976). *Peasants into Frenchmen: The Modernization of Rural France, 1870–1914* (1st ed.). Stanford, CA: Stanford University Press.

Williams, J. (2017). *Games Without Frontiers: Football, Identity and Modernity*. New York: Routledge.

Yoshino, K. (1992). *Consuming Ethnicity and Nationalism: Asian Experiences*. London: Wiley.

Zimmer, O. (2003). Boundary Mechanisms and Symbolic Resources: Towards a Process-Oriented Approach to National Identity. *Nations and Nationalism, 9*(2), 173–193. https://doi.org/10.1111/1469-8219.00081

7

Conclusions on French Muslims

7.1 Situating Conclusions in the Broader Field of Muslim Studies in the Diaspora

This book set out to open up the discussion of the contemporary situation of French Muslims by contrasting the highly exceptional with the extraordinarily banal. This set up a contrasting picture during the Charlie Hebdo shooting of two French Muslims committing an act of mass killing, while millions of others went about their daily business and performed far more banal and positive social roles in France. As such, this point of departure was designed to demonstrate that the acts of the very few can discursively obscure the integration of the many. Thus in the aftermath of this, and other, Islamist attacks in France, the whirlwind of social media campaigns such as #jesuischarlie, discussions of the need to defend liberty, and marches by world leaders can obscure the fact that there are many more French Muslims serving in the French security services than there are French Muslim jihadis (Roy, 2015). This is partially attributable to the need for the news media to report the exceptional as by definition this is their job. However, from a sociological perspective it is necessary to understand that French Muslims are not only an extremely

© The Author(s) 2019
J. Downing, *French Muslims in Perspective*,
https://doi.org/10.1007/978-3-030-16103-3_7

diverse group but also that they are actually very well integrated and play a wide range of important roles in French society. Building on this observation of their diversity and banality, they cannot be simple understood by examining overtly 'Muslim' or 'Islamic' themes, events or issues.

Paradoxically, attempting to study Muslims simply through the lens of them as Muslims, with Muslim concerns, who express their identity and concerns through Islamic idioms is in fact highly essentialising and quite dangerous. This is because, like any other identity category, being a 'Muslim' will only ever be one aspect of an individual's experiences, identity and social relations, and trying to 'flatten' the question of European Muslims into one plane misses the importance of the multidimensional nature of the continent's Muslim populations. In a similar vein, it would not make sense to study any aspect of 'Frenchness' or the 'English' only using either remarkable events, such as acts of violence, or simply when they mobilise or express themselves in nationalist idioms. This would likely seriously skew the population studied towards those of quite extreme political and nationalist views. The same is true of minority populations, and therefore to understand French Muslims in any kind of meaningful way it is necessary to understand not only how discourse is constructed around them as Muslims, but also as citizens of France, football supporters, music fans and public servants. This book has sought to purposely cast its empirical net as wide as possible to consider this diversity of social roles which Muslims occupy. Additionally, it has been a central conceptual underpinning of this book that to understand French Muslims, one must consider the class, ethno-racial and gendered ways which intersect to not only objectively constitute a diverse population, but also which subjectively go into the means by which they are, and have been, socially constructed within the broader national narrative. This demonstrates the far more important point that the way in which minorities are constructed over time changes dramatically. One of the key inspirations for the genesis of my academic career, when I was seeking to write a PhD proposal on Marseille in 2008, was the then newly published book by Alec Hargreaves (2007), *Multi-Ethnic France*. In this, Hargreaves' focus on ethnicity, and the diversity of it, as the primary means of analysing the contemporary French situation was not only extremely insightful, but also mirrored the discourse in France up to that point, which had been dominated by ethnicity as a key means by which the future of France was debated. Here, the Marche des Beurs in 1983, which led to the founding of 'SOS Racisme', and the use of the term 'racaille' by Sarkozy to describe the rioters in 2005, demonstrate the primacy of race and class in the discussion of diversity in France at that point. Fast forward ten years and added to this mix has been a focused discussion of the same diversity, and the broader issue it poses for the future of France is framed as 'Islamic' and 'Muslim'.

This does not mean that the class and ethno-racial aspects of the discourse have disappeared, rather they have had a layer of religion grafted on top of them as a way to modernise and unify the subjective and unproven threat that 'diversity' poses to France under the Islamic banner. This also plays directly into the French system where the specificities of the secular system enable those of minority religions to be particularly vulnerable to marginalisation (Alba, 2005). Indeed, in constructing French Muslims as Muslim first and foremost, and as highly attached to their religion, it almost seems that the concerns of xenophobes such as Marine Le Pen and Éric Zemmour about French Muslims are actually legitimate objective commentaries on how to preserve a secular system in the face of religious zealotry. Two observations emerge from this that are key in challenging these voices, which unfortunately shout rather loud in France—being Catholic did not stop the xenophobic construction of an 'Italian Invasion' in the nineteenth century in France, and otherness and threat have been constructed in a variety of ways historically in France. This is an observation that was not lost on the French Jews such as Alfred Dreyfus, who brought French anti-semitism into focus four decades before French collaborators would aid the Nazis in exterminating French Jewry. Secondly, it has been precisely to subvert this discourse around the exceptional, and threat-posing nature of French Muslims that this book has chosen to speak of French Muslims over and above other means to discuss this diverse social group. It is hoped that through a wide-ranging discussion of the ways in which French Muslims play important roles in French society has demonstrated that they are not quite so exceptional or threatening after all. Thus, the key take-home message is that French

Muslims, like any other social group are sociologically very interesting—but 'exceptional', 'other' and 'threatening' they are not.

7.2   Conclusions on the State and the Republic

These assertions about the lack of exceptionality find an important reflection in an unexpected place in this book—the relations between the French state and notions of religious and ethnic difference. This is because, while France is often still constructed as a unique case of a democracy that is very strictly assimilationist, the reality is actually much more complex. This is not to say that this book makes the argument that the republic does explicitly recognise these kinds of differences, but on close inspection neither does it strictly *not* do so. Here it is important to think not of a single 'republic' that has a position on ethno-religious difference as it may seem on the surface, but rather as a situation where a plurality of semi-autonomous 'republics' find themselves in a variety of political, social and economic situations that require them to formulate policies on ethnic and religious differences in a variety of ways, but overwhelmingly in positions of political solitude. Thus, here many republics exist in a situation of many political solitudes. Indeed, a good starting point when seeking to understand why there is such a diversity of means by which the French state deals with questions of ethnicity and religion can actually be traced back to the provision in the constitution which is the central legal edict from which assimilation stems. Here, laïcité and a ban on the collection of ethnic statistics both come from the constitutional commitment to 'ensure the equality of all citizens before the law, without distinction of origin, race or religion. It shall respect all beliefs' (Assemblé Nationale, 2018). This is actually a foundational statement that is remarkable for being extremely vague from its outset and thus open to significant differences in interpretation in the abstract, let alone when it is used in an applied setting such as the daily political and social practices of a complex polity.

Previous conceptions of the diversity of state policy responses at the national level are limited in their scope (Raymond & Modood, 2007).

Even when scholars have taken into account the particularly diverse local level of the French state, conceptualising policy innovation as territorial affirmative action (Doytcheva, 2007), bureaucratic pluralism (Dunn, 1995) or 'multiple states, multiple republics' (Downing, 2015), they still fail to capture the complex political solitudes that exist between these levels of governance and the national level of the republic. Here, because policy innovations are overwhelmingly occurring in complete isolation from each other, they can be seen as examples of political solitudes (inter alia Oliver, 1999; Rice, 2009). On a more macro level, this more nuanced understanding of many republics existing in situations of many solitudes seeks to challenge and nuance grander ideas in the political field that saw France as the archetype of the civic nation (Safran, 1991; Todorov & Anzalone, 1989). Clearly, this book is not unique here as much of this work has been done already (a particularly insightful example can be found in Zimmer, 2003). However, much of this previous work ignores other breaks in colour-blind republicanism, such as the persecution of Jews during the Second World War and the racial hierarchies which were created under the French empire (Camiscioli, 2009). These are often neglected in both 'official' state accounts of French nationalism as well as nationalism scholarship, but these are important examples of how this vague commitment to equality is far more malleable and tenuous than it seems on the surface. Thus, not only is French assimilation more flexible in the contemporary era than it seems, but also has been very malleable historically, with disastrous consequences for those in Africa considered unable to 'evolve' into Frenchmen, for the internal other Jews who quickly found that colour-blind equality could also exclude them, and for the women that the original 'rights of man' did not see as fit for universal suffrage. Thus, rather than being an unflinching crusader for universal justice, the French republic, like any other political system, has its historical failings and contradictions, which should be kept in mind by those who seek to defend its eternal usefulness and socio-political perfection in the present day.

Moving back to more contemporary dynamics of the many republics, the analysis of state bodies does offer some important insights in the contemporary era into how the republic continues to change, morph and bend, depending on the contingencies of the time and the more general fickle tastes of successive governments. Here, the creation of France's first national Muslim and Black associations in collaboration with the central government are important means by which we can see that, given the political will, the republic can show some multicultural tendencies (Modood, 2007). However, these analyses miss the complexity of the dynamics of assimilation at the national level. Various incarnations of the French state operate with significant autonomy at the national level, and even come into conflict with other parts of the republic and overturn local interpretations of laïcité in rare instances where different facets of the republic intrude into each other's solitudes. The national council of state overturning the regional 'burkini bans' is an example of this, where it ruled that these bans were unconstitutional.

Examining the local level of state shows that this ability of the many republics to be flexible in the ways that it facilitates difference oriental policies is quite remarkable. However, the local level of the many republics also demonstrates that paradoxically with the freedom provided by solitude comes much vulnerability. Those that benefit from close relations with the local republic to implement policy innovation do so in an extremely risky setting where, should the winds of fortune change direction, they find that their political solitude leaves them with little to no recourse to political, financial and or logistical support. From a discursive perspective this is particularly important as an example discussed here shows that simply a polemic around financial irregularities, with no judicial findings of wrong-doing, was enough to bring a voluntary association to its closure and France's only public commemoration of Eid Al Kabir to an end. The clientelist relationship between the UFM13 and a socialist politician, and the resulting unfounded allegations of corruption, resulted in the retrenchment of the L'Aïd dans la Cité festival. This was not only unique in France as a public commemoration of Eid, but also unique because it was funded by the local state. It was not even issues around violating secularism and assimilation that sunk this initiative, but rather the murky nature of local politics in the Bouches-du-Rhône.

However, operating locally in political solitude also brings with it other kinds of vulnerabilities. Discursively, it can be enough to be the subject of a polemic concerning your theoretical violation of assimilation to derail a local project which previously had political support. Again, here operating in conditions of solitude, even with the direct support of the local mayor, policy innovators have no recourse to real or rhetorical support of higher authorities. This kind of discursive vulnerability has been demonstrated by the association Les Oranges of Nanterre. Here, even when operating with significant material and political support from the local mayor, discursive and polemical allegations of violating assimilation resulted in the cancelling of the naming of a high school after a French Algerian sociologist. This would have been the first high school in France named after someone of North African origin. This retrenchment did not even require the accusation of breaking any formal law—just that this action in some diffuse and ill-defined way went against assimilationist dogma. Thus, we can see here how assimilation is discursively a double-edged sword whereby one can violate it when using the name of a Frenchman of Muslim origin, whereas such an allegation would be implausible for a similar situation with a man of Breton or Basque origin, even though technically recognising those differences would also be in violation of assimilation.

Adding to this complexity are the political solitudes created by the intrusion of European government and norms into France, which are in some important ways in direct opposition to assimilation. It is worth noting that France stands as an anomaly in Europe for not implementing European legislation for the protection of national minority rights for linguistic and regional minority groups. However, such legislation at the European level is ill conceived when it comes to the issue of when 'migrant' communities become national minorities in a formal sense, as those of post-colonial origin, while numbering the millions, would still not be considered national minorities even if they have ancestry in the country for more than half a century. However, like the many republics, there are also many Europes, which engage with questions of ethnic and religious difference in varying ways, and there are indeed forms of European government which take post-migration difference as not only of central importance in discussions of diversity, but also which make funding for large projects conditional on recognising and valorising these forms of difference.

This is relevant because difference in norms extends into more immediate daily practices of statehood. This is because local parts of the French state or local NGOs must engage with and satisfy these norms when seeking to access European funding as a means to engage local minority and migrant communities, a number of whom are French Muslims. This can take extremely diverse forms, both in terms of the institutional set-ups involved and in the scale of European spending, whether at the micro or macro level. These two scales of analysis generate paradoxical results. It forces some of the many republics to engage with pluralist norms, but European involvement is no panacea because although it does allow the local state or local NGOs to exit political solitudes, it rather works to trap them in new forms of solitude. The joining of the Intercultural Cities programme by Lyon is an important example of how this works on a large scale, where the city joined a CoE programme whose basic principle is to not only recognise different cultures, but also to celebrate and valorise cultural diversity. However, this resulted in significant conflict with the local bureaucratic cultures for whom the idea of valorising diversity is alien. While this was expressed in the frustration of a local NGO who took part in this work to valorise local diversity, it did not render their work nor the ICP involvement in Lyon completely moribund. It did, however, mean that the NGO was not able to transcend their local audience and spread their work further, and rather left them entrapped in a new form of political solitude where European involvement briefly brought them into the wider public realm, but then did not allow them to fully transcend into the mainstream. At the micro level, the project analysed here as an example of a small-scale European involvement in policy towards French Muslims demonstrates the issues with the onerous conditions placed on small-scale projects by the weight of European audit norms. While EU funding enabled BGE PaRIF to employ two enterprise advisers to give minority communities advice on setting up businesses as a way around unemployment, the precarity of such funding and the significant administrative burden incurred in applying for, and even in getting, such funding significantly limited the ability of this form of policy innovation to transcend the political solitude of the local.

In light of these findings, it is necessary to remain nuanced in one's understanding and analysis of how the republic relates to the French Muslim population. It is also clear that the republic relates to French Muslims in a number of ways—whether ethnically in terms as them as black, or culturally as Algerians or geographically through forms of territorial affirmative action. Thus, not only are the many republics not the ideal types of civic governance that they may seem, but the ways by which they defy the civic typology are also varied, dynamic but all too often confined to the solitude of their specific setting.

7.3   Conclusions on War, Colonies and Security Forces

This idea of the many republics existing in many solitudes could also be applied to the experience of Muslims serving in the French security forces. This is because the army is one of the only institutions with a formal exception from laïcité. However, this observation merely skims the surface of the much greater analytical challenges that the analysis of the role of French Muslims in security forces in both a contemporary and historical perspective poses. Pertinent and building on the numerical demographic questions that are never far away from discussions of French Muslims, it has been asserted that there are many more French Muslims today serving the republic's security needs than have joined jihadist groups, which Roy (2015) estimates is at least an order of magnitude larger. This is, however, historically nothing remarkable as Muslim troops have defended the physical integrity and ideological basis of the republic for several centuries—in roles as diverse as fighting for the territorial integrity of the French empire and also being central to the liberation of mainland France from the Nazis. It should be noted that while a number of those of white French origin collaborated with the Nazis to undermine French values and deport French Jews to concentration camps, it was Muslim soldiers alongside those white French of the Resistance and soldiers from other French colonies that liberated the hexagon and restored liberty, equality and fraternity. This does not mean, however, that the commemoration of Muslim service to the republic has been straightforward, or that the French army itself did not contain notions of racial hierarchy and the inferiority of the colonial other— which it did.

This is where the primary focus turned to analysing the discourses created by the commemoration of Muslim service to the French security services, both in historical and contemporary incarnations, ranging from imperial stone monuments to the narratives created in contemporary news and social media. It is fundamental here to acknowledge the difficulties and nuances present in doing this, because it is not enough to understand just the circumstances around the Muslims that served and continue to serve in the French security services, it has also been important to understand how the meanings, contexts of, and indeed location of such commemorations have changed over time.

This is particularly relevant in the current epoch, where public recognition of religious or ethnic difference is such a taboo because many of the historical sites of commemoration that exist to Muslim troops in France, particularly those erected in the wake of the Muslim contribution to the effort in the First World War, also demonstrate that at times France has not been so hostile to publicly acknowledging religious and ethnic differences. This is rendered even more paradoxical, given that the racial hierarchies of the colonies constructed those African Muslims that served the republic as less equal and therefore less free than Europeans, while their service received significant attention in the works of bronze and stone that were created in France and its overseas colonies. There have also been significant contributions made by French Muslims which have gone un-commemorated or have received commemoration many years after the fact. Perhaps most tragically concerning the Harkis, Muslim soldiers that fought for the French in Algeria, who were prevented from migrating to France on Algerian independence with many being tortured to death—while the French state spent large amounts of money repatriating bronze and stone war memorials from Algeria. Thus, while the formal hierarchies of the colonial order saw the North African Muslim as the least likely to be able to 'evolve' into a Frenchman, the informal racial hierarchy created by these events demonstrates that they were also considered to be below pieces of metal and stone in their importance to the mid-twentieth-century French state. The dynamics of this process is illustrated here with the journey of the monument of the dead of Oran, erected in Oran and then moved to a suburb of Lyon on independence, while humans that had served the imperial interests of the French empire were left behind to die. However, this does not mean that these monuments are merely contemporary incarnations of the tragedies of imperial wars, but rather are redefined and re-appropriated by French Muslims as symbols of home and place making. The monument to the dead of the orient on the corniche of Marseille demonstrates this by being included on the cover of an album of a Muslim French rap group as a key symbol of their home city. As such, the meanings and connotations of memorials to those of Muslim origin who gave their life for France remain dynamic and ever changing.

The broader conceptual discussion of the commemoration of Muslims in service of the republic was then opened up by going beyond stone and bronze to examining the way that contemporary contributions of Muslims to the security of France are constructed in new forms of media. Given that the state does not formally count or release statistics about the number or nature of the current Muslim contribution to the defence and security of France, the unfortunate fact of death in service is one of the few ways that discourse about Muslims emerges in this domain. This represents one of the only times where the discursive monochrome of the republic slips, and colour and richness is in the forms of names, origins and personal details of those serving the republic. This process, while important and insightful, does not come without its own problems. This is because those Muslims who die in the service of the republic in the contemporary era risk being constructed as 'ideal' Muslim victims, against which other less ideal Muslims can be judged—thus re-enforcing the good/bad Muslim dichotomy. Nowhere is this perhaps more problematic than in the Twitter data analysed for #jesuisahmed, which emerged during the Charlie Hebdo attacks to commemorate the Muslim police officer who died while on duty. These 'bottom-up' creations of vernacular commemorative memory draw heavily on notions of Ahmed being defined by his service to the French nation, and upholding the liberal ideals of democracy and free speech. These are three features of France which French Muslims are frequently charged with undermining and thus justifying narratives that have depicted French Muslims as some kind of problem that needs control and regulation. However, once again the posthumous construction of Ahmed in this way risks the creation of the ideal victim—a 'good' Muslim against whom other Muslims can be measured. These discussions of terror and victimhood, however, have far larger relevance to contemporary French politics because of the wave of jihadist attacks in France that began with Mohammed Merah in 2012 and reached its crescendo with the horrific Paris attacks on 13 November 2015.

7.4   Conclusions on Jihadism, Causality, Victimhood and French Muslims

This book has also sought to demonstrate that understanding French jihadism, and indeed the discursive constructions around it, is no simple task, regardless of the arguments made by politicians, xenophobes and worryingly academics to the contrary. To understand the complexities and nuances of the recent wave of jihadist violence in France it is necessary to move away from the problem-solving orientation of early terrorism studies and embrace the uncertainties around causality. One would be quite justified in making an argument that, given the ineffectiveness of the huge amount of resources expended in diverse programmes trying to understand and eradicate Islamist terrorism in the past decades, a magical 'silver bullet' solution does not exist. Bringing this observation back to the French context, the first step in this analysis is to deconstruct the theories that have emerged to explain French jihadism which seek to make erroneous casual claims. Using the deconstructivist tools of CTS demonstrates that paternalistic explanations relying on France's colonial history and structural arguments about jihadism being a function of France's dysfunctional domestic politics do not hold water. This stems from these theories essentialising and homogenising the French Muslim population, which is actually extremely diverse socially, culturally and doctrinally. Thus, it is not sufficient to say that all Muslims, like all French people, receive and respond to social situations of historical wrongs in the same way, least not in ways that lead to mass violence. The huge number of French people, Muslims and non-Muslims, who experience poverty, racism and disagree with France's colonial history demonstrate that jihadism remains a statistical anomaly in France which defies broad generalisations. Making broad causal claims inadvertently securitises French Muslims even further, because these arguments are centred on the idea that the root cause of politically motivated mass murder inadvertently makes every socially marginalised Muslim a potential terrorist, waiting for a cue to self-radicalise and commit acts of violence.

Turning this causal equation on its head, this book's discussion of French jihadism also seeks to highlight how one of the reasons that recent attacks have been so brutally effective in creating mass casualties is because of the far more banal failings of the French state in the realm of security. This can be understood by outlining the more general features of the security landscape that contribute to French jihadism operating and being so deadly and effective. Institutionally, the French state was overly complex and bureaucratic in its approach to monitoring a range of terror threats, which enabled the networks involved, transnational in nature as they were, to plan and carry out attacks on French soil. Additionally, the French state has an extremely poor record in dealing with banal security concerns and has thus presided over the proliferation of heavy-grade military weapons onto the streets of French cities through organised crime networks. Thus, without the availability of Kalashnikov assault rifles it is unlikely that the gunmen in the Charlie Hebdo and the 2015 Paris attacks would have been able to inflict such mass casualties on the French public.

A discussion of casualties also opens up a discussion of another way that jihadi terrorism can be nuanced in France by examining the narratives created by Muslim victimhood in these attacks. In a similar way to death in service being one of the few ways in which narratives about French Muslims in the security services emerge, victimhood in terror events is one of the ways in which the biographical details of French Muslims emerge in the broader media narrative. These banal details of French Muslim lives exposed by victimhood open up significant aspects for the nuancing of Muslim group identity in a context where both those on the far right of European politics and the fringes of Muslim extremism set up a dichotomy where Islamic values do not allow Muslims to integrate into European society. The opposite is demonstrated by the biographical details which emerge, because they demonstrate the lack of peculiarity of Muslims in professional positions in society.

These profiles in text and pictures demonstrate, as a collection, the 'broad church' of everyday activities that Muslims undertake in Europe, which goes a long way to nuancing group identity and thus making it difficult for a 'Muslim terrorists versus European society' dichotomy to be plausible and sustained in popular discourse. This does not mean that these are not assertions that can be made in unproblematic ways. Rather, this analysis opened up a broader discussion about how class can contribute to the construction/deconstruction of the good/bad Muslim dichotomy. This further demonstrates that it is not possible to understand Muslims in the diaspora without examining a range of social categories including class and gender. An example of this is how the 'good' economically active Muslim who dies in central Paris during a terror attack can contrast sharply with those in suburbs without such economic opportunities who may be forced to rely on the grey or black economy to survive. This is of particular relevance when the life histories of several notable French jihadists demonstrate a life trajectory not necessarily replete with religious piety, but one that has involved significant time spent committing petty crimes. Thus, discursively discussing the question of the good/bad Muslim dichotomy goes beyond religious piety and political views, and also needs to be considered from a far broader range of social positions. This is also relevant when thinking about the role of gendered norms and how the images which connect to these profiles depict the Muslim victims of jihadist violence. The death in these attacks of women who wear the Muslim veil, in addition to working-class men who bear resemblance to jihadists, further demonstrates that Muslim victimhood complicates both understandings of these events but also how French Muslims are related to them. Highlighting these women as victims of jihadi violence alongside a diverse range of their co-citizens, in their roles as mothers and active participants, goes against the grain of narratives which situate the wearing of the veil as a means of expressing one's separateness from French society.

7.5   Conclusions on Gender and French Muslims

However, it is again extremely limiting to examine gender and French Muslims from the perspective of the overtly Muslim, such as discussing issues around the headscarf. This is not to say that these debates lack significance, but rather that they only tell one small part of the story of the way that gender and Muslimness come together in French context. Even mainstream forms of political organisation by French Muslim women, such as the founding of NPNS, occur outside of an overt framing as forms of Islamic mobilisation. This further demonstrates issues with discussions of forms of 'Islamic' feminism which are deeply essentialising. Indeed, more recent forms of mobilisation around feminist platforms of anti-racism, in the case of the Parti des Indigènes de la République, which directly address issues such as the banning of the veil, do so from a position which fuses anti-colonial ideas with Islamic concerns. Thus, even here a far broader range of influences and frames are applied to Muslim issues than simply understanding such movements as forms of 'Islamic' feminism can provide. Rather these are specific mobilisations, that while involving Muslims and directly engaging with overtly Muslims issues, are very much products of the specifics of the French context. These observations set up the broader analytical point about gender that seeking to understand it requires casting the net much wider than simply overtly Muslim-framed issues. Popular culture provides an important means by which further understanding can be gleaned about how orientalist forms of gender construction occur, and how ideas about culture being a key lens through which one can gaze at the other can be applied in a very contemporary sense. In this case, it is an internal other, which rather than existing in exotic poses in hammams, harems and deserts, does so against a backdrop of the concrete forms of the French suburban estate. This context, which is as much constituted by geographical, class and ethnoracial markers, exists as a world apart that mainstream French society is fascinated with, but has no direct experience of, nor is ever likely to have. Wacquant (2007) discusses this in terms of Paris being a 'dual city' of city proper and poor suburbs which exist apart, and which create a line across which few transgress. This operates in an imaginary sense, where the curiosity about this parallel, 'savage' world creates a market for cultural forms which offer the outside the ability to gaze into this weird and mysterious world through the safety of a screen.

This is highlighted by the popularity of pornography in France, which allows the viewer to gaze on the erotic nature of the 'beurette' or the French-born women of North African origin. However, examining these films does not just enable, as scholars have argued for many years (inter alia Williams, 1989), an understanding of the nature of contemporary sexual relations. Analysing these films in the vein of the critical cultural turn in society enables a much broader analysis of the power and cultural relations in society. Here, digging deeper than just the erotic nature of these films enables an understanding of the ways in which Muslim women are constructed in a much wider sense, even when they are not name checked as 'Muslim', but rather are presented in ethnic and classed based terms as the young, sexually exploitable and available women of the housing estates. The plot lines situate these women as highly sexualised and using their sexuality to escape the immediate surroundings of the socio-economically deprived housing estate, while at the same time showing their passivity vis-à-vis Muslim men. However, in other contexts more is overtly made of their exotic origins, where the women discuss their origins and perform belly dances to exhibit their oriental eroticism. This demonstrates that Muslim femininity and eroticism contain a number of properties where class, geographical residency and form of exotified North African culture all come to typify the erotic appeal of the feminine form of the internal other.

However, it is not just feminine forms which are exotified in ways which echo previous orientalist gendered themes. Masculinities are also important in creating narratives about contemporary French Muslims, but in rather different ways. Here, even in erotic films the men are not eroticised per se, but are rather constructed in ways which reflect nineteenth-century orientalist themes about the savage nature of the oriental man. While men play marginal roles compared to the women in these films, owing to them being produced for a heterosexual market, they do however perform roles which show them being controlling and misogynistic. They verbally harass, exploit and control the Muslim women, demonstrating how such films reproduce the problematic stereotypes of Muslim men in France as something women need to be protected from (Guénif-Souilamas & Macé, 2006).

These themes of the savage oriental man are further deployed in more 'mainstream' forms of French culture. Analysing season two of the hit TV series 'Engranages' offers an insight into how forms of masculine criminality, long constructed vis-à-vis ethnic minorities in France, have become 'Islamised'. While the idea of the working-class, minority ethnic criminal 'racaille' has long been a common trope in France, even used by Nicolas Sarkozy during his tenure as interior minister, it was one which was largely secular. Here, while these young men were criminal and of minority ethnic extraction, they were not specifically 'Muslim' per se. As scholars have discussed both the Islamisation of Muslim communities in France (G. Kepel, 2012) and the increased focus on 'Muslims' in the discourse as security threats (Jocelyne Cesari, 2013), it appears that cultural output is also following suit in constructing minority ethnic origin criminals as 'Muslim gangsters'. The criminals in the material analysed are not just of North African origin, but also give money to an Imam to build a new mosque, and are seen torturing a rival in the basement while a family gathering goes on upstairs. As such, following on from other cultural contexts where criminals have been constructed as having specific backgrounds, such as the African-American and Italian-American gangster in the USA (Chan, 1998; Mason, 2002), in the French cultural landscape there is an emergence of a particularly Muslim form of gangster. Linking this back to themes from the orientalist paintings of the nineteenth century, the 'savage' Arab cavalry man in the desert has been replaced by the 'savage' criminal of the concrete suburbs. This discussion of both masculinity and femininity in relation to French Muslims demonstrated that orientalism is not only alive and well, but also is a dynamic process which has adapted and changed in form, if not substance, when constructions are made about Muslims as the internal other in the diaspora. Although contemporary forms of culture have replaced the harem, hammam and desert with the concrete housing estate, this does not render the depictions any less problematic.

7.6 Conclusions on French Muslims and Cultural Nationalism

This discussion of gendered forms of discourse vis-à-vis French Muslims opens up a much broader discussion about the wide range of ways in which they are constructed. The penultimate chapter of this book demonstrated that there is a far broader range of ways that French Muslims feature in the re-creation of French national identity than simply when they are name checked as 'Muslims'. Rather, the widespread participation in all facets of French society, from the creation and dissemination of popular culture to playing key roles in the French national football team, demonstrates that French Muslims are enmeshed in the very fabric of Frenchness. Thus, they are not simply an 'add on' that features in marginal discussions that clearly signpost themselves as instances of discussing Muslim integration but are rather central in a range of domains. The paradoxes of the construction of French national identity thus operate in exclusionary ways for French Muslims alongside, and at the same time as, other post-colonial minority groups. When examining the re-creation of nationhood at the intersection of politics and culture, Zimmer (2003) demonstrates the range of ways that these paradoxes of nationhood can be observed and analysed. This was an important observation because it takes this book in a cyclical way back to build on the observations of the second chapter on French Muslims and the state. This is because an analysis of the state only as the means by which narratives of exclusion or inclusion from the national narrative is extremely limited, and therefore this analysis of how processes which occur at the intersection of politics and culture sits as complementary to the earlier analysis in Chap. 1. Thus, as the state can work in contradictory ways in accommodating religious and ethnic difference in ways that contravene certain interpretations of laïcité, public culture, which is not governed by the formal rules of the state, nevertheless can work to exclude French Muslims.

The three examples discussed show the multitude of ways in which these paradoxes of French national identity reconstruction take place, demonstrating the diversity of ways in which narratives of exclusion emerge around themes that in other contexts have paradoxically been integrated as important parts of the French national story. The key differences are not necessarily in the substance but rather in the form—namely that those contexts in which phenomena are constructed as outside the norms of the national story are those which involve participation by those who are French of minority ethnic origin. This is important to understand because marginalisation in France occurs for much more diverse groups than French Muslims. The rioters of 2005 were extremely diverse in their social and ethnic make up. However, the paradox of national identity emerges in the reaction to, and coverage of, these riots. On the surface it seems clear that such an anti-systemic action would be, and possibly even normatively should be, condemned and constructed as outside of the national narrative. However, the paradox here can only be seen in comparative perspective, where other events of anti-systemic direct political action, from the revolution of 1789 to the riots of May 1968, have been incorporated in a history that defines such direct action as a key part of Frenchness. Additionally, it is not just the fact that the 2005 riots have not found their place alongside these other events in the national narrative that demonstrates the de facto ethnicisation of Frenchness in the public cultural sphere, but rather the racialised way in which they were covered. This demonstrates the primacy of the 'othering' of the rioters in 2005 on ethnic, racial and religious grounds, even when white French rioters took part and that mobilisation did not occur around religious or ethnic concerns. Indeed, the rioters of 2005 shared many of the revolutionary ideals that are celebrated in France in their detestation of oppression and socio-economic marginalisation.

The paradoxes of French national identity construction for those of minority ethnic origin, French Muslims among them, was demonstrated in the construction of French rap as a threat to social order when France has traditionally accepted and celebrated a diversity of cultural expression. France has never shied away from embracing and celebrating artists who produce controversial material or lead controversial lives—whether this is epitomised in the 'belle époque' lives of painters such as Henri de Toulouse-Lautrec, or the more contemporary lives of controversial artists of immigrant origin such as Serge Gainsbourg. The paradox emerges here in the reception and coverage of French rap music, which has been one of the commercially most popular art forms in contemporary France. However, it has been the subject of several legal cases about the freedom of expression of rap artists in ways that other art forms have not. While clearly not all French rappers are of French Muslim origin, a number of the most prominent are. Additionally, rap has been an important form of public culture which has been one of the few open to expressions of Islamic idioms and themes, and where it has been possible to make commentaries on multicultural French life. Thus, here politics has got involved in a field of culture outside of the boundaries of the state to attempt to define French rap, its subjects, idioms and artists as legally unacceptable to the norms of French artistic expression.

This marginalisation of French Muslims on ethnic grounds continues in the paradoxical discussions around the French national football team. In the 20 years between its two World Cup triumphs in 1998 and 2018, the ethnic origin of the team members has been questioned both in success and defeat. Again, not a solely French Muslim domain, a number of the great and good of both French World Cup winning teams were born or converted French Muslims. Additionally, when victorious, the French national team has been constructed as an almost exceptional vehicle of socio-economic and personal advancement to those of post-migrant origin, especially those of poor socio-economic status. However, closer inspection of the time of the World Cup wins and also the 'lean' years when the team was not successful, demonstrates the paradoxical means whereby even the national team is subject to critique and construction that marginalises those of non-white backgrounds. While the cases of this paradoxical construction of national identity are unfortunately plural, one that stands out is the controversial proposal to have quotas for ethnic minority players to limit their number in the team. The irony of such a proposal made in such an important national body, while refusing to create positive quotas to fight socio-economic discrimination, is clear. However, going deeper it is emblematic of broader existential discussions around the national team and its 'Frenchness' being compromised by being 'too black'. Here we can see another way in which cultural and politics intersect to create a national identity which is de facto racialising and exclusionary under the de jure umbrella of radical colour-blind equality.

The discussion of the paradoxes of French national identity construction was the final empirical example that points to the bigger theoretical contribution that this book seeks to make to the broader discussion of the sociology of Muslims in the diaspora. Rather than studying French Muslims simply as the subject of 'securitised' forms of narratives and emergency politics, this book has aimed to show that the key concerns facing French Muslims, and indeed those that are likely to face them, and France itself over the next 20 years are deeply rooted in the banal. Whether this is in discussions of the construction of gender in popular culture or why jihadism has been able to exploit the vectors of insecurity which exist in France to such deadly ends, these problems and the solutions to them are rooted in the daily. Whether this is the construction of French Muslims in orientalist ways in public culture, or the ongoing pervasive daily insecurity in the French suburbs, neither rely on, nor indeed confirm, a grand narrative that France and its Muslims are indeed locked in an unending 'intifada'. Just as the clash of civilisations has proved to be overstated in the international system, the current situation in France is not an internal 'clash of civilisations', but rather Muslims are integral parts of French society in a range of roles. Directions for future research could go many ways from here, but this book has sought to be a kind of rallying call to scholars to think outside the box and to look for Muslims in the diaspora in places where they may not be obviously labelled as such to demonstrate their striking normality in Western societies. While there may well be clear political, economic and even academic incentives to sensationalise the Muslim presence in Western countries, and indeed even present the current situation as an 'intifada' with a clear historical and cultural trajectory from the Kasbah of Algiers to the Bataclan concert hall, we should be careful before we embark on the creation of such narratives. Rather than being locked in confrontation, French Muslims have been defining their relationship to their Frenchness for hundreds of years, and continue to define it, as liberty, equality and fraternity—just like other French citizens. Taking this back to one of the first examples used in this book, and one that is particularly close to my heart, demonstrates that an intifada or a long war between France and 'its Arabs' is myth and not reality. This example is the warm relations between the staff and customers in the couscous restaurants of my adopted home city of Marseille. Here, in one of the great social institutions of daily French life, French, Muslim, Christian, Jewish and atheist sit arm to arm to arm, enjoying a simple meal and perhaps even complaining that the merguez were better last week in that other place just around the corner.

Bibliography

Alba, R. (2005). Bright vs. Blurred Boundaries: Second-Generation Assimilation and Exclusion in France, Germany, and the United States. *Ethnic and Racial Studies, 28*(1), 20–49.

Assemblé Nationale. (2018). *Welcome to the English Website of the French National Assembly – Assemblée Nationale.* Retrieved August 21, 2018, from http://www2.assemblee-nationale.fr/langues/welcome-to-the-english-website-of-the-french-national-assembly

Camiscioli, E. (2009). *Reproducing the French Race: Immigration, Intimacy and Embodiment in the Early Twentieth Century.* Durham, NC: Duke University Press.

Cesari, J. (2013). European Conundrum: Integration of Muslims or Securitisation of Islam? *World Review.* Retrieved from https://berkleycenter.georgetown.edu/essays/european-conundrum-integration-of-muslims-or-securitisation-of-islam

Chan, K. (1998). The Construction of Black Male Identity in Black Action Films of the Nineties. *Cinema Journal, 37*(2), 35–48. https://doi.org/10.2307/1225641

Downing, J. (2015). Understanding the (Re) Definition of Nationhood in French Cities: A Case of Multiple States and Multiple Republics. *Studies in Ethnicity and Nationalism, 15*(2), 336–351.

Doytcheva, M. (2007). *Une discrimination positive à la Française? Ethnicité et territoire dans les politiques de la ville.* Paris: Broché.

Dunn, J. (1995). The French Highway Lobby: A Case Study in State-Society Relations and Policymaking. *Comparative Politics, 27,* 3–275.

Guénif-Souilamas, N., & Macé, E. (2006). *Les féministes et le garçon arabe.* La Tour-d'Aigues (Vaucluse): Editions de l'Aube.

Hargreaves, A. (2007). *Multi-Ethnic France: Immigration, Politics, Culture and Society* (2nd ed.). New York; London: Routledge.

Kepel, G. (2012). *Banlieue de la République.* Paris: Institut Montaigne.

Mason, F. (2002). *American Gangster Cinema: From 'Little Caesar' to 'Pulp Fiction'.* Berlin: Springer.

Modood, T. (2007). *Multiculturalism: A Civic Idea.* London: Polity Press.

Oliver, P. (1999). Canada's Two Solitudes: Constitutional and International Law in Reference re Secession of Quebec. *International Journal on Minority and Group Rights, 6*(1), 65–95. https://doi.org/10.1163/15718119920907640

Raymond, G., & Modood, T. (2007). *The Construction of Minority Identities in France and Britain*. London: Palgrave.

Rice, K. (2009). *Must There Be Two Solitudes? Language Activists and Linguists Working Together*. J. Reyhner & L Lockard (eds.), Indigenous Language Revitalization: Encouragement, Guidance, and Lessons Learned, pp. 37–59. Flagstaff, AZ: Northern Arizona University. http://jan.ucc.nau.edu/~jar/ILR/ILR-4.pdf.

Roy, O. (2015, January 10). *There Are More French Muslims Working for French Security Than for Al Qaeda*. Retrieved September 1, 2018, from https://www.huffingtonpost.com/olivier-roy/paris-attack-muslim-cliches_b_6445582.html

Safran, W. (1991). State, Nation, National Identity, and Citizenship: France as a Test Case. *International Political Science Review/Revue Internationale de Science Politique, 12*(3), 219–238.

Todorov, T., & Anzalone, J. (1989). Nation and Nationalism: The French Variant. *Salmagundi, 84*, 138–153.

Wacquant, L. (2007). *Urban Outcasts: A Comparative Sociology of Advanced Marginality*. Retrieved from https://www.amazon.co.uk/Urban-Outcasts-Comparative-Sociology-Marginality/dp/0745631258/ref=sr_1_3?ie=UTF8&qid=1517652872&sr=8-3&keywords=wacquant

Williams, L. (1989). *HARDCORE: Power, Pleasure and the 'Frenzy of the Visible'*. Los Angeles: University of California Press.

Zimmer, O. (2003). Boundary Mechanisms and Symbolic Resources: Towards a Process-Oriented Approach to National Identity. *Nations and Nationalism, 9*(2), 173–193. https://doi.org/10.1111/1469-8219.00081

Bibliography

Abdi, M., & Amara, F. (2006). *La Racaille de la République... Ni Putes ni Soumises*. Paris: Le Seuil.

Abrahamic Group of La Duchère. (2012). *Inter-Religious Declaration of the Abrahamic Group of La Duchère* [Online]. Retrieved from http://www.christianismesocial.org/Declaration-du-Groupe.html

Agence France-Press. (2007). *L'Aïd dans la Cité, un festival qui monte, qui monte à Marseille*. Retrieved from http://www.tv5.org/TV5Site/cinema/afp_article.php

Ageron, C.-R. (2000). Le 'Drame des harkis': Mémoire ou histoire? *Vingtième Siècle. Revue d'histoire, 68*, 3–15. https://doi.org/10.2307/3772174

Ahearne, J. (Ed.). (2002). *French Cultural Policy Debates: A Reader*. London: Routledge.

Alba, R. (2005). Bright vs. Blurred Boundaries: Second-Generation Assimilation and Exclusion in France, Germany, and the United States. *Ethnic and Racial Studies, 28*(1), 20–49.

Aldrich, R. (2005). *Vestiges of Colonial Empire in France*. Retrieved from http://www.palgrave.com/us/book/9781403933706

Almato, A. (1979). *Monuments en exil*. Editions l'Atlantrope. Retrieved from https://www.amazon.fr/Monuments-en-exil-Amato-Alain/dp/2864420066

© The Author(s) 2019
J. Downing, *French Muslims in Perspective*,
https://doi.org/10.1007/978-3-030-16103-3

Al-Saji, A. (2008). Voiles racialisés: la femme musulmane dans les imaginaires occidentaux. *Les ateliers de l'éthique/The Ethics Forum, 3*(2), 39–55. https://doi.org/10.7202/1044595ar

Amnesty International. (2016). *France: Upturned Lives: The Disproportionate Impact of the State of Emergency*. Retrieved October 1, 2018, from https://www.amnesty.org/en/documents/document/?indexNumber=eur21%2f3364%2f2016&language=en

Amos, D. (2005). *Sarkozy at the Centre of French Riot Debate* [Online]. Retrieved from http://www.npr.org/templates/story/story.php

Amra, F., & Zappi, S. (2004). *Ni Putes Ni Soumises*. Paris: La Découverte.

Anderson, B. (Ed.). (2006). *Imagined Communities: Reflections on the Origin and Spread of Nationalism*. London: Verso.

Arfi, F., Mathieu, M., & Hajdenberg, M. (2011). *Les quotas discriminatoires dans le foot français*. Retrieved October 9, 2018, from https://www.mediapart.fr/journal/france/dossier/les-quotas-discriminatoires-dans-le-foot-francais

Arnau, M. (2018). Les Porn Studies, qu'est-ce que c'est? *Playboy France,* (8), 38–39.

Aslam, M. (2012). *Gender-Based Explosions: The Nexus Between Muslim Masculinities, Jihadist Islamism and Terrorism*. UNU Press. Retrieved from https://collections.unu.edu/view/UNU:2519

Assemblé Nationale. (2018). *Welcome to the English Website of the French National Assembly – Assemblée Nationale*. Retrieved August 21, 2018, from http://www2.assemblee-nationale.fr/langues/welcome-to-the-english-website-of-the-french-national-assembly

Bachman, C., & Basier, L. (1985). Junior s'entraine tres fort, ou le smurf comme mobilisation symbolique. *Langage et société, 34*, 57–68.

BBC. (2011). French Football Suspends Official. *BBC News*. Retrieved from https://www.bbc.com/news/world-europe-13236864

BBC. (2014, January 20). French Players in Prostitution Trial. *BBC News*. Retrieved from https://www.bbc.com/news/world-europe-25802279

BBC. (2017). African-Caribbean War Memorial Opened. *BBC News*. Retrieved from https://www.bbc.com/news/uk-england-london-40372063

de Beauvoir, S. (2011). *The Second Sex* (C. Borde & S. Malovany-Chevallier, Trans.) (1st ed.). New York: Vintage.

Beer, D. (2014). Hip-Hop as Urban and Regional Research: Encountering an Insider's Ethnography of City Life. *International Journal of Urban and Regional Research, 38*(2), 677–685. https://doi.org/10.1111/j.1468-2427.2012.01151.x

Begag, A. (2011). *Arithmétique migratoire, Azouz Begag: Il y a 15 à 20 millions de musulmanes en France*. Retrieved January 5, 2018, from https://www.daily-motion.com/video/xiwsnc

Bel Hadi, F. (2007). *Un Collége Abdelmalek Sayad, pour le symbole, Libération* [Online]. Retrieved from http://www.liberation.fr/societe/010118809-un-college-abdelmalek-sayad-pour-le-symbole

Bellil, S. (2003). *Dans l'enfer des tournantes*. Paris: Folio.

Bennet, A. (1999). *Hip Hop Am Main: The Localization of Rap Music and Hip Hop Culture*. Media.

Berger, P. L., & Luckman, T. (1966). *The Social Construction of Reality* (Later Reprint ed.). New York: Anchor Books.

Bertossi, C., & Wihtol de Wenden, C. W. D. (2007). *Les couleurs du drapeau*. Paris: Robert Laffont.

BFMTV. (2018). *Mai 68, gilets jaunes: une comparaison qui a ses limites*. Retrieved February 9, 2019, from https://www.bfmtv.com/societe/mai-68-gilets-jaunes-une-comparaison-qui-a-ses-limites-1583488.html

Bhabha, H. K. (2006). Cultural Diversity and Cultural Differences. In B. Ashcroft, H. Griffiths, & F. Tiffin (Eds.), *The Post-Colonial Studies Reader*. London: Routledge.

Bhaskar, P. R. (2008). *A Realist Theory of Science*. London; New York: Verso.

Billig, M. (1995). *Banal Nationalism*. London: Sage.

Blanchard, E. (2004). La dissolution des Brigades nord-africaines de la Préfecture de police: la fin d'une police d'exception pour les Algériens de Paris (1944–1958)? *Bulletin de l'IHTP, 83*, 70–82.

Bleich, E. (2011). Social Research and 'Race' Policy Framing in Britain and France. *The British Journal of Politics & International Relations, 13*(1), 59–74. https://doi.org/10.1111/j.1467-856X.2010.00439.x

Body-Gendrot, S. (2013). Urban Violence in France and England: Comparing Paris (2005) and London (2011). *Policing and Society, 23*(1), 6–25. https://doi.org/10.1080/10439463.2012.727608

Bongiovanni, F. M. (2018). *Europe and the End of the Age of Innocence*. Cham: Springer.

Booth, K. (2007). *Theory of World Security* (1st ed.). Cambridge; New York: Cambridge University Press.

Bougarel, X., Branche, R., & Drieu, C. (2017). *Combatants of Muslim Origin in European Armies in the Twentieth Century: Far From Jihad*. London: Bloomsbury Publishing.

Bourmeau, S. (2015, January 2). *Scare Tactics: Michel Houellebecq Defends His Controversial New Book*. Retrieved February 7, 2019, from https://www.theparisreview.org/blog/2015/01/02/scare-tactics-michel-houellebecq-on-his-new-book/

Bouteldja, H. (2016). *Les Blancs, les Juifs et nous: Vers une politique de l'amour révolutionnaire*. Paris: La Fabrique Editions.

Bouteldja, H., Khiari, S., Ewanjé-Epée, F. B., & Magliani-Belkacem, S. (2012). *Nous sommes les indigènes de la République*. Paris: Editions Amsterdam.

Bouvet, L. (2015). *L'insécurité culturelle*. Paris: Fayard.

Bouzar, D., Caupenne, C., & Valsan, S. (2014). *La Metamorphose Operée Chez Le Jeune Par Les Nouveaux Discours Terroristes – CPDSI*. Retrieved from http://www.cpdsi.fr/articles-et-rapports/la-metamorphose-operee-chez-le-jeune-par-les-nouveaux-discours-terroristes/

Brenner, E., & Bensoussan, G. (2015). *Les territoires perdus de la République* (3rd ed., amended and enlarged). Paris: Fayard/Pluriel.

Breuilly, J. (1994). *Nationalism and the State*. University of Chicago Press. Retrieved from https://www.press.uchicago.edu/ucp/books/book/chicago/N/bo3619074.html

Brown, M. D. (2006). Comparative Analysis of Mainstream Discourses, Media Narratives and Representations of Islam in Britain and France Prior to 9/11. *Journal of Muslim Minority Affairs, 26*(3), 297–312. https://doi.org/10.1080/13602000601141216

Brubaker, R. (1998). *Citizenship and Nationhood in France and Germany*. Cambridge, MA: Harvard University Press.

Brubaker, R. (2001). The Return of Assimilation? Changing Perspectives on Immigration and Its Sequels in France, Germany, and the United States. *Ethnic and Racial Studies, 24*(4), 531–548.

Bruckner, P. (2006). *La tyrannie de la pénitence*. Paris: Grasset.

Bruckner, P. (2018). *An Imaginary Racism: Islamophobia and Guilt*. Medford, MA: Polity Press.

Bulmer, S., & Radaelli, C. (2004). *The Europeanisation of National Policy?* Queens Papers on Europeanisation (p0042). Belfast, UK: Queens University Belfast.

Burgot, F. (2016). *Comprendre l'islam politique*. Retrieved October 1, 2018, from http://www.editionsladecouverte.fr/catalogue/index-Comprendre_l_islam_politique-9782707192134.html

Burnett, J., & Whyte, D. (2005). Embedded Expertise and the New Terrorism. *Journal for Crime, Conflict and the Media, 1*, 1–18.

Butler, J. (2006). *Precarious Life: The Power of Mourning and Violence* (Reprint ed.). London; New York: Verso Books.

Buzan, B., Waever, O., & de Wilde, J. (1997). *Security: A New Framework for Analysis* (UK ed.). Boulder, CO: Lynne Rienner Publishers.

Caeux, P., Haget, H., Saubaber, D., & Thiolay, B. (2012). *Ils s'appelaient Mohamed… Deux jeunesses françaises*. Retrieved September 4, 2018, from https://www.lexpress.fr/actualite/societe/ils-s-appelaient-mohamed-deux-jeunesses-francaises_1098162.html

Caillet, R., & Puchot, P. (2017). *Le combat vous a été prescrit*. Retrieved from http://www.editions-stock.fr/livres/essais-documents/le-combat-vous-ete-prescrit-9782234082502

Caldwell, C. (2014). *Une révolution sous nos yeux: Comment l'islam va transformer la France et l'Europe (Poche)*. Paris: L'artilleur.

Calhoun, C. (2007). *Nations Matter: Culture, History, and the Cosmopolitan Dream*. London: Routledge.

Camiscioli, E. (2009). *Reproducing the French Race: Immigration, Intimacy and Embodiment in the Early Twentieth Century*. Durham, NC: Duke University Press.

Canet, R., Pech, L., & Stewart, M. (2015). France's Burning Issue: Understanding the Urban Riots of November 2005. In M. T. Davis (Ed.), *Crowd Actions in Britain and France from the Middle Ages to the Modern World* (pp. 270–292). London: Palgrave Macmillan UK. https://doi.org/10.1057/9781137316516_17

Carrera, S., Guild, E., Vosyliūtė, L., & Bard, P. (2017). *Towards a Comprehensive EU Protection System for Minorities*, p. 182. European Parliament.

Carroll, J. S., Padilla-Walker, L. M., Nelson, L. J., Olson, C. D., Barry, C. M., & Madsen, S. D. (2008). Generation XXX: Pornography Acceptance and Use Among Emerging Adults. *Journal of Adolescent Research, 23*(1), 6–30. https://doi.org/10.1177/0743558407306348

Centre Resource Prospective du Grand Lyon. (2012). *Groupe Abraham de La Duchère*. Retrieved from http://www.millenaire3.com/Affichage-de-la-ressource.122+M51a10fb25bd.0.html

Cesari, J. (2005). *Ethnicity, Islam and les Banlieues: Confusing the Issues* [Online]. Brooklyn, NY: Social Science Research Council. Retrieved from http://riots-france.ssrc.org/Cesari/

Cesari, J. (2009). *The Securitisation of Islam in Europe*. Vol. 15. CEPS. Retrieved from http://aei.pitt.edu/10763/1/1826.pdf

Cesari, J. (2013a). European Conundrum: Integration of Muslims or Securitisation of Islam? *World Review*. Retrieved from https://berkleycenter. georgetown.edu/essays/european-conundrum-integration-of-muslims-or-securitisation-of-islam

Cesari, J. (2013b). Securitization of Islam in Europe: The Embodiment of Islam as an Exception. In *Why the West Fears Islam: An Exploration of Muslims in Liberal Democracies* (pp. 83–105). New York: Palgrave Macmillan US. https://doi.org/10.1057/9781137121202_5

Chakraborti, N. (2013, June 17). *Policing Muslim Communities*. https://doi. org/10.4324/9781843926504-10

Chan, K. (1998). The Construction of Black Male Identity in Black Action Films of the Nineties. *Cinema Journal, 37*(2), 35–48. https://doi.org/10.2307/1225641

Chieze, G. (2017). *Police: un ancien fiché S est devenu gardien de la paix*. Retrieved September 1, 2018, from https://www.rtl.fr/actu/debats-societe/police-un-ancien-fiche-s-est-devenu-gardien-de-la-paix-7790220004

Chrisafis, A. (2015). Charlie Hebdo Attackers: Born, Raised and Radicalised in Paris. *The Guardian*. Retrieved from https://www.theguardian.com/world/2015/jan/12/-sp-charlie-hebdo-attackers-kids-france-radicalised-paris

Chrisafis, A. (2016). *Paris Attacks Inquiry Finds Multiple Failings by French Intelligence Agencies*. Retrieved from https://www.theguardian.com/world/2016/jul/05/paris-attacks-inquiry-multiple-failings-french-intelligence-agencies

Christie, N. (1986). The Ideal Victim. In *From Crime Policy to Victim Policy* (pp. 17–30). London: Palgrave Macmillan. https://doi.org/10.1007/978-1-349-08305-3_2

Chua, D. (2008). Orientalism as Cultural Practices and the Production of Sociological Knowledge. *Sociology Compass, 2*(4), 1179–1191.

CoE. (2018). *The European Charter for Regional or Minority Languages Is the European Convention for the Protection and Promotion of Languages Used by Traditional Minorities*. Retrieved August 28, 2018, from https://www.coe. int/en/web/european-charter-regional-or-minority-languages/home

Cohen, W. B. (2002). The Algerian War, the French State and Official Memory. *Historical Reflections/Réflexions Historiques, 28*(2), 219–239.

Cole, A. (2008). *Governing and Governance in France*. Cambridge, UK: Cambridge University Press.

Connell, R. W. (2005). *Masculinities*. Cambridge: Polity.

Cornevin, C., & Piquet, C. (2016). *Attentats: la longue traque d'une nebuleuse terroriste franco-belge*. Retrieved from http://www.lefigaro.fr/actualite-france/2016/03/25/01016-20160325ARTFIG   00296-attentats-la-longue-traque-d-une-nebuleuse-terroriste-franco-belge.php

Coskun, B. B. (2011). *Analysing Desecuritisation: The Case of the Israeli-Palestinian Peace Education and Water Management.* Cambridge Scholars Publishing. Retrieved from https://www.amazon.co.uk/Analysing-Desecuritisation-Israeli-Palestinian-Education-Management/dp/1443827312

Council of Europe. (2008). *Intercultural Cities Joint Action of the Council of Europe and the European Commission Lyon, France 2008.* Retrieved from https://rm.coe.int/1680482a84

Couvelaire, L. (2019, February 12). *Antisémitisme: en France, les différents visages d'une haine antijuive insidieuse et banalisée.* Retrieved from https://www.lemonde.fr/societe/article/2019/02/12/en-france-les-differents-visages-d-une-haine-anti-juive-insidieuse-et-banalisee_5422326_3224.html

Crenshaw, K. (1989). Demarginalizing the Intersection of Race and Sex: A Black Feminist Critique of Antidiscrimination Doctrine, Feminist Theory and Antiracist Politics. *University of Chicago Legal Forum, 1989*, 139.

Crettiez, X., Sèze, R., Ainine, B., & Lindemann, T. (2017). *Saisir les mécanismes de la radicalisation violente: pour une analyse processuelle et biographique des engagements violent, Rapport de recherche pour la mission de recherche droit et justice.* Retrieved from http://www.gip-recherche-justice.fr/wp-content/uploads/2017/08/Rapport-radicalisation_INHESJ_CESDIP_GIP-Justice_2017.pdf

Croucher, S. (2008). French-Muslims and the Hijab: An Analysis of Identity and the Islamic Veil in France. *Journal of Intercultural Communication Research, 37*, 3.

Dagistanli, S., & Grewal, K. (2016). Perverse Muslim Masculinities in Contemporary Orientalist Discourse: The Vagaries of Muslim Immigration in the West. In *Global Islamophobia: Muslims and Moral Panic in the West.* Routledge, London, UK.

Dagorn, G. (2018, June 12). Le rappeur Médine au Bataclan: la polémique en quatre questions. *Le Monde.* Retrieved from https://www.lemonde.fr/politique/article/2018/06/12/le-rappeur-medine-au-bataclan-la-polemique-en-quatre-questions_5313815_823448.html

Davidson, N. (2009). La mosquée de Paris. Construire l'islam français et l'islam en France, 1926–1947. *Revue des mondes musulmans et de la Méditerranée, 125*, 197–215. https://doi.org/10.4000/remmm.6246

Dearden, L. (2016). *Why France Is in Uproar over the Burkini – and Why It Matters.* Retrieved August 26, 2018, from http://www.independent.co.uk/news/world/europe/burkini-ban-why-is-france-arresting-muslim-women-for-wearing-full-body-swimwear-and-why-are-people-a7207971.html

Delbecque, E. (2017). *Une 'task force' anti-terroiste à l'Elysée peut elle empêcher des attentats?* Retrieved from http://www.huffingtonpost.fr/eric-delbecque/task-force-macron-terrorisme_a_22108783/

Dell'Oro, J. L. (2015). Combien y a-t-il de djihadistes en France et quels sont leurs profils? – *Challenges.* Retrieved October 1, 2018, from https://www.challenges.fr/france/combien-y-a-t-il-de-djihadistes-en-france-et-quels-sont-leurs-profils_45504

Dely, R. (1998). Le Pen: 'la Coupe du monde, est un détail de l'histoire'. *Nouvelle diatribe provocatrice du leader du FN.* – *Libération.* Retrieved October 9, 2018, from https://www.liberation.fr/france/1998/07/13/le-pen-la-coupe-du-monde-est-un-detail-de-l-histoire-nouvelle-diatribe-provocatrice-du-leader-du-fn_243689

Dikeç, M. (2007). *Badlands of the Republic: Space, Politics and Urban Policy.* Oxford: Blackwell Publishing.

Doran, M. (2004). Negotiating Between Bourge and Racaille: Verlan as Youth Identity Practice in Suburban Paris. In *Negotiation of Identities in Multilingual Contexts.* Clevedon: Multilingual Matters.

Dorlin, E. (2010). 33. Le grand strip-tease: féminisme, nationalisme et burqa en France. In *Ruptures postcoloniales* (pp. 429–442). La Découverte. Retrieved from https://www.cairn.info/resume.php?ID_ARTICLE=DEC_BANCE_2010_01_0429

Dot-Pouillard, N. (2007). Les recompositions politiques du mouvement féministe français au regard du hijab. Le voile comme signe et révélateur des impensés d'un espace public déchiré entre identité républicaine et héritage colonial. *SociologieS.* Retrieved from http://journals.openedition.org/sociologies/246

Douet, E. (2015). *Des armes utilisées par les terroristes identifiées en Serbie.* Retrieved October 1, 2018, from https://www.rtl.fr/actu/debats-societe/attentats-a-paris-des-armes-utilisees-par-les-terroristes-identifiees-en-serbie-7780673680

Downing, J. (2015). Understanding the (Re) Definition of Nationhood in French Cities: A Case of Multiple States and Multiple Republics. *Studies in Ethnicity and Nationalism, 15*(2), 336–351.

Downing, J. (2016). Fighting Cultural Marginalisation with Symbolic Power in a Parisian Banlieue: Post-colonial Culture and the Voluntary Association Les Oranges. *International Journal of Sociology and Social Policy, 36*(7/8), 516–530.

Doytcheva, M. (2007). *Une discrimination positive à la Française? Ethnicité et territoire dans les politiques de la ville.* Paris: Broché.

Drissel, D. (2009). Hip-Hop Hybridity for a Glocalized World: African and Muslim Diasporic Discourses in French Rap Music. *The Global Studies*

Journal, *2*(3). Retrieved from https://www.academia.edu/1591080/Hip-Hop_Hybridity_for_a_Glocalized_World_African_and_Muslim_Diasporic_Discourses_in_French_Rap_Music

Dunn, J. (1995). The French Highway Lobby: A Case Study in State-Society Relations and Policymaking. *Comparative Politics*, *27*, 3–275.

Durand, A.-P. (2002). *Black, Blanc, Beur: Rap Music and Hip-Hop Culture in the Francophone World*. Lanham, MD: Scarecrow Press.

El Hamel, C. (2002). Muslim Diaspora in Western Europe: The Islamic Headscarf (Hijab), the Media and Muslims' Integration in France. *Citizenship Studies*, *6*(3), 293–308. https://doi.org/10.1080/1362102022000011621

Elder-Vass, D. (2013). *The Reality of Social Construction* (Reprint ed.). Cambridge: Cambridge University Press.

Erlanger, S. (2010, July 13). Parliament Moves France Closer to a Ban on Facial Veils. *The New York Times*. Retrieved from https://www.nytimes.com/2010/07/14/world/europe/14burqa.html

Eroukhmanoff. (2015). The Remote Securitisation of Islam in the US Post-9/11: Euphemisation, Metaphors and the "Logic of Expected Consequences" in Counter-Radicalisation Discourse. *Critical Studies on Terrorism*, *8*, 246–265.

Europe1. (2017). *Pour Nasri, Benzema, Ben Arfa et lui sont victimes d'un racisme ambiant*. Retrieved November 24, 2018, from http://www.europe1.fr/sport/pour-nasri-benzema-ben-arfa-et-lui-sont-victimes-d-un-racisme-ambiant-3458684

Evans, M., & Lunn, K. (1997). *War and Memory in the Twentieth Century*. Berg Publishers. Retrieved from https://researchportal.port.ac.uk/portal/en/publications/war-and-memory-in-the-twentieth-century(67f47f22-7690-43ae-9517-8981a7e00b17).html

Flores. (2000). *From Bomba to Hip-Hop: Puerto Rican Culture and Latino Identity*. New York: Colombia University Press.

Fogarty, R. S. (2012). *Race and War in France: Colonial Subjects in the French Army, 1914–1918*. Baltimore, MD: Johns Hopkins University Press.

Foot Mercato. (2017). *Equipe de France: Karim Benzema règle ses comptes avec Didier Deschamps*. Retrieved October 9, 2018, from http://www.footmercato.net/equipe-de-france/equipe-de-france-karim-benzema-regle-ses-comptes-avec-didier-deschamps_214107

Forman, M. (2004). Represent: Race, Space and Place in Rap Music. In M. Forman & M. A. Neal (Eds.), *That's the Joint! The Hip-Hop Studies Reader*. New York: Routledge.

Fournier, L. (2008). Le 'féminisme musulman' en Europe de l'Ouest: le cas du réseau féminin de Présence musulmane. *Amnis. Revue de civilisation contemporaine Europes/Amériques, 8.* https://doi.org/10.4000/amnis.593

France 24,. (2016). Des attentats déjoués "tous les jours" en France et 15 000 personnes radicalisées. Retrieved from https://www.france24.com/fr/20160911-terrorisme-franceattentats-dejoues-tous-jours-15000-personnes-radicalisees-valls

Franceinfo. (2016). *Attentats terroristes en France: quelles armes ont été utilisées?* Retrieved October 1, 2018, from https://www.francetvinfo.fr/faits-divers/terrorisme/attaques-du-13-novembre-a-paris/enquete-sur-les-attentats-de-paris/attentats-terroristes-en-france-quelles-armes-ont-ete-utilisees_1374239.html

Fredette, J. (2014). *Constructing Muslims in France: Discourse, Public Identity, and the Politics of Citizenship.* Temple University Press. Retrieved from https://www.amazon.co.uk/Constructing-Muslims-France-Discourse-Citizenship-ebook/dp/B00HSFS6V0/ref=sr_1_1?ie=UTF8&qid=1538397208&sr=8-1&keywords=Muslims+in+France+%E2%80%93+Discourse%2C+Public+Identity%2C+and+the+Politics+of+Citizenship

Future.fr. (2011). *IAM sort un triple album pour célébrer ses 20 ans.* Retrieved from http://joga.future.fr/actualites/article-886-iam-sort-un-triple-album-pour-celebrer-ses-20-ans.html

Geisser, V. (2007). Des Voltaire, des Zola musulmans…? Réflexion sur les 'nouveaux dissidents' de l'islam. *Revue internationale et stratégique, 65,* 143–156. https://doi.org/10.3917/ris.065.0143

Geisser, V., & Lorcerie, F. (2011). *Rapport Les Marseillais Musulmans.* New York: Open Society Foundation.

Gellner, E. (Ed.). (1983). *Nations and Nationalism.* London: Blackwell.

Gellner, E. (Ed.). (1988). *Plough, Sword and Book: The Structure of Human History.* London: Collins Harvill.

Gelman, S. A. (2003). *The Essential Child: Origins of Essentialism in Everyday Thought.* New York: Oxford University Press.

Ghaill, M. A. (1994). *The Making of Men: Masculinities, Sexualities and Schooling.* Milton Keynes: McGraw-Hill Education (UK).

Gilroy, P. (2002). *There Ain't no Black in the Union Jack: The Cultural Politics of Race and Nation.* London: Routledge.

Ginio, R. (2017). *The French Army and Its African Soldiers: The Years of Decolonization.* Lincoln: University of Nebraska Press.

Giry, S. (2006, September 1). France and Its Muslims. *Foreign Affairs* (September/ October). Retrieved from https://www.foreignaffairs.com/articles/ france/2006-09-01/france-and-its-muslims

Gnedovsky, M. (2009). *Intercultural Cities Program Report on the Visit to Lyon, France*. Council of Europe. Retrieved from http://www.coe.int/t/dg4/cul- tureheritage/culture/cities/GnedovskyICCLyonReport_en.pdf

Gorski, P. S. (2013). What Is Critical Realism? And Why Should You Care? *Contemporary Sociology, 42*(5), 658–670. https://doi.org/10.1177/ 0094306113499533

Guénif-Souilamas, N., & Macé, E. (2006). *Les féministes et le garçon arabe*. La Tour-d'Aigues (Vaucluse): Editions de l'Aube.

Gunning, J., & Jackson, R. (2011). What's So 'Religious' About 'Religious Terrorism'. *Critical Studies on Terrorism, 4*, 369–388.

Hackett, C. (2017). *5 Facts About the Muslim Population in Europe*. Retrieved October 1, 2018, from http://www.pewresearch.org/fact-tank/2017/11/29/5- facts-about-the-muslim-population-in-europe/

Hacking, I. (2000). *The Social Construction of What?* (Revised ed.). Cambridge, MA: Harvard University Press.

Hagopian, P. (2009). *The Vietnam War in American Memory: Veterans, Memorials, and the Politics of Healing*. Amherst: University of Massachusetts Press.

Hall, S., Roberts, B., Clarke, J., Jefferson, T., & Critcher, C. (1978). *Policing the Crisis: Mugging, the State, and Law and Order*. Macmillan. Retrieved from https://www.amazon.co.uk/Policing-Crisis-Mugging-Critical-Studies/ dp/0333220617

Hamilton, C. (1998). *Terrific Majesty: The Powers of Shaka Zulu and the Limits of Historical Invention* (1st ed., 3rd ed.). Cambridge, MA: Harvard University Press.

Hammou, K. (2014). *Une histoire du rap en France*. Paris: Editions Découverte.

Hamoumou, M. (1990). Les harkis, un trou de mémoire franco-algérien. *Esprit (1940–), 161*(5), 25–45.

Hansen, L. (2011). Theorizing the Image for Security Studies: Visual Securitization and the Muhammad Cartoon Crisis. *European Journal of International Relations, 17*(1), 51–74. https://doi.org/10.1177/1354066110388593

Hansen, L. (2018). Images and International Security. *The Oxford Handbook of International Security*. https://doi.org/10.1093/oxfordhb/9780198777854. 013.39

Hargreaves, A. (2007). *Multi-Ethnic France: Immigration, Politics, Culture and Society* (2nd ed.). New York; London: Routledge.

Hargreaves, A., & McKinney, M. (Eds.). (1997). *Post-Colonial Cultures in France* (1st ed.). London; New York: Routledge.

Haskins, E. (2007). Between Archive and Participation: Public Memory in a Digital Age. *Rhetoric Society Quarterly, 37*(4), 401–422. https://doi.org/10.1080/02773940601086794

Hayward, K., & Yar, M. (2006). *The 'Chav' Phenomenon: Consumption, Media and the Construction of a New Underclass.* Retrieved February 15, 2018, from http://journals.sagepub.com/doi/abs/10.1177/1741659006061708

Heneghan, T. (2007, November 29). *Why We Don't Call Them 'Muslim Riots' in Paris Suburbs.* Retrieved October 20, 2018, from http://blogs.reuters.com/faithworld/2007/11/29/why-we-dont-call-them-muslim-riots-in-paris-suburbs/

Herring, E. (2008). Critical Terrorism Studies: An Activist Scholar Perspective. *Critical Studies on Terrorism, 1*(2), 197–211. https://doi.org/10.1080/1753915 0802187507

Hess, A. (2007). In Digital Remembrance: Vernacular Memory and the Rhetorical Construction of Web Memorials. *Media, Culture & Society, 29*(5), 812–830. https://doi.org/10.1177/0163443707080539

Hobsbawm, E., & Ranger, T. O. (1984). *The Invention of Tradition.* Cambridge: Cambridge University Press.

Hooghe, L. (Ed.). (1996). *Cohesion Policy and European Integration: Building Multi-Level Governance.* Oxford, UK: Oxford University Press.

Hooks, B. (1987). *Ain't I a Woman: Black Women and Feminism.* Retrieved March 23, 2018, from https://www.amazon.co.uk/Aint-Woman-Black-Women-Feminism/dp/0861043790/ref=sr_1_cc_1?s=aps&ie=UTF8&qid=1521806924&sr=1-1-catcorr&keywords=Ain%27t+I+a+Woman%3A+black+women+and+feminism

Hopkins, P. E. (2006). Youthful Muslim Masculinities: Gender and Generational Relations. *Transactions of the Institute of British Geographers, 31*(3), 337–352. https://doi.org/10.1111/j.1475-5661.2006.00206.x

Horne, A. (2006). *A Savage War of Peace: Algeria 1954–1962.* New York: NYRB Classics.

Houellebecq, M. (2017). *Soumission.* Paris: J'AI LU.

Human Rights Watch. (2016). *France: Abuses Under State of Emergency | Human Rights Watch.* Retrieved October 1, 2018, from https://www.hrw.org/news/2016/02/03/france-abuses-under-state-emergency

Huntingdon, S. (1993, Summer). The Clash of Civilisations? *Foreign Affairs, 72*(3), 22–49.

Hussey, A. (2014). *The French Intifada: The Long War Between France and Its Arabs.* London: Granta.

Hutchingson, J. (1982). *The Dynamics of Cultural Nationalism: The Gaelic Revival and the Creation of the Irish Nation State*. Crows Nest, Australia: Allen and Unwin.

Huysmans, J. (1998). The Question of the Limit: Desecuritization and the Aesthetics of Horror in Political Realism. *Millennium – Journal of International Studies, 27*, 569–589.

Hytner, D. (2010). World Cup 2010: France Revolt Leaves Raymond Domenech High and Dry. *The Guardian*. Retrieved from https://www.theguardian.com/football/2010/jun/20/france-raymond-domenech-nicolas-anelka

Ibn Ziaten, L. (2014). *Mort pour la France – Mohamed Merah a tué mon fils*. Paris: J'ai lu témoignage. Retrieved from https://www.amazon.fr/Mort-pour-France-Latifa-Ziaten/dp/2290076007

INSEE. (2016). *Ethnic-Based Statistics | Insee*. Retrieved August 21, 2018, from https://www.insee.fr/en/information/2388586

Ireland, S. (2001). Negotiating Gender in the Work of Women Writers of Maghrebi Immigrant Descent. *Nottingham French Studies, 40*(1), 52–62. https://doi.org/10.3366/nfs.2001.007

Jackson, R. (2007a). Constructing Enemies: 'Islamic Terrorism' in Political and Academic Discourse. *Government and Opposition, 42*, 394–426.

Jackson, R. (2007b). The Core Commitments of Critical Terrorism Studies. In *European Consortium for Political Research*. Retrieved from https://www.researchgate.net/publication/32031958_The_Core_Commitments_of_Critical_Terrorism_Studies

Jackson, R., Gunning, J., & Breen Smyth, M. (2007). The Case for a Critical Terrorism Studies. *Paper of the American Political Science Association*.

Jackson-Preece, J. (2005). *Minority Rights: Between Diversity and Community*. London: Polity.

Jacob, E. (2016). *La population musulmane largement surestimée en France*. Retrieved from http://www.lefigaro.fr/actualite-france/2016/12/14/01016-20161214ARTFIG 00214-la-population-musulmane-largement-surestimee-en-france.php

Jarvis, L. (2011). 9/11 Digitally Remastered? Internet Archives, Vernacular Memories and WhereWereYou.org. *Journal of American Studies, 45*(4), 793–814. https://doi.org/10.1017/S002187581100096X

Jobard, F. (2006). Chapitre 2: Sociologie politique de la 'racaille'. In *Émeutes urbaines et protestations* (pp. 59–80). Presses de Sciences Po (P.F.N.S.P.). Retrieved from https://www.cairn.info/emeutes-urbaines-et-protestations-une-singularite%2D%2D9782724609921-p-59.htm

Jobard, F. (2009). An Overview of French Riots: 1981–2004. In D. Waddington, F. Jobard, & M. King (Eds.), *Rioting in the UK and France. A Comparative Analysis* (pp. 27–38). Willan Publishing. Retrieved from https://hal.archives-ouvertes.fr/hal-00550788

Johnson, N. (1995). Cast in Stone: Monuments, Geography, and Nationalism, Environment and Planning D. *Society and Space, 13*(1), 51.

Kader Hamadi, A. (2006). Mémoire des lieux: les 'camps' ouverts aux 'harkis' dans le sud de la France (Places of Memory: 'Camps' of 'Harkis' in the South of France). *Bulletin de l'Association de Géographes Français, 83*(1), 105–120. https://doi.org/10.3406/bagf.2006.2497

Kalra, V. S. (2009). Between Emasculation and Hypermasculinity: Theorizing British South Asian Masculinities. *South Asian Popular Culture, 7*(2), 113–125. https://doi.org/10.1080/14746680902920874

Kapaló, J. A. (2013). Folk Religion in Discourse and Practice. *Journal of Ethnology and Folkloristics, 7*(1), 3–18.

Kattago, S. (2009). War Memorials and the Politics of Memory: The Soviet War Memorial in Tallinn. *Constellations, 16*(1), 150–166. https://doi.org/10.1111/j.1467-8675.2009.00525.x

Katz, E. (2012). Did the Paris Mosque Save Jews? A Mystery and Its Memory. *The Jewish Quarterly Review, 102*(2), 256–287.

Kaya, A. (2009). *Islam, Migration and Integration: The Age of Securitization.* Reston, VA: AIAA.

Kazi-Tani, S. (2018). *Sports | Football: de la cité de la Castellane aux étoiles du Real, Zinédine Zidane ce héros made in Marseille | La Provence.* Retrieved October 9, 2018, from https://www.laprovence.com/article/sports/4988951/de-la-castellane-au-real-zinedine-zidane-un-heros-made-in-marseille.html

Kemp, A. (2009). Marianne d'aujourd'hui?: The Figure of the beurette in Contemporary French Feminist Discourses. *Modern & Contemporary France, 17*(1), 19–33. https://doi.org/10.1080/09639480802639751

Kepel, G. (2012). *Banlieue de la République.* Paris: Institut Montaigne.

Kepel, G. (2017). *Terreur dans l'Hexagone: Genèse du djihad français.* Folio.

Kepel, G., & Jardin, A. (2017). *Terror in France: The Rise of Jihad in the West.* Princeton, NJ: Princeton University Press. Retrieved from https://www.amazon.fr/Terror-France-Rise-Jihad-West-ebook/dp/B01M3XAUKO/ref=sr_1_fkmr0_1?ie=UTF8&qid=1538394128&sr=8-1-fkmr0&keywords=kepel++jardin+2015

Khosrokhavar, F. (2014). *Radicalisation (fiche technique).* Les éditions de la maison des sciences de l'home. Retrieved from http://www.editions-msh.fr/livre/?GCOI=27351100399910&fa=details

Kimlicka. (2010). The Rise and Fall of Multiculturalism: New Debates on Inclusion and Accommodation in Diverse Societies. In S. Vertovec & S. Wessendorf (Eds.), *The Multiculturalism Backlash: European Discourses, Policies and Practice*. London: Routledge.

Knill, C. (2001). *The Europeanisation of National Administrations: Patterns of Institutional Change and Persistence*. Cambridge, UK: Cambridge University Press.

Kohn, H. (2005). *The Idea of Nationalism*. New Brunswick, NJ: Transaction Publisher.

Krims, A. (2000). *Rap Music and the Poetics of Identity*. Cambridge: Cambridge University Press.

Kymlicka, W. (1996). *Multicultural Citizenship*. Oxford: Oxford University Press.

Kymlicka, W. (2002). *'Multiculturalism' in Contemporary Political Philosophy: An Introduction* (2nd ed.). Oxford: Oxford University Press.

La Dépêche. (2017). *Profanation de la stèle d'Abel Chennouf: 'J'ai chialé comme un môme', raconte son père*. Retrieved September 4, 2018, from https://www.ladepeche.fr/article/2017/12/08/2700620-profanation-stele-abel-chennouf-ai-chiale-comme-mome-raconte-pere.html

La Région Auvergne-Rhône-Alpes. (2007). Monument aux morts d'Oran online at https://patrimoine.auvergnerhonealpes.fr/dossier/monument-aux-mortsd-oran/2f0a2558-1574-498b-ac0dc61012cbc8aa

Lacroix, A. (2005). Alain Finkielkraut: 'The Illegitimacy of Hatred'. *Le Figaro*. Retrieved from http://www.lefigaro.fr/debats/2005/11/17/01005-20051117 ARTFIG90264-alain_finkielkraut_the_illegitimacy_of_hatred.php

Landais, É. (2014). Porn studies et études de la pornographie en sciences humaines et sociales. *Questions de Communication*, (26), 17–37.

Landes, X., & Nielsen, M. E. J. (2018). Racial Dodging in the Porn Industry: A Case with No Silver Bullet. *Porn Studies*, 1–16. https://doi.org/10.1080/232 68743.2018.1435302

Laurent, S. (2015). Terrorisme: qu'est-ce que la 'fiche S'? *Le Monde*. Retrieved from http://www.lemonde.fr/les-decodeurs/article/2015/08/31/terrorisme-peut-on-sanctionner-les-personnes-faisant-l-objet-d-une-fiche-s_4741574_4355770.html

Lawther, C. (2014). The Construction and Politicisation of Victimhood. In *Victims of Terrorism: A Comparative and Interdisciplinary Study*. London: Routledge.

Le Monde. (2015). *Le mémorial du 'Monde' aux victimes des attentats du 13-Novembre*. Retrieved from http://www.lemonde.fr/attaques-a-paris/visuel/2015/11/25/enmemoire_4817200_4809495.html

Le Monde. (2016). *Le mémorial du 'Monde' aux victimes de attentats de Nice*. Retrieved from http://www.lemonde.fr/grands-formats/visuel/2016/10/06/le-memorial-du-monde-aux-victimes-des-attentats-de-nice_5009546_4497053.html

Leerssen, J. (2015). The Nation and the City: Urban Festivals and Cultural Mobilisation. *Nations and Nationalism, 21*(1), 2–20. https://doi.org/10.1111/nana.12090

Levinas, E. (1985). *Ethics and Infinity: Conversations with Philippe Nemo*. Pittsburgh: Duquesne University Press.

Lichfield, J. (2016, May 31). France Accused of Excluding Players of North African Origin from Euro 2016 Squad. *The Independent*. Retrieved from http://www.independent.co.uk/sport/football/international/euro-2016-france-accused-of-excluding-players-of-african-origin-from-squad-for-tournament-a7058371.html

Londres, A. (1926). *Marseille porte du Sud*. Paris: Arléa.

Lutrand, M.-C., & Yazdekhasti, B. (2011). Laïcité et présence musulmane en France: des dynamiques d'influence réciproque. *Cahiers de la Méditerranée, 83*, 327–335.

Maira, S. (2009). 'Good' and 'Bad' Muslim Citizens: Feminists, Terrorists, and U. S. Orientalisms. *Feminist Studies, 35*(3), 631–656.

Maktouf, S. (2017). *Je défendrai la vie autant que vous prêchez la mort*. Neuilly-sur-Seine: Michel Lafon.

Malešević, S. (2007). *Ernest Gellner and Contemporary Social Thought*. Cambridge, UK: Cambridge University Press. https://doi.org/10.1017/CBO9780511488795

Mamdani, M. (2008). Good Muslim, Bad Muslim: A Political Perspective on Culture and Terrorism. *American Anthropologist, 104*(3), 766–775. https://doi.org/10.1525/aa.2002.104.3.766

Mamou, Y. (2018). *Le grand abandon: Les élites françaises et l'islamisme*. Paris: L'artilleur.

Marc, J. (2010). *Finkielkraut: 'L'équipe de France est une bande de voyous avec une morale de mafia'*. Retrieved October 9, 2018, from http://www.agoravox.tv/tribune-libre/article/finkielkraut-l-equipe-de-france-26725

Marianne. (2016). *Comment le débat sur l'équipe de France de football s'est racialisé depuis 1998*. Retrieved October 9, 2018, from https://www.marianne.net/societe/comment-le-debat-sur-lequipe-de-france-de-football-sest-racialise-depuis-1998

Martin, L. (2013). La démocratisation de la culture en France: une ambition obsolète? In M. Poirrier (Ed.). Retrieved from http://tristan.u-bourgogne.fr/CGC/publications/democratiser_culture/Democratiser_culture.html

Mason, F. (2002). *American Gangster Cinema: From 'Little Caesar' to 'Pulp Fiction'*. Berlin: Springer.

Mavelli, L. (2013). Between Normalisation and Exception: The Securitisation of Islam and the Construction of the Secular Subject. *Millennium, 41*(2), 159–181. https://doi.org/10.1177/0305829812463655

Max, A. (2017). Plan Anti-Kebab à Marseille reportage dans le centre-ville, entre boboïsation et «repas du pauvre». Retrieved from https://www.20minutes.fr/marseille/2097739-20170702-plan-anti-kebab-marseille-reportage-centre-ville-entre-boboisation-repas-pauvre

Mayo, J. M. (1988). War Memorials as Political Memory. *Geographical Review, 78*(1), 62–75. https://doi.org/10.2307/214306

McCoy, T. S. (1988). Hegemony, Power, Media: Foucault and Cultural Studies. *Communications, 14*(3), 71–90. https://doi.org/10.1515/comm.1988.14.3.71

McCulloch, J., & Pickering, S. (2009). Pre-Crime and Counter-Terrorism: Imagining Future Crime in the 'War on Terror'. *The British Journal of Criminology, 49*, 628–645.

McGowan, W. (2016). Critical Terrorism Studies, Victimisation, and Policy Relevance: Compromising Politics or Challenging Hegemony? *Critical Studies on Terrorism, 9*(1), 12–32. https://doi.org/10.1080/17539153.2016.1147772

McLennan, G. (2014). Sociology, Cultural Studies and the Cultural Turn. In J. Holmwood & J. Scott (Eds.), *The Palgrave Handbook of Sociology in Britain* (pp. 510–535). London: Palgrave Macmillan UK. https://doi.org/10.1007/978-1-137-31886-2_23

Mechaï, H. (2018). *French-Algerian Activist Houria Bouteldja: 'The Left Is Struggling in France'*. Retrieved October 6, 2018, from https://www.middleeastmonitor.com/20180319-french-algerian-activist-houria-bouteldja-the-left-is-struggling-in-france/

Med'in Marseille. (2010). *L'Aïd dans La Cité: Une Fête Pour Tous*. Retrieved from http://www.med-in-marseille.info/L-Aid-dans-la-Cite-une-fete-pour.html

Menucci, P. (2013). *Nous Les Marseillais*. Paris: Pygmalion.

Merchet, J.-D. (2009). *Exclusif: l'armée reconnait que quelques soldats musulmans refusent de partir en Afghanistan*. Retrieved September 1, 2018, from http://secretdefense.blogs.liberation.fr/2009/01/14/exclusif-larme/

Messerschmidt, J. W., Tomsen, S., & Tomsen, S. (2018, April 9). *Masculinities and Crime*. https://doi.org/10.4324/9781315622040-8

Meynier, G., & Vidal-Naquet, P. (1981). *L'Algérie révélée: La guerre de 1914–1918 et le premier quart du XXe siècle*. Geneva: Librairie Droz.

Ministère des armées. (2013). *25 septembre: 'Journée nationale d'hommage aux harkis et autres membres des formations supplétives'*. Retrieved November 12, 2018, from https://www.defense.gouv.fr/actualites/memoire-et-culture/25-septembre-journee-nationale-d-hommage-aux-harkis-et-autres-membres-des-formations-suppletives3

Mitchell, K. (2011). Marseille's Not for Burning: Comparative Networks of Integration and Exclusion in Two French Cities. *Annals of the Association of American Geographers, 101*(2), 404–423.

Modood, T. (2007). *Multiculturalism: A Civic Idea*. London: Polity Press.

Modood, T. (2010). *Still Not Easy Being British: Struggles for a Multicultural Citizenship*. Stoke-on-Trent: Trentham Books.

Monumentum.fr. (2018). 'Monument aux héros de l'armée d'Orient et des terres lointaines, square Lieutenant-Danjaume à Marseille'. Retrieved from https://monumentum.fr/monument-aux-herosarmee-orient-des-terres-lointaines-squarelieutenant-danjaume-pa13000057.html

Moon, J. (1975). *The Logic of Political Inquiry: A Synthesis of Opposed Perspectives*. Reading, MA: Addison-Wesley.

Moore, D. (2001). *Ethnicité et Politique de la ville en France et en Grande-Bretagne*. Paris: Editions L'Harmattan.

Moran, M. (2011). Sarkozy Versus the Banlieues: Deconstructing Urban Legend. *Journal of Franco-Iberian Studies*, Special Issue: 'Beyond Hate: Representations of the Parisian Banlieue'.

Moser, K. (2014). *A Practical Guide to French Harki Literature*. Lanham: Lexington Books.

Mosse, G. L. (1991). *Fallen Soldiers: Reshaping the Memory of the World Wars*. New York: Oxford University Press.

Muggs, J. (2005). *Should French Hip Hop Take the Rap for Rioting* [Online]. Retrieved from http://www.telegraph.co.uk/culture/music/rockandjazzmusic/3648576/Should-hip-hop-take-the-rap-for-rioting.html

Musées Gadagne. (2013). *Les Minorités Religieuses à Lyon de Moyen Age à Nos Jours* [Online]. Retrieved from http://www.gadagne.musees.lyon.fr/index.php/histoire_fr/Histoire/Programmation/Conferences-colloques/Histoire-de-Lyon/Histoire-des-eglises-a-Lyon

Nash, K. (2001). The 'Cultural Turn' in Social Theory: Towards a Theory of Cultural Politics. *Sociology, 35*(1), 77–92. https://doi.org/10.1177/00380385 01035001006

Ni Putes Ni Soumises. (2005). *Le guide du respect*. Paris: Cherche Midi.

Nielsen, K. (1996). Cultural Nationalism, Neither Ethnic Nor Civic. *Philosophical Forum, 28*(1–2), 42–52.

Noiriel, G. (1988). *Le Creuset français: Histoire de l'immigration XIXe-XXe Siècles*. Paris: Seuil.

Oliver, P. (1999). Canada's Two Solitudes: Constitutional and International Law in Reference re Secession of Quebec. *International Journal on Minority and Group Rights, 6*(1), 65–95. https://doi.org/10.1163/15718119920907640

Ouest France. (2018). Braquage à la Kalachnikov: 500 000 E de bijoux volés. Retrieved from https://www.ouest-france.fr/societe/faits-divers/saint-tropez-braquage-l-arme-lourde-500-000-eu-de-bijoux-voles-5481474

Pascual, J., Courouble, E., & Bonniel, J. (2009). *Interculturalism in the Cultural Policies of European Cities*. Retrieved from http://www.coe.int/t/dg4/culture-heritage/culture/cities/CULTURAL.policy_en.pdf

Pateman, C. (Ed.). (1989). Feminist Critiques of the Public/Private Dichotomy. In *The Disorder of Women: Democracy, Feminism and Political Theory*. Stanford, CA: Stanford University Press.

Paveau, M.-A. (2014). Un objet de discours pour les études pornographiques. *Questions de Communication, 2*(26), 7–15.

Pecqueux, A. (2007). *Voix du rap: Essai de sociologie de l'action musicale*. Paris: Editions L'Harmattan.

Perrier, J. (2010). *Rap Francais: Dix Ans Après*. Paris: Poche.

Pervis, A. (2007). *Marseille's Ethnic Bouillabaisse: Some View Europe's Most Diverse City as a Laboratory of the Continent's Future*. Smithsonian Magazine.

Poirrier, P. (Ed.). (2013). *La Politique culturelle en débat: Anthologie 1955–2012*. Paris: Comité d'histoire du Ministère de la culture/La Documentation française.

Prévos, A. (2001). Post-Colonial Popular Music in France: Rap Music and Hip-Hop Culture in the 1980s and 1990s. In *Global Noise: Rap and HipHop outside of the USA*. Middletown, CT: Wesleyan University Press.

Prévos, J. M. (1996). The Evolution of French Rap Music and Hip Hop Culture in the 1980s and 1990s. *The French Review, 69*(5), 713–725.

Procter, J. (2004). *Stuart Hall*. London: Routledge.

Pulham, S. (2005, November 8). *Inflammatory Language*. Retrieved February 15, 2018, from http://www.theguardian.com/news/blog/2005/nov/08/inflammatoryla

Rafter, N. H. (2006). *Shots in the Mirror: Crime Films and Society*. Oxford: Oxford University Press.

Ramdani, K. (2011). Bitch and Beurette: When Femininity Rhymes with Freedom. *Volume !, 8*(2), 13–39.

Raymond, G., & Modood, T. (2007). *The Construction of Minority Identities in France and Britain*. London: Palgrave.

Reece, R. L. (2015). The Plight of the Black Belle Knox: Race and Webcam Modelling. *Porn Studies, 2*(2–3), 269–271. https://doi.org/10.1080/232687 43.2015.1054672

Rice, K. (2009). *Must There Be Two Solitudes? Language Activists and Linguists Working Together*. J. Reyhner & L Lockard (eds.), Indigenous Language Revitalization: Encouragement, Guidance, and Lessons Learned, pp. 37–59. Flagstaff, AZ: Northern Arizona University. http://jan.ucc.nau.edu/~jar/ILR/ILR-4.pdf.

Richardson, E. (2006a). *Hiphop Literacies*. Retrieved from https://www.amazon.co.uk/Hiphop-Literacies-Elaine-Richardson/dp/0415329272

Richardson, J. (Ed.). (2006b). *European Union: Power and Policy-Making*. London: Routledge.

Rioux, J.-S. (2004). Two Solitudes: Quebecers' Attitudes Regarding Canadian Security and Defence Policy. *Journal of Military and Strategic Studies, 7*(3). Retrieved from https://jmss.org/jmss/index.php/jmss/article/view/143

Roe, P. (2004). Securitization and Minority Rights: Conditions of Desecuritization. *Security Dialogue, 35*, 279–292.

Rose, T. (1994). *Black Noise: Rap Music and Black Culture in Contemporary America*. Hanover, NH: Wesleyan University Press.

Rothenbuhler, Eric W. (2002). Chapter 17: Ground Zero, the Firemen, and the Symbolics of Touch on 9-11 and After. In Eric W. Rothenbuhler & Mihai Coman (Eds.), *Media Anthropology*. London: Sage.

Roy, O. (2004). *Globalised Islam: The Search for a New Ummah*. London: C Hurst & Co Publishers Ltd.

Roy, O. (2005). Intifada des banlieues ou émeutes des jeunes déclassés? *Esprit*, (12).

Roy, O. (2015, January 10). *There Are More French Muslims Working for French Security Than for Al Qaeda*. Retrieved September 1, 2018, from https://www.huffingtonpost.com/olivier-roy/paris-attack-muslim-cliches_b_6445582.html

Roy, O. (2017). *Jihad and Death: The Global Appeal of Islamic State*. London: Hurst and Co. Retrieved from https://www.amazon.co.uk/Jihad-Death-Global-Appeal-Islamic/dp/1849046980

RTL. (2018). *VIDÉO – Les gilets jaunes mènent-ils un combat historique?* Retrieved February 9, 2019, from https://www.rtl.fr/actu/debats-societe/video-1789-mai-1968-les-gilets-jaunes-menent-ils-un-combat-historique-7795794100

Rumelili, B. (2013). Identity and Desecuritisation: The Pitfalls of Conflating Ontological and Physical Security. *Journal of International Relations and Development, 18,* 52–74.

Safran, W. (1991). State, Nation, National Identity, and Citizenship: France as a Test Case. *International Political Science Review/Revue Internationale de Science Politique, 12*(3), 219–238.

Sagemen, M. (2014). The Stagnation in Terrorism Research. *Terrorism and Political Violence, 26,* 565–580.

Sahlins, P. (2006). *Civil Unrest in the French Suburbs.* New York: Brooklyn.

Said, E. (1978). *Orientalism.* New York: Pantheon Books.

Samers, M. E. (2003). Diaspora Unbound: Muslim Identity and the Erratic Regulation of Islam in France. *International Journal of Population Geography, 9*(4), 351–364. https://doi.org/10.1002/ijpg.292

Sayad, A. (1999). *La double absence: des illusions de l'émigré aux souffrances de l'immigré.* Paris: Liber.

Sayare, S. (2009, August 26). French Rap as a Flash Point. *The New York Times.* Retrieved from https://www.nytimes.com/2009/08/27/arts/27iht-rap.html

Sberna, B. (Ed.). (2008). *Une sociologie du rap à Marseille.* Broché.

Schmid, A. P. (2013). Radicalisation, De-Radicalisation, Counter-Radicalisation: A Conceptual Discussion and Literature. *Review, ICCT Research Paper.* Retrieved from https://www.icct.nl/download/file/ICCT-Schmid-Radicalisation-De-Radicalisation-Counter-Radicalisation-March-2013.pdf

Sellami, S. (2016). Le vrai visage du narco-banditisme. *Marseille, Le Parisien* online at http://www.leparisien.fr/faits-divers/le-vrai-visage-du-narco-banditisme-a-marseille-02-05-2016-5760745.php

Senni, A. (2016). *Les banlieues, des fabriques de djihadistes? La faute aux politiques. Il est temps d'agir.* Retrieved October 1, 2018, from http://leplus.nouvelobs.com/contribution/1500213-les-banlieues-des-fabriques-de-djihadistes-la-faute-aux-politiques-il-est-temps-d-agir.html

Settoul, E. (2015). 'You're in the French Army Now!' Institutionalising Islam in the Republic's Army. *Religion, State and Society, 43*(1), 73–84. https://doi.org/10.1080/09637494.2015.1022400

Sharp, D. (2013). Policing After Macpherson: Some Experiences of Muslim Police Officers. In B. Salek (Ed.), *Islam, Crime and Criminal Justice*. https://doi.org/10.4324/9781843924586-10

Simmons, S. (2001). *An Extract from Serge Gainsbourg: A Fistfull of Gitanes* [Online]. Retrieved from http://www.guardian.co.uk/books/2001/feb/02/culture.features

Simpson, D. (2006). *9/11: The Culture of Commemoration*. Chicago: University of Chicago Press.

Singer, D. (2002). *Prelude to Revolution: France in May 1968*. Cambridge, MA: South End Press.

Sirin, S. R., & Fine, M. (2007). Hyphenated Selves: Muslim American Youth Negotiating Identities on the Fault Lines of Global Conflict. *Applied Developmental Science, 11*(3), 151–163. https://doi.org/10.1080/10888690701454658

Smith, A. D. (2005). The Genealogy of Nations: An Ethno-Symbolist Approach. In A. Ichijo & G. Uzelac (Eds.), *When Is the Nation?* London: Routledge.

Smith, J. G., & Luykx, A. (2017). Race Play in BDSM Porn: The Eroticization of Oppression. *Porn Studies, 4*(4), 433–446. https://doi.org/10.1080/23268743.2016.1252158

Souilamas, G. (1999). *Des beurettes aux descendantes d'immigrants nord-africains*. Paris: Grasset.

Sports Journalist Association. (2010). *Regis on Big Ron, Racism and Death Threats Sent with a Bullet*. Sports Journalists' Association. Retrieved September 13, 2018, from https://www.sportsjournalists.co.uk/other-bodies/football-writers/regis-on-big-ron-racism-and-death-threats-wrapped-in-a-bullet/

Sweedenburg, T. (2001). Islamic Hip-Hop vs. Islamophobia: Aki Nawaz, Natacha Atlas, Akhenaton. In *Global Noise: Hip Hop Outside of the USA*. Middletown, CT: Wesleyan University Press.

Tarrow, S. (1993). Social Protest and Policy Reform: May 1968 and the Loi d'Orientation in France. *Comparative Political Studies, 25*(4), 579–607. https://doi.org/10.1177/0010414093025004006

Taylor, C. (1994). *Multiculturalism: Examining the Politics of Recognition*. Princeton, NJ: Princeton University Press.

Temime, E. (Ed.). (1999). *Migrance: Histoire des migrations à Marseille*. Paris: Editions Jeanne Laffite.

Tervé, C. (2018). *Des familles de victimes du Bataclan dénoncent la récupération de leurs portraits contre la venue de Médine*. Retrieved September 12, 2018, from https://www.huffingtonpost.fr/2018/07/04/medine-au-bataclan-des-familles-de-victimes-denoncent-la-recuperation-de-leurs-portraits-pour-la-deprogrammation-du-concert_a_23474648/

Tilly, C. (1998). *Durable Inequality*. Berkeley, CA: University of California Press.

Todorov, T., & Anzalone, J. (1989). Nation and Nationalism: The French Variant. *Salmagundi, 84*, 138–153.

Tomlinson, A., & Young, C. (2006). *National Identity and Global Sports Events: Culture, Politics, and Spectacle in the Olympics and the Football World Cup*. Albany: SUNY Press.

Tribalat, M. (2017). *Assimilation: la fin du modèle français: Pourquoi l'Islam change la donne*. Paris: L'artilleur.

Tyler, I. (2008). Chav Mum Chav Scum. *Feminist Media Studies, 8*(1), 17–34. https://doi.org/10.1080/14680770701824779

Vale, L. (1999). Mediated Monuments and National Identity. *The Journal of Architecture, 4*(4), 391–408.

Valette, N. (2018). *Un homme tué par des tirs de Kalachnikov à Marseille le soir du réveillon*. Retrieved October 1, 2018, from https://www.francebleu.fr/infos/faits-divers-justice/un-homme-tue-par-des-tires-de-kalachnikov-a-marseille-le-soir-du-nouvel-1514771178

Valnet, J., Cachin, O., AKA, & Maéro, J.-P. (2013). *M.A.R.S. Histoires et légendes du hip-hop marseillais* (1st ed.). Paris: Wildproject Editions.

Van den Avenne, C., Gascquet-Cyrus, M., & Kosmicki, G. (1999). *Paroles et Musiques à Marseille: Les voix d'une Ville*. Paris: Editions L'Hartmann.

Van Puyvelde, D. (2015). *We Can't Expect Intelligence Services to Prevent Every Terrorist Attack*. Retrieved from https://theconversation.com/we-cant-expect-intelligence-services-to-prevent-every-terrorist-attack-36676

Vertovec, S. (2007). Super-Diversity and Its Implications. *Ethnic and Racial Studies, 30*(6), 1024–1054. https://doi.org/10.1080/01419870701599465

Vice Media. (2018). *Zinedine Zidane Shares His World Cup Memories – VICE Video: Documentaries, Films, News Videos*. Retrieved from https://video.vice.com/en_uk/video/vice-zinedine-zidane-shares-his-world-cup-memories/5b3b81eebe407726cc522301

Vidacs, B. (2011). Banal Nationalism, Football, and Discourse Community in Africa. *Studies in Ethnicity and Nationalism, 11*(1), 25–41. https://doi.org/10.1111/j.1754-9469.2011.01105.x

Vigouroux, R., & Ouaknin, J. (2005). *Laïcité + Religions: Marseille Espérance*. Marseille: Transbordeurs.

Ville de Lyon. (2011). *'Our Cultures in the City' Days Program* [Online]. Retrieved from http://www.polville.lyon.fr/polville/sections/fr/les_thematiques/culture/les_journees_nos_cu/

Ville de Lyon. (2012). *Charte de Coopération Culturelle* [Online]. Retrieved from http://www.polville.lyon.fr/static/polville/contenu/Culture/CHARTE%20%203.pdf

Vince, N. (2015). *Our Fighting Sisters: Nation, Memory and Gender in Algeria, 1954–2012*. Retrieved March 23, 2018, from https://www.amazon.co.uk/Our-Fighting-Sisters-Algeria-1954-2012-ebook/dp/B012DLLXWM/ref=sr_1_1?ie=UTF8&qid=1521805565&sr=8-1&keywords=Our+Fighting+Sisters%3A+Nation%2C+Memory+and+Gender+in+Algeria%2C+1954-2012

Vinocur, N. (2016). *French Court Strikes Down Burkini Ban*. Retrieved August 26, 2018, from https://www.politico.eu/article/french-court-strikes-down-burkini-ban/

Vörös, F. (2015). *Cultures pornographiques: Anthologie des Porn Studies*. Paris: Editions Amsterdam.

Wacquant, L. (2007). *Urban Outcasts: A Comparative Sociology of Advanced Marginality*. Retrieved from https://www.amazon.co.uk/Urban-Outcasts-Comparative-Sociology-Marginality/dp/0745631258/ref=sr_1_3?ie=UTF8&qid=1517652872&sr=8-3&keywords=wacquant

Waizenegger, A., & Hyndman, J. (2010). Two Solitudes: Post-tsunami and Post-conflict Aceh. *Disasters, 34*(3), 787–808. https://doi.org/10.1111/j.1467-7717.2010.01169.x

Weber, E. (1976). *Peasants into Frenchmen: The Modernization of Rural France, 1870–1914* (1st ed.). Stanford, CA: Stanford University Press.

Weber, T. (2005). *Time of Two Solitudes Has Passed: Jean*. Retrieved from https://www.theglobeandmail.com/news/national/time-of-two-solitudes-has-passed-jean/article20426310/

Weil, P. (2008). *How to Be French: Nationality in the Making Since 1789* (C. Porter, Trans.). Durham, NC: Duke University Press.

Wihtol de Wenden, C. (2004). Multiculturalism in France. In *The Governance of Multiculturalism*. Palgrave. Retrieved from http://spire.sciencespo.fr/hdl:/2441/46mbanhapncmp6s99itam92a8/resources/contentserver.asp-1.pdf

Wihtol de Wenden, C. (2010). L'armée française face à la diversité: une réflexion sur la citoyenneté. *Migrations Société, 131*, 201–214. https://doi.org/10.3917/migra.131.0201

Winter, J. (1998). *Sites of Memory, Sites of Mourning: The Great War in European Cultural History*. Cambridge: Cambridge University Press.

Williams, J. (2017). *Games Without Frontiers: Football, Identity and Modernity*. New York: Routledge.

Williams, L. (1989). *HARDCORE: Power, Pleasure and the 'Frenzy of the Visible'.* Los Angeles: University of California Press.

Williams, L. (2014). Pornography, Porno, Porn: Thoughts on a Weedy Field. *Porn Studies, 1*(1–2), 24–40. https://doi.org/10.1080/23268743.2013.863662

Williams, M. C. (2003). Words, Images, Enemies: Securitization and International Politics. *International Studies Quarterly, 47*(4), 511–531. https://doi.org/10.1046/j.0020-8833.2003.00277.x

Wolak, J., Mitchell, K., & Finkelhor, D. (2007). Unwanted and Wanted Exposure to Online Pornography in a National Sample of Youth Internet Users. *Pediatrics, 119*(2), 247–257. https://doi.org/10.1542/peds.2006-1891

Wood, P. (2004). *The Intercultural City: A Reader.* London: Comedia.

Wood, P. (2010). *Intercultural Cities: Towards a Model for Intercultural Integration: Insights from the Intercultural Cities Programme, Joint Action of the Council of Europe and the European Commission.* Strasbourg: Council of Europe.

Woodhead, L. (2009). The Muslim Veil Controversy and European Values. Research Portal | Lancaster University. *Swedish Missiological Themes, 97*(1), 17.

Yoshino, K. (1992). *Consuming Ethnicity and Nationalism: Asian Experiences.* London: Wiley.

Young, I. (2009). Structural Injustice and the Politics of Difference. In T. Christiano & J. Christman (Eds.), *Contemporary Debates in Political Philosophy.* Oxford: Blackwell.

Young, J. E. (1993). *The Texture of Memory: Holocaust Memorials and Meaning.* London: Yale University Press.

Zappi, S. (2015, October 22). Le djihadiste, nouvel épouvantail des banlieues françaises. *Le Monde.* Retrieved from https://www.lemonde.fr/banlieues/article/2015/10/22/le-djihadiste-nouvel-epouvantail-des-banlieues-francaises_4794877_1653530.html

Zemmour, E. (2009). *Le premier sexe.* Paris: J'AI LU.

Zemmour, E. (2014). *Le Suicide français.* Paris: Albin Michel.

Zemmour, E. (2018). *Destin français.* Paris: Albin Michel.

Zemouri, A. (2013). *Marseille: soupçon de favoritisme sur la suppléante de Patrick Menucci.* Retrieved from http://www.lepoint.fr/societe/marseille-soupcon-de-favoritisme-sur-la-suppleante-de-patrick-menucci-27-09-2013-1735968_23.php

Zillmann, D. (1989). Effects of Prolonged Consumption of Pornography. In *Pornography: Research Advances and Policy Considerations.* Hillsdale, NJ: Lawrence Erlbaum Associates.

Zimmer, O. (2003). Boundary Mechanisms and Symbolic Resources: Towards a Process-Oriented Approach to National Identity. *Nations and Nationalism, 9*(2), 173–193. https://doi.org/10.1111/1469-8219.00081

Index

© The Author(s) 2019
J. Downing, *French Muslims in Perspective*,
https://doi.org/10.1007/978-3-030-16103-3

Printed by Printforce, the Netherlands